看護医療学校受験

オープンセサミシリーズ 問題集 アクセス ❸

英語

平成30年告示 学習指導要領対応

東京アカデミー 編

東京アカデミー七賢出版

はじめに

オープンセサミ・シリーズは，看護・医療系学校入試に完璧に対応できるよう，入試問題を分析し作成した看護・医療系専用の問題集です。この問題集をマスターすることで，基礎を確実に固めながら，同時に自然に入試傾向をつかむことができるよう構成されています。

あなたがこのシリーズを十分に活用し，目的を達成されることを念願します。

東京アカデミー看護医療試験研究室スタッフ一同

CONTENTS

第 6 章　実践問題

■ 解答・解説は別冊

看護医療学校受験参考書オープンセサミシリーズ③英語の準拠問題集です。あわせてご利用いただくと、より効果的です。
A は基本問題、**B** は標準問題、**C** は応用問題となっています。

Open Sesame Series

第1章　文

1　文　型

A

1　次の文と文型の等しい文をそれぞれあとの**ア**～**オ**，**カ**～**コ**から選び，記号で答えよ。また，第何文型かを答えよ。

(1)　When in Rome do as the Romans do.
(2)　I think that he is poor but he is honest.
(3)　Will you tell me the way to the station?
(4)　She will get well soon after taking this medicine.
(5)　What makes you so sad?

ア　How to read is as important as what to read.
イ　She bought her daughter a new bag.
ウ　I want you to go to the hospital.
エ　The thief ran away.
オ　Could you make out what she said?

(6)　She smiled happily.
(7)　He is a baseball player.
(8)　My father bought a car last month.
(9)　Ms. Tanaka teaches us math.
(10)　My mother calls me Libby.

カ　Michael made his daughter a dress.
キ　Sally looks sad.
ク　One of my friends lives in London.
ケ　Jack made his son a doctor.
コ　Anne likes to read books.

2 次の各文が，あとの**ア**～**オ**のどの文型であるか答えよ。

(1) It gets dark in the evening.
(2) The train stopped suddenly.
(3) I don't like loud music.
(4) The present made me happy.
(5) His mother told him an interesting story.
(6) She has lived in the country.
(7) It looks like an egg.
(8) Keep it a secret, please.
(9) He made his family a log cabin.
(10) I wonder who told you that thing.
(11) I hope to get there at six.
(12) He named his dog John.

ア S+V　**イ** S+V+C　**ウ** S+V+O　**エ** S+V+O+O
オ S+V+O+C

B

3 次の各組の文が同じ意味になるように(　　)に適する語句を入れよ。

(1) I asked him some questions. [第 4 文型]
I asked some questions (　　) him. [第 3 文型]
(2) There are five rooms in this house. [第 1 文型]
This house (　　) five rooms. [第 3 文型]
(3) We think it very strange. [第 5 文型]
We think that (　　) (　　) very strange. [第 3 文型]
(4) We have much rain in June. [第 3 文型]
(　　) (　　) much here in June. [第 1 文型]

4 次の第 4 文型の各文を第 3 文型に書き換えよ。

(1) He gave me some flowers.
(2) My father bought me a new dictionary.
(3) Ms. Suzuki teaches us English.
(4) May I ask you a favor?
(5) My sister made me a doll.
(6) Please lend me this bicycle.

第1章　文

2　文の種類

A

5　次の各文を指示に従って書き換えよ。

(1)　He is an ambitious boy.［否定文に］

(2)　You can play tennis.［疑問文に］

(3)　George doesn't know her address.［疑問文に］

(4)　I will do my homework tonight.［否定文に］

(5)　You are the best skier in my class.［付加疑問文に］

6　次の各文を，下に与えられた**ア**～**オ**の語句を適当に並べ換えて完成させよ。

(1)　If (　　) (　　) (　　) (　　), (　　) have caught the train.

ア　I could　　**イ**　only I　　**ウ**　earlier

エ　five minutes　　**オ**　had come

(2)　She takes (　　) (　　) (　　) (　　) (　　) in hospitals.

ア　mothers　　**イ**　are employed　　**ウ**　care of

エ　children　　**オ**　whose

(3)　When Margaret was a young girl, she (　　) (　　) (　　) (　　) (　　).

ア　of politics　　**イ**　to the study　　**ウ**　herself

エ　decided　　**オ**　to devote

(4)　You are (　　) (　　) (　　) (　　) (　　) anyone else.

ア　win　　**イ**　more　　**ウ**　likely to

エ　than　　**オ**　the speech contest

(5)　I (　　) (　　), (　　) (　　) (　　) I have read as yet.

ア　of　　**イ**　neither　　**ウ**　which　　**エ**　bought　　**オ**　two books

B

7 次の(　　　)に適する語句を補い英文を完成させよ。

(1) 彼女が何歳か知っていますか。
Do you know (　　　) (　　　) (　　　) (　　　)?

(2) ここから駅までの距離はどのくらいありますか。
How (　　　) (　　　) (　　　) (　　　) (　　　) to the station?

(3) かぜをひかないように注意しなさい。
(　　　) careful (　　　) (　　　) (　　　) a cold.

(4) あの方はどこの国の人だと思いますか。
What country (　　　) (　　　) think he is (　　　)?

8 次の各組で日本文と同じ意味の英文になるように，(　　　)に適する語句を入れよ。

(1) だれでもほしい人に私の本をあげます。
I'll give my book (①) (②) wants it.

(2) 昨日その市の見物をした。
I saw (③) (④) of the city yesterday.

(3) まもなく彼は自分のしたことを後悔するだろう。
It won't be long (⑤) he feels sorry for (⑥) he has done.

(4) 今日はずっと気分がよい。
I feel (⑦) (⑧) today.

(5) 今年は例年より雪が少なかった。
We had (⑨) snow than (⑩) this year.

9 次の各組の英文が同じ意味になるよう(　　　)に適する語句を入れよ。

(1) Whenever I see this album, I remember my happy high school days.
This album always (①) me (②) my happy high school days.

(2) After we walked thirty minutes, we got to the beach.
Thirty minutes' walk (③) us (④) the beach.

(3) Thanks to his good health, he could accomplish his plan.
Good health (⑤) him (⑥) accomplish his plan.

(4) If she sleeps well, she will feel better tomorrow.
A good sleep will (⑦) her (⑧) better tomorrow.

(5) Because my father was sick, I couldn't go to the party.
My father's sickness (⑨) me (⑩) going to the party.

10 次の各文の下線部が答えの中心となる疑問文を書け。

(1) This bag cost twelve thousand yen.
(2) I like summer better than winter.
(3) He borrowed Tom's pen yesterday.
(4) This is John's helmet.
(5) I met him in the park yesterday.
(6) I met him in the park yesterday.
(7) I met him in the park yesterday.

11 次の各組の英文が同じ意味になるよう(　　　)に適する語句を入れよ。

(1) Do you mind if I call you tonight?
Do you mind (　　　) (　　　) you tonight?

(2) He is so kind that he does not do such a thing.
He is (　　　) kind (　　　) do such a thing.

(3) Change of air will make him well.
(　　　) he gets change of air, (　　　) will be well.

(4) If you don't take a vacation, you will get sick.
Take a vacation, (　　　) you will get sick.

(5) Who knows what will happen in the future?
(　　　) knows what will happen in the future.

12 次の各文を指示に従って書き換えよ。

(1) Let's go right now.［否定文に］
(2) It lasted a very long time.［感嘆文に］
(3) The car came running very quickly.［感嘆文に］
(4) I like tea better than coffee.［下線部が答えの対象となる疑問文に］
(5) You must not drink too much.［命令文に］

第2章　動詞

3　動詞の種類・活用，時制

A

13 次の動詞の語形変化のうち誤っているものを３つ選び，番号で答えよ。

	原形	過去形	過去分詞	現在分詞
(1)	carry	carried	carried	carrying
(2)	cut	cut	cut	cutting
(3)	die	died	died	diing
(4)	fly	flew	flown	flying
(5)	hope	hoped	hoped	hoping
(6)	hid	hid	hidden	hiding
(7)	leave	left	left	leaving
(8)	lie	lay	lain	lying
(9)	sink	sank	sank	sinking
(10)	ski	skied	skied	skiing
(11)	throw	threw	thrown	throwing
(12)	wear	wore	worn	wearing

B

14 次の(　　　)の動詞を正しい形に書き換えよ。ただし１語になるとは限らない。

(1) I will stay at home and read books if it (rain) tomorrow.

(2) Mrs. Jones surprised me by (use) the computer the way experienced people do.

(3) My father usually (get) up at seven, but he (get) up half an hour later this morning.

(4) My brother (be) ill in bed since last week.

(5) I expect that you (do) your best next time.

(6) She showed me the watch which her father (give) her.

(7) What language (speak) in Canada ?

15 次の各文の(　　　)に入る適当な語句を**ア**～**エ**から選び，記号で答えよ。

(1) We enjoyed (　　　) in the country.

ア stay　**イ** staying　**ウ** stayed　**エ** to stay

(2) Did you have your shirts (　　　) yesterday?

ア wash　**イ** washing　**ウ** washed　**エ** to wash

(3) He cannot be an honest man (　　　) such a thing.

ア does　**イ** doing　**ウ** did　**エ** to do

(4) Any fish (　　　) in the bay is dangerous to eat.

ア catch　**イ** catching　**ウ** caught　**エ** to catch

(5) I don't like you (　　　) him that way.

ア help　**イ** helping　**ウ** helped　**エ** to help

16 次の各文の(　　　)内に入っている動詞の原形を正しい形に変えよ。必要ならばほかの語を補ってもよい。

(1) Lucy is in charge of (organize) the meeting.

(2) My parents (be) to Europe three times.

(3) It is hot in this room because the window (close).

(4) My sister is busy (prepare) for her wedding.

(5) Nearly everyone (invite) came to the party.

17 次の各文の(　　　)に入る適当な語句を**ア**～**エ**から選び，記号で答えよ。

(1) As it threatens to rain, you had better (　　　) an umbrella with you.

ア take　**イ** took　**ウ** taking　**エ** to take

(2) I was very surprised to hear my name (　　　) in the dark.

ア call　**イ** called　**ウ** calling　**エ** to call

(3) Don't forget (　　　) me tomorrow morning, or I may oversleep and be late for an important meeting.

ア call　**イ** called　**ウ** calling　**エ** to call

(4) She concluded her letter by writing "I'm looking forward (　　　) you soon."

ア to see　**イ** to have seen　**ウ** to be seen　**エ** to seeing

(5) The dog (　　　) on the sofa seems lazy, but he has an experience in rescuing a baby from drowning.

ア lay　**イ** laying　**ウ** lying　**エ** lied

18 次の各組の英文が同じ意味になるよう(　　　)に適する語句を入れよ。

(1) His uncle died five years ago.
His uncle has been (　　　) for five years.

(2) Ten people are reported to have been killed in the explosion.
It is reported that ten people (　　　) killed in the explosion.

(3) Ten years have passed since she came here.
It (　　　) ten years since she came here.

(4) She seemed to be rich.
It seemed that she (　　　) rich.

19 次の各文の(　　　)に入る適当な語句を選び，記号で答えよ。

(1) Florence Nightingale (　　　) in 1910.
ア died　**イ** has died　**ウ** was died　**エ** dead

(2) The street is wet. (　　　) while we were watching the movie.
ア It must be rain　**イ** It must have rained
ウ It must have raining　**エ** It might have rain

(3) Since 1988, there (　　　) no earthquakes here.
ア have been　**イ** are　**ウ** is　**エ** were being

(4) Most of the people who attended the audition yesterday (　　　) currently students at acting schools.
ア is　**イ** are　**ウ** was　**エ** has been

(5) When I dropped in at Bob's office, he (　　　) home.
ア has already gone　**イ** has been going
ウ had already gone　**エ** had been going

20 次の英文をそれぞれあとの指示に従ってほぼ同じ意味になるように書き換えよ。

(1) It seems that he heard the news. [He で始めて単文で]

(2) Two hours have passed since I began to study. [I で始めて単文で]

第2章　動詞

4　受動態

A

21　次の各文を和訳し，さらに態を変えた英文をつくり，それを和訳せよ。

(1)　Columbus discovered America in 1492.

(2)　What do you call this flower in English?

(3)　The whole crowd laughed at him.

(4)　Tom made Susie go there.

22　次の各組の英文が同じ意味になるよう(　　　)に適する語句を入れよ。

(1) { Mr. Tanaka teaches us English.
We (　　　) taught English (　　　) Mr. Tanaka.

(2) { We often heard her sing.
She was often (　　　) (　　　) sing.

(3) { His sudden death greatly shocked us.
We were greatly (　　　) (　　　) his sudden death.

(4) { The story did not interest me.
I was not (　　　) (　　　) the story.

(5) { Everybody in the room knows the man.
The man is (　　　) (　　　) everybody in the room.

23　次の各文を能動態に変えよ。

(1)　A long novel is being written by Jane.

(2)　She will be surprised at the news.

(3)　By whom was he brought up?

(4)　French is spoken in Canada.

B

24 次の各組の英文が同じ意味になるよう(　　)に適する語句を入れよ。

(1) { They don't sell gym shoes at that store.
  { Gym shoes (　　) (　　) (　　) at that store.

(2) { They saw John enter the room.
  { John (　　) (　　) (　　) enter the room.

(3) { She dislikes people looking at her.
  { She dislikes (　　) looked at.

(4) { They may ask you to show them your passport.
  { You may (　　) (　　) to show them your passport.

(5) { Every Japanese knows his name.
  { His name is known (　　) every Japanese.

(6) { The news surprised me.
  { I was (　　) (　　) the news.

(7) { She didn't come in till the officers were seated.
  { When she came in, the officers (　　) already (　　) (　　).

(8) { The writer was writing an interesting story.
  { An interesting story (　　) (　　) (　　) by the writer.

25 次の各組の英文が同じ意味になるよう(　　)に適する語句を入れよ。

(1) { Everybody loves him.
  { He is (　　) (　　) everybody.

(2) { My camera was stolen.
  { I (　　) my camera stolen.

(3) { Do the work carefully.
  { (　　) the work (　　) (　　) carefully.

(4) { He was seen (　　) climb the fence.
  { We (　　) him climb the fence.

(5) { They looked up to him as their leader.
  { He was (　　) (　　) (　　) as their leader.

(6) { People believed that he had been a millionaire.
  { He (　　) (　　) to (　　) (　　) a millionaire.

26 次の各文の態を変えよ。

(1) I saw him enter the room.
(2) Who showed you the way?
(3) People believe that he was lazy.
(4) No one ever took me for my twin brother.
(5) They put off the departure till the next morning.
(6) The answer didn't surprise his teacher.
(7) They say that John and Jenny have been married for five years.
(8) An American spoke to me.

27 次の日本文を，受動態を使って英訳せよ。

(1) この本は彼によって書かれた。
(2) その列車は大雪のために遅れた。
(3) 彼女は街で知らない人に話しかけられた。
(4) 英語は世界中で話されている。

第2章　動詞

5　助動詞

A

28　次の各組で日本文と同じ意味の英文になるように，(　　　)に適する語句を入れよ。

(1) あなたはこの本を読めますか？
(　　　) you (　　　) (　　　) read this book?

(2) あなたはすぐに医者に診てもらうべきです。
You (　　　) (　　　) see your doctor at once.

(3) あなたはすぐに自分の宿題をやらなければならない。
You (　　　) (　　　) do your homework soon.

(4) あなたは映画に行ってもよいが，妹を連れて行かなければならない。
You (　　　) go to the cinema, but you (　　　) take your sister.

(5) 君がそのニュースを聞いて驚くのも当然だ。
You (　　　) (　　　) be surprised at the news.

(6) 健康にはいくら注意しても注意しすぎることはない。
We (　　　) be (　　　) careful of our health.

29　次の英文を和訳せよ。

(1) *Prior to the spread of *mammography, such women might have died of other causes before their breast cancer was diagnosed.

* **prior to**　～より前　　**mammography**　乳房レントゲン検査

(2) They used to call her 'the Lady of the Lamp' because at night she would go round the hospital with a lamp to see that they were all right.

B

30 次の(　　)に適する語句をあとのア～エから選び，記号で答えよ。

(1) "Which shoes did your wife buy?"
"The green ones, but I (　　) bought the brown ones."
ア rather had　イ will rather have
ウ would rather have　エ would have rather

(2) She (　　) in London about this time tomorrow.
ア must have arrived　イ must be arrived
ウ should have arrived　エ will have arrived

(3) You had (　　) there alone.
ア not better go　イ not better to go
ウ better not go　エ better not to go

(4) "Must I finish this report by tomorrow?" "No, you (　　)."
ア may not　イ must not　ウ can't
エ don't have to

(5) I don't know when he (　　) back.
ア comes　イ will come　ウ come
エ has come

(6) I suggested (　　) start early.
ア him to　イ for him to　ウ that he
エ of him to

31 次の各文の(　　)に適する助動詞を選び，記号で答えよ。

(1) She expressed her wish that I (ア might　イ ought　ウ should　エ would) succeed.

(2) (ア Can　イ May　ウ Must　エ Should) it be true that the patient died last night?

(3) If you (ア are not　イ had not been　ウ were not　エ would like) feeling well, go and lie down for a while.

(4) (ア I had　イ I suppose　ウ Were I　エ Would I) you, I would do the same.

(5) He suggested to me that we (ア would　イ should　ウ might　エ could) wait until she came.

(6) Let's play tennis, (ア will　イ shall　ウ must　エ can) we?

32

(1)　次の英文の(　　　)に適する語句を選び，記号で答えよ。

①　Now John is no longer what he (　　　) be.

(ア　would　　イ　used to　　ウ　was used to　　エ　had to)

②　(　　　) had he begun to speak than the audience interrupted him.

(ア　Hardly　　イ　Scarcely　　ウ　No sooner　　エ　As soon as)

(2)　次の各文を書き換えるとき，下線部に入れるのに最も適当な語句を選び，記号で答えよ。

This way of thinking saves me from judgment.

⇒ When I think in this way, I ＿＿＿＿＿＿＿＿＿＿.

ア　cannot avoid judging　　イ　don't have to judge

ウ　won't fear to judge　　エ　must remember to judge

33　次の会話を読み，あとの各問いに答えよ。

Cabin Crew : What are you doing, dear?　You know we can't stop the departure now.

Passenger : (　①　) I have got to be in Los Angeles in two hours. [a]I can't not be there. (　②　)

Cabin Crew : Let me see your ticket then.

Passenger : I don't have a ticket.　But I promise I'll buy one when I arrive.

Cabin Crew : (　③　) We have another flight in two hours.　Let me help you with that.

Passenger : My daughter is very ill.　She is going in for surgery in three hours in L.A.　I have to be there!　I must be with her!

Cabin Crew : But you can't, for you have no ticket.

Passenger : I promise I'll buy a ticket when I arrive. [b]Don't let an airline ticket stand in the way of my being there for my daughter, please!

(1)　空欄(　①　)～(　③　)に入る最も適切なものをそれぞれあとの**ア**～**オ**から１つ選び，記号で答えよ。

ア　Yes, you may get on that plane.

イ　But you must.

ウ　I have to get on that plane.

エ　Impossible.

オ　I can't get on that plane.

(2) 下線部 a，b と同じ意味の文をそれぞれ 1 つ選び，記号で答えよ。

a ア It is impossible for me to be there.

イ It is absolutely necessary for me to be there.

ウ I am unable to get to Los Angeles if I miss the plane.

エ I am unable to get on the plane.

b ア Don't put off getting an airline ticket, for the plane is standing in the way.

イ Don't bother me by selling an airline ticket in the way.

ウ Don't make an airline ticket an obstacle to my being there.

エ Don't lose an airline ticket for my being there.

34 次の英文を和訳せよ。

Many great men have tried to show the world how pictures ought to be painted, but everything that they are able to say was said by Leonard da Vinci. What he wrote about art is the foundation of the artist's knowledge.

第2章　動詞

6　不定詞

A

35　次の文の不定詞に線を引き，その用法を述べよ。

(1)　I began to learn English at the age of twelve.
(2)　There was nobody to help her.
(3)　She will be happy to see me.
(4)　It is important to keep quiet in a hospital.
(5)　To master a foreign language is not easy.

36　次の各文の(　　　)の中から，適当なものを答えよ。

(1)　I want you (play, to play) the guitar.
(2)　I made him (go, to go) there.
(3)　He was made (go, to go) there by me.
(4)　Takako had him (mend, to mend) her bag.
(5)　I saw him (get, to get) on the train.

B

37 次の各組の英文が同じ意味になるよう(　　　)に適する語句を入れよ。

(1) She was so strong as to lift the barbell.
She was strong (　　　) to lift the barbell.

(2) Nobody could be seen in the office.
Nobody was (　　　) (　　　) (　　　) in the office.

(3) Do you mind not singing in the room?
Would you be kind (　　　) (　　　) to (　　　) in the room?

(4) It seems that you were in poor health last week.
You seem (　　　) (　　　) (　　　) in poor health last week.

(5) Father made him work very hard.
He was (　　　) (　　　) (　　　) very hard by Father.

(6) I could not help laughing at the strange sight.
I could not but (　　　) at the strange sight.

38 「be 動詞＋to-不定詞」は，**ア**予定，**イ**義務，**ウ**可能，**エ**意図，**オ**運命などを表すが，次の各文の下線部はそのいずれであるか答えよ。

(1) Uncle Kondo is to meet us at the airport.
(2) If you are to pass the exam, you must study hard.
(3) Not a trace of him was to be discovered.
(4) He was to die in a foreign land.
(5) It is to be remembered that though education has a beginning, there is no end of it.

39 次の英文を和訳せよ。

(1) All you have to remember is to write what you would say to the person as if you were in the same room talking to him.
(2) Most Americans can find no reason why it is necessary to remain in the place where one is born.

40 日本文と同じになるように，次の(　　　)内の語句を正しく並べ換えよ。

(1) 伊藤さんとお会いになるのは，今度が初めてですか。
Is this (for, first, the, you, to meet, time) Mr. Ito ?

(2) 我々はトムに歌を歌ってもらった。
We (song, Tom, a, had, sing).

(3) その問題の解き方はそれほど難しくない。
It (the question, not, how, difficult, to solve, is, so).

(4) 彼女を気の毒に思わないではいられない。
I (feel, for, sorry, but, can't, her).

(5) 我々がその山をそちら側から登ることは不可能に思えた。
It (us, seemed, that side, impossible, climb, for, to, of, the mountain).

(6) 彼は全員に聞こえるくらいの大声でしゃべった。
He (by, be, loudly, everyone, spoke, enough, heard, to).

(7) ある日，おばあさんは川へ洗濯に行きました。
One day, the (woman, the river, old, to, went, to, do) the laundry.

(8) 彼女は大きな桃が流れてくるのを見て驚きました。
She (was, to, a, see, surprised, big, peach, flowing) down the river.

(9) 彼女はその桃をつかもうとしましたが，うまくいきませんでした。
She (grab, to, tried, peach, the), but she couldn't.

41 次の文を不定詞を用いて書き換えよ。

(1) It is strange that he should say so.
(2) It seems that she was absent from school yesterday.
(3) The stone was so heavy that Jim could not move it.
(4) Shigeo is so rich that he can buy anything.

42 次の日本文を英訳せよ。

(1) 私の夢はゆっくり時間をとってヨーロッパの博物館巡りをすることです。
(2) 私は彼に窓を開けないように言った。

第2章　動詞

7　動名詞

A

43 次の各文の(　　　)内から正しい語を選べ。

(1) I have finished (to pack, packing).

(2) She promised (to come, coming) here again.

(3) I remember (to see, seeing) her twice.

(4) I could not avoid (to say, saying) that.

(5) Would you mind (to lend, lending) me your dictionary?

B

44 次の各組の英文が同じ意味になるよう(　　　)に適する語句を入れよ。

(1) Do you mind if I join you?
Do you mind (　　　) joining you?

(2) I did not go out, but stayed at home.
Instead (　　　) going out, I stayed at home.

(3) He is proud that he was educated in England.
He is proud (　　　) having (　　　) educated in England.

(4) I couldn't go to his party because I was ill.
I couldn't go to his party (　　　) (　　　) illness.

(5) It is impossible to know what she will do.
There is (　　　) (　　　) what she will do.

(6) The man insisted that she should be innocent of the crime.
The man insisted on (　　　) (　　　) innocent of the crime.

45 次の(　　)内の語句を並べ換えて英文を完成させよ。ただし，文頭にくるものも小文字で示してある。

(1) 彼は釣りに行くときはいつも息子を連れて行く。
He (ア without　イ never　ウ taking　エ goes　オ fishing) his son.

(2) その本は二度読む価値がある。
(ア is　イ the　ウ twice　エ book　オ worth　カ reading).

(3) 少し熱があったので仕事に行けなかった。
A slight (ア to　イ me　ウ going　エ fever　オ kept　カ work　キ from).

(4) ストレスの管理には定期的な運動が重要な役割を果たすことは言うまでもない。
It (ア plays　イ regular　ウ goes　エ an　オ role　カ without　キ important　ク that　ケ exercise　コ saying) in the stress management.

(5) 我々は皆あなたに会えるのを楽しみにしています。
We are (ア forward　イ looking　ウ seeing　エ all　オ to) you again.

46 次の文を動名詞を用いて書き換えよ。

(1) He is proud that he is rich.
(2) It is impossible to return on the road of life.
(3) Whenever they meet, they quarrel.
(4) I regret that I didn't see the movie.

47 次の文を意味が通るように左右を結びつけよ。

(1) It goes without saying	ア of being poor
(2) You should be careful	イ for reading
(3) I'm not ashamed	ウ skiing and skating
(4) Autumn is the best season	エ that health is above wealth
(5) In winter we enjoy	オ in crossing the road

48 次の各文の下線部が動名詞であるのはどれか。番号で答えよ。

(1) How long have you been studying English?

(2) The girl standing by the door is Mary.

(3) Did you enjoy reading the book?

(4) Picking up a stone, he threw it at the dog.

49 次の各組の文を意味の相違がわかるように和訳せよ。

(1) ① He remembers doing the work today.
② He must remember to do the work today.

(2) ① Miho is sure to pass the exam.
② Miho is sure of passing the exam.

(3) ① He stopped smoking.
② He stopped to smoke.

第2章　動詞

8　分　詞

B

50　次の各文の(　　　)に入る最も適当な語句を1つずつ選べ。

(1) The mother looked (　　　) at the sight.
ア shock　イ shocked　ウ shocking　エ to shock

(2) Amy couldn't make herself (　　　) because of the noise of the approaching train.
ア hear　イ to be heard　ウ heard　エ hearing

(3) I found myself in an (　　　) situation last night.
ア embarrassing　イ embarrassment
ウ embarrassedly　エ embarrass

(4) Many high school students (　　　) a foreign language.
ア interested with　イ interest by
ウ are interesting to　エ have an interest in

(5) My health (　　　), I will spend the coming summer traveling through America.
ア permit　イ permits　ウ permitting
エ being permitted　オ to permit

(6) Please remain (　　　) for another minute.
ア seat　イ seating　ウ seated　エ to seat

(7) We often hear it (　　　) that ours is an essentially tragic age.
ア say　イ to say　ウ said　エ saying

(8) All things (　　　) into consideration, my mother's life was a happy one.
ア taken　イ took　ウ taking　エ take

(9) Look! There's a cat in the house. Someone must have left the door (　　　).
ア be opened　イ to open　ウ open　エ opening

(10) (　　　) so many students chatting, it was impossible to hear what the teacher was trying to say.
ア When　イ With　ウ On　エ Because

51 次の文の(　　　)内の語を適当な形に直せ。

(1) Shuichi has had his wallet (steal).
(2) A (drown) man will catch at a straw.
(3) He takes it for (grant) that people are honest.
(4) Can you make yourself (understand) in French ?
(5) Can you smell something (burn) ?
(6) After a long search, we found the boy (lie) on a sofa in the basement.

52 次の各文を分詞構文を用いて書き換えよ。

(1) The girl was dressed in poor clothes, and she was ashamed of herself.
(2) When Mr. Tanaka arrived at the station, he found his train gone.
(3) When many days had passed, people forgot all about it.
(4) If we judge from the look of the sky, it may rain this afternoon.

53 次の各文の下線部の誤りを１つずつ指摘し，訂正せよ。

(1) The movie was so interested that I couldn't stop laughing.
1 2 3 4

(2) Seeing from the top of the mountain, the lake looks very beautiful.
1 2 3 4

(3) I didn't like yesterday's speech making by the president, but at least
1 2 3
it was nice and short.
4

54 次の文の(　　　)内の語句を並べ換えて意味の通る文にせよ。

(1) She was (place, at, on, appointed, the, time).
(2) Jim (for, me, waiting, an, kept, hour).
(3) I (a parking lot, a terrible time, had, finding).
(4) He (out, without, never, taking, goes, fishing) his son.

55 次の各文の(　　)に入る適当な語句を答えよ。

(1) 彼はとても急いで書いたので，彼の２番目の本は最初の本よりも少しも良くなかった。

His second book, (　　) (　　) (　　) (　　), was not in the least as good as his first one.

(2) 陽が沈んだ後，私たちは夜を通してそこにいた。

The sun (　　) (　　), we stayed there for the night.

(3) 彼はどうしたら良いのかわからなかったので，父にアドバイスを求めた。

(　　) (　　) (　　) (　　) (　　), he asked for his father's advice.

(4) 私は先週自転車を盗まれた。

I (　　) (　　) (　　) (　　) (　　) week.

56 次の(　　)内の語句を並べ換えて英文を完成させよ。ただし，文頭にくるものも小文字で示してある。また，(5)～(7)は不要な語が１つずつ入っている。

(1) 時計は専門店で直してもらったのですか。

(you, your watch, did, at the clock shop, fixed, have)?

(2) 朝９時にこの駅を出る急行があると聞いています。

I hear there is (nine, an, leaving, at, express, this station) in the morning.

(3) ２時間かそこら待たされて，ジムはとても怒っていた。

Jim was very (because, for, he, hours, kept, two, waiting, was, angry) or so.

(4) 私はいつも犬を庭の木につないでおきます。

I (to, keep, always, dog, tied, my) a tree in the garden.

(5) 空席がなかったので立ち続けた。

(no, being, as, seat, vacant, there), I kept standing.

(6) 戸口に立ってはいけません。入るのを待っている人がいます。

Don't stand in the doorway. There are some people (come, who, to, waiting) in.

(7) トムは目を閉じたままベンチに座っていた。

(sitting, a bench, Tom, closed, his, was, on, eyes, in, with).

57 次の日本文を分詞を用いて英訳せよ。

(1) あまりに寒かったので，だれも外に出ていく者はなかった。

(2) 彼はいつもテレビを見ながら勉強する。

C

58 次の英文の(　　　)内から最も適切な語句を選べ。

A cruel battle was (1)(being, been, to have) fought. The ground was covered with dead and (2)(die, dying, have died) men. The air was hot and stifling. The sun (3)(shone, shown, shoned) without pity on the (4)(wound, wounded, winded) soldiers (5)(lying, lieing, laying) in the blood and dust.

One of these soldiers was a nobleman, (6)(who, whom, that) everybody loved for his gentleness and kindness. Yet now he was no (7)(good, better, well) off than the poorest man in the field. He had been wounded, and would die; and he was (8)(suffering, suffered, suffer) much with pain and thirst.

When the battle was (9)(overed, over, overing), his friends hurried to his aid. A soldier came (10)(run, running, to be run) with a cup in his hand. But the nobleman gave the water to another soldier.

第3章　構文

9　関係詞

A

59 次の各組の英文を意味の違いがわかるように和訳せよ。

(1) ① He has two sons who are doctors.
　　② He has two sons, who are doctors.

(2) ① The doll has one eye which is closed.
　　② The doll has one eye, which is closed.

(3) ① He became a magician who surprised us.
　　② He became a magician, which surprised us.

B

60 次の各文の(　　)に入る適当な語句を選び，記号で答えよ。

(1) You can see a hospital (　　) was built many years ago.
　ア it　イ which　ウ who　エ what

(2) The artist (　　) works made the greatest impression on me was Monet.
　ア who　イ which　ウ whose　エ of which

(3) The earth (　　) we live is pulling all nearby objects towards its center.
　ア which　イ where　ウ why　エ what

(4) That is the castle (　　) yesterday.
　ア I talked about　イ which I talked
　ウ which I talked about it　エ about whom I talked

(5) Robert Brown, (　　), has won first prize.
　ア that I was at school with　イ I was at school with
　ウ with who I was at school　エ with whom I was at school

(6) Though he was poor, he did all he (　　) for his son.
　ア had　イ did　ウ could　エ worked

(7) Spring is (　　) leaves and plants start to grow again.
ア when　　イ where　　ウ why　　エ how

(8) They give the map to (　　) is not familiar with the country.
ア whoever　　イ wherever　　ウ whomever　　エ whatever

(9) My brother died of cancer when I was young. That is (　　) I decided to be a doctor.
ア because　　イ why　　ウ how　　エ what

(10) Would you mind repeating (　　) you've just said?
ア what　　イ which　　ウ to which　　エ of which

61 次の(　　)に適する関係詞を補い英文を完成させよ。

(1) He has a friend (　　) name is the same as his.
(2) All the flowers (　　) are blooming in our garden are roses.
(3) (　　) visits Los Angeles goes to Disneyland.
(4) There is no mother (　　) loves her children.
(5) Let me know the time (　　) you'll arrive at the airport.
(6) We stopped at a gas station, (　　) we bought a road map.
(7) (　　) is good for one person is not always good for another.
(8) The man (　　) I thought was her father was actually a visitor.
(9) Jim came home yesterday, (　　) was a pleasant surprise to us.
(10) The treatment of the disease today is different from (　　) it was in the 19th century.

62 次の各組の英文が同じ意味になるよう(　　)に適する語句を入れよ。

(1) Tell me why you told a lie.
Tell me the reason (　　) (　　) you told a lie.

(2) My uncle bought me a nice red dress two weeks ago, but I lost it.
I lost a nice red dress which my uncle (　　) (　　) me two weeks before.

(3) However hard you study, you can't pass the examination.
No (　　) (　　) hard you study, you can't pass the examination.

(4) Whenever they get together, they quarrel.
They (　　) get together (　　) quarreling.

(5) Thanks to that coach the player succeeded.
That coach has made the player (　　) he is now.

63 次の(　　　)内の語を並べ換えて英文を完成させよ。ただし，文頭にくるものも小文字で示してある。

(1) 彼女に私が持っているなけなしのお金をあげた。
I (had, what, her, little, I, gave, money).

(2) 今こそ彼のような偉大な政治家が必要です。
Now (such, when, we, time, the, need, is) a great stateman as he.

(3) 私の知り合いで君ほど有能な人はいない。
There is (efficient, know, I, is, that, nobody, as) as you.

(4) 今日できることを明日まで延ばすべきではありません。
You should not (what, can, put, you, off, till, do, tomorrow) today.

(5) 食べるものがほとんどない人々がいる。
(are, eat, have, little, people, some, there, to, who).

(6) 外国語を習得する手っ取り早い方法は，その言葉が話されている国で数年過ごすことである。
The quickest way (a foreign language, in the country, is, it is, master, several years, spend, to, to, where) spoken.

64 次の各文の下線部のうち，誤りを含むものを指摘し，訂正せよ。

(1) This $\underset{1}{\underline{\text{is}}}$ $\underset{2}{\underline{\text{which}}}$ I $\underset{3}{\underline{\text{have wanted}}}$ $\underset{4}{\underline{\text{for}}}$ a long time.

(2) $\underset{1}{\underline{\text{Do you remember}}}$ $\underset{2}{\underline{\text{the place}}}$ $\underset{3}{\underline{\text{which}}}$ we $\underset{4}{\underline{\text{first met}}}$?

(3) My father $\underset{1}{\underline{\text{gave}}}$ me a book, $\underset{2}{\underline{\text{what}}}$ I $\underset{3}{\underline{\text{found}}}$ very $\underset{4}{\underline{\text{interesting}}}$.

(4) $\underset{1}{\underline{\text{This}}}$ is the athlete $\underset{2}{\underline{\text{whom}}}$ everyone $\underset{3}{\underline{\text{says}}}$ $\underset{4}{\underline{\text{will win}}}$ the gold medal at the Olympic Games.

(5) It $\underset{1}{\underline{\text{was}}}$ $\underset{2}{\underline{\text{the most beautiful picture}}}$ $\underset{3}{\underline{\text{that}}}$ $\underset{4}{\underline{\text{she had}}}$ $\underset{5}{\underline{\text{never seen}}}$ in her life.

65 次の日本文を英訳せよ。

(1) 2か月前に私があなたに貸した本を返して下さい。

(2) わたしたちは彼女を待つより仕方がない。
(All, can do, to wait をそのままの形で用いよ)

C

66 次の英文を和訳せよ。

(1) Water carries body heat to the surface of the skin, where the heat is lost through perspiration.

(2) Patients were asked to let their thoughts wander and say whatever came into their minds.

(3) Helen Keller, an American author and lecturer, who, though physically handicapped, inspired millions with her life of achievement, was born in Alabama in 1880.

(4) It is at the family dinner table that children learn (or don't learn) the table manners that will stay with them throughout their lives.

(5) The large part of our thoughts and feelings that we do not know and cannot control he called the unconscious.

第3章　構文

10　比　　較

A

67　次の各文の(　　　)内に適する語句をあとのア～キから選び，記号で答えよ。

(1)　Five (　　　) three is fifteen.

(2)　Bill is (　　　) of the two boys.

(3)　Come as early (　　　).

(4)　You will look (　　　) in this dress.

(5)　Our lessons will become (　　　) difficult.

ア　more than　　イ　times　　ウ　more and more　　エ　better

オ　the taller　　カ　as I can　　キ　as possible

68　次の文の意味を考えて，下線部を正しい形にせよ。

(1)　The sooner, the happy.

(2)　Mitsuru runs fast in his class.

(3)　To catch the last train, Yuko must come back by 8:00 p.m. at late.

(4)　Everybody thinks Mami is much pretty than Keiko.

(5)　Paris is one of the most beautiful city in the world.

B

69　次の各文の(　　　)に入る適当な語句を選び，記号で答えよ。

(1)　The light travels (　　　) than the sound.

ア　slower　　イ　faster　　ウ　longer　　エ　higher

(2)　She is taller than I am (　　　) a head.

ア　on　　イ　in　　ウ　by　　エ　over

(3)　She works (　　　) than her brother.

ア　much more hardly　　イ　very hardlier

ウ　much more hard　　エ　much harder

(4)　The more you have, (　　　) you want.

ア　do as　　イ　so much　　ウ　more　　エ　the more

(5) Tokyo being first, Geneva is said to have (　　　) cost of living in the world.
ア the second of the　　イ of the second highest
ウ the second highest of the level　　エ the second highest

(6) He knows little of mathematics, (　　　) of physics.
ア still more　　イ still less　　ウ as well　　エ no less than

(7) There're (　　　) girls as boys in this high school.
ア three times as many　　イ three times more
ウ more than three times　　エ three more times

(8) To our surprise, (　　　) 207 students have applied for next week's English test.
ア as many　　イ as many as　　ウ as much as
エ much as　　オ so much

(9) You are not an expert at this (　　　) than I am.
ア no more　　イ so much　　ウ any more　　エ much more

(10) "Mr. Brooks, what should I do to improve my ability to read English ?"
"Tim, first of all, you should read (　　　) you can."
ア as English books many as　　イ as many English books as
ウ English books as many as　　エ many English books as

70 次の各組の英文が同じ意味になるよう(　　　)に適する語句を入れよ。

(1) She is younger than I by three years.
I am three years (　　　) to her.

(2) No other boy in his class is so clever as he.
He is (　　　) (　　　) (　　　) in his class.

(3) This computer is more expensive than that one.
That computer is not (　　　) expensive (　　　) this one.

(4) I will go there no more.
I won't go there (　　　) more.

(5) I have never seen such a fine picture as this.
This is (　　　) (　　　) picture I have ever seen.

(6) He saved as much as one million yen.
He saved no (　　　) than one million yen.

(7) He is not so foolish as to lend money to a man like that.
He knows (　　　) (　　　) to lend money to a man like that.

71 次の各文の下線部のうち，誤りを含むものを指摘し，訂正せよ。

(1) I suppose[1] the boy is very[2] younger than[3] my brother[4].

(2) Japan is said to be[1] more safe[2] than any[3] other country[4] in the world.

(3) You are the[1] kindest[2] person I've[3] never[4] met.

(4) I am as anxious to hear[1] the election[2] results than[3] you are[4].

72 次の(　　　)内の語句を正しい順序に並べ換えよ。ただし，文頭にくるものも小文字で示してある。

(1) 富士山が日本で一番高い山だ。
No (is, other, Mt. Fuji, than, higher, mountain in Japan).

(2) アルバイトで彼女は私の３倍稼ぐ。
She (three, much as, times, as, earns, I) do at her part-time job.

(3) タクシーで行くくらいなら歩いた方がましだ。
(walk, by taxi, would, than, I, go, rather).

(4) ダイエットするとは，体重を減らすために普段より少なく食べることです。
If you go on a diet, (less, eat, usual, food, you, than) in order to lose weight.

(5) 私も名選手というわけではないが，彼だって同じだ。
He is (a, player, more, good, no) than I am.

(6) その本を読んだら，思っていたよりずっとおもしろかった。
I found (book, much, had, more, the, interesting, I, than) expected.

(7) 彼ほどの正直者はこの世にいません。[不要な語を１つ含む]
He's as (man, lived, a, as, ever, so, honest).

(8) 湖はこの地点が一番深い。[不要な語を１つ含む]
The lake (at, deepest, this, is, the, point).

73 次の英文を和訳せよ。

(1) She can paint much better than she could last year.

(2) My income is twice as large as yours.

(3) Try to swim as fast as possible.

(4) Sooner or later the flowers will be opening.

(5) Americans are less likely than Japanese, for example, to feel middle-aged once they reach a certain age.

(6) Soon computers will be smarter than we mere human beings, at least in some ways. And at the leading position of this computer revolution are Japan and America, each racing to develop more intelligent computers.

74 次の日本文を英訳せよ。

(1) あの女の子はクラスの誰よりも泳ぎがうまい。[比較級を使って]

(2) ゴミを減らす効果的な方法をできるだけ早く見つけなければならない。

第3章　構文

11　接続詞

A

75　次の各文の(　　　)に入る適当な語句をあとの**ア**～**コ**から選び，記号で答えよ。ただし同じ語を2度使ってはいけない。

(1)　Please do your homework (　　　) I am cleaning.
(2)　We couldn't go hiking (　　　) it was raining.
(3)　I have been playing tennis (　　　) I was ten years old.
(4)　The milkman comes to the house (　　　) I get up, so I never see him.
(5)　(　　　) you study hard, you will succeed.
(6)　He lost his money, (　　　) he couldn't buy a present for his mother.
(7)　He said (　　　) he was going to visit his grandfather.
(8)　It is raining heavily, (　　　) I must go.
(9)　You'll never make it (　　　) you try.
(10)　The doctor got up, (　　　) then he went to the hospital immediately.

ア　since　　**イ**　if　　**ウ**　while　　**エ**　unless
オ　because　　**カ**　before　　**キ**　that　　**ク**　so
ケ　and　　**コ**　but

76　次の各文の(　　　)に，and, or, for, so, nor のいずれかを入れよ。

(1)　Are you going to Tokyo by Shinkansen (　　　) by plane ?
(2)　She was very amiable, (　　　) I employed her.
(3)　Twist the handle to the right, (　　　) hot water will come out.
(4)　I have not seen him, (　　　) have I heard of him.
(5)　I am very thirsty, (　　　) I ran all the way.

B

77 次の各組の英文が同じ意味になるよう(　　)に適する語句を入れよ。

(1) Stop smoking, (　　) you will die of lung cancer.
(　　) you stop smoking, you will die of lung cancer.

(2) This problem is too difficult for me to solve.
This problem is (　　) difficult (　　) I (　　) solve (　　).

(3) As soon as he opened the cage, the bird flew out of it.
No (　　) had he opened the cage than the bird flew out of it.

(4) I never speak English without making a mistake.
(　　) I speak English, I make a mistake.

(5) I brought my watch to the store in order to have it fixed.
I brought my watch to the store so (　　) I (　　) have it fixed.

(6) I am sure of his winning the race.
I am sure (　　) (　　) will win the race.

(7) Jack went out in spite of the heavy rain.
Jack went out (　　) it was (　　) (　　).

78 次の各文の(　　)に入る適当な語句をあとのア～サから選び，記号で答えよ。

(1) (　　) hard you may try, you won't win her heart.
(2) It was not long (　　) the conductor appeared again.
(3) We don't know the value of health (　　) we lose it.
(4) Not only I (　　) also my wife was warmly welcomed.
(5) Make another mistake, (　　) you'll be disqualified.

ア Wherever　イ Whenever　ウ However　エ but
オ after　カ until　キ before　ク as
ケ because　コ and　サ or

79 次の各文の(　　)に入る適当な語句を選び，記号で答えよ。

(1) If it (　　) tomorrow, I will stay home.
ア rain　イ rains　ウ will rain　エ would rain

(2) The food on the plane was (　　) bad that I couldn't eat it.
ア too　イ so　ウ such　エ quite

(3) Any book will do as (　　) as it is interesting.
ア only　イ if　ウ long　エ far

(4) The (　　　) he heard the news, he turned pale.
　ア sooner　　イ instance　　ウ time　　エ moment
(5) I am not sure (　　　) he will come late or not.
　ア what　　イ whom　　ウ if　　エ which
(6) (　　　) you are pregnant, you have to eat for two.
　ア Not only　　イ Now that　　ウ In order that　　エ The sooner

80 日本文の意味に合うように次の(　　　)内の語を並べ換えよ。ただし，文頭にくるものも小文字で示してある。
(1) 彼女はとても急いでいたので，私と立ち話できなかった。
　She was (in, a, that, such, hurry) she couldn't stop to talk with me.
(2) 父はもうすぐよくなるでしょう。
　(be, it, my father, long, not, will, before) gets well.
(3) その時になってはじめて私はその危険な状況に気がついた。
　Not (then, the danger, I, till, realize, of, did) the situation.
(4) メアリは１年間メキシコに住んでいたけれども，スペイン語を学ばなかった。
　Mary didn't learn Spanish even (in, she, Mexico, though, lived) for a year.
(5) バスに乗り遅れることのないよう，早く行きなさい。
　(that, leave, won't, the bus, early, so, miss, you).

81 次の各文に続く文として適当なものをそれぞれあとの**ア**～**オ**，**カ**～**コ**より選び，記号で答えよ。
(1) He was very proud when
(2) I think I dropped the letter
(3) The batteries have run out,
(4) The ice cream is in the freezer
(5) I can hardly remember
　ア where it won't melt.
　イ the first house I lived in.
　ウ as I was getting out of the car.
　エ his father appeared on TV.
　オ so I can't listen to my personal stereo.
(6) I like him all the better
(7) You should do
(8) Do not put off till tomorrow
(9) Once you have made up your mind

(10) Scarcely had he said so

カ what you can do today.

キ you should do your best.

ク for his faults.

ケ before he began to cry.

コ as you are told.

82 次の各文の下線部の語の用法と同じものを選び，記号で答えよ。

(1) As I know, he is a man of ability.

ア Do as you are told.

イ Rich as he is, he is not happy.

ウ He came into the room as I was sleeping.

エ He treated me as a child.

(2) The study have shown the fact that 80% of mothers hold their infants in their left arms.

ア I need the book that you bought yesterday.

イ He said that you were right.

ウ Who lives in that house ?

エ We cannot change his belief that he is right.

83 次の英文を和訳せよ。

(1) As a result of these and of other pollutants, some lakes and rivers have become so contaminated that the fish in them die.

(2) Learning to write kanji had always been the center of Japanese education and ought to be continued no matter what machines are invented.

84 次の各文をあとの指示に従って書き換えよ。

(1) Not only you but also he was surprised at the news.

［as well as を用いて］

(2) She is believed to have known the fact. ［It～ を書き出しに］

(3) As soon as he went to bed, he heard the strange sound.

［下線部を on を用いて］

第3章 構文

12 仮定法

A

85 次の各文を仮定法を使って書き換えよ。

(1) Since I have no money, I cannot buy my own house.
(2) I'm sorry that I did not propose marriage to her.
(3) As I didn't know your address, I did not write to you.

86 次の英文を和訳せよ。

(1) But for her careful nursing, he would have died.
(2) If it had not been for your advice, I should have made a great mistake.
(3) I was busy, otherwise I would have called you.

B

87 次の各文の(　　　)の動詞を適当な形に変えよ。

(1) If I (have) a car, I could have taken you for a drive.
(2) He speaks as if he (be) an Englishman.
(3) I wish I (realize) earlier how seriously ill my mother was.
(4) It is high time we (stop) working.
(5) Had he (know) my trouble, he would have helped me.

88 次の各組の英文が同じ意味になるよう(　　　)に適する語句を入れよ。

(1) {But for your help, he would not be successful.
If it (　　　) (　　　) (　　　) your help, he would not be successful.

(2) {Without your help, I would have been killed in the accident.
If it (　　　) (　　　) (　　　) for your help, I would have been killed in the accident.

(3) {I am sorry you did not tell me the truth.
I wish you (　　　) (　　　) me the truth.

(4) His attendance at the party would have encouraged them.
(　　) he (　　) attended the party, they would have been encouraged.

(5) This medicine will make you feel better.
(　　) you take this medicine, you will feel better.

(6) I'm sorry it won't stop raining.
If only it (　　) (　　) raining!

89 次の各文の(　　)に入る適当な語句を選び，記号で答えよ。

(1) Had your father wanted to go to the cinema yesterday, he (　　) you.
ア told　イ had told　ウ would tell　エ would have told

(2) (　　) more diligence, you could have succeeded in the project.
ア If you had　イ After　ウ If you have had　エ With

(3) If anything (　　) happen, please let me know.
ア should　イ would　ウ might　エ must

(4) I felt (　　) they were cheating me.
ア as far as　イ as though　ウ even if　エ if any

(5) If I had followed your advice, I (　　) in bad health now.
ア won't be　イ wouldn't be　ウ wouldn't have been
エ wouldn't been

(6) I suggested (　　) go for it.
ア him to　イ for him to　ウ that he　エ on him to

(7) If she had enough time, she (　　) a boat to China.
ア takes　イ will take　ウ would take　エ could have taken

90 次の(　　)内の語句を日本文と同じ意味になるように並べ換えよ。ただし，文頭にくるものも小文字で示してある。

(1) あなたは，もっと早く私にそのことを知らせるべきであった。
You (have, to, should, it, tell, come) to me earlier.

(2) 彼らは仕事の量を抑えて，子供と過ごす時間をもう少し作った方が良かっただろうに。
They would have been happier if they had been able to work (more, with, to, spend, less, time, and) their children.

(3) アケミがその事実を知っていたらどうしていただろうか。
(what, Akemi, done, I, have, wonder, would) if she had known the fact.

(4) 万一デイビッドの妻が亡くなったら，一体彼はどうなるだろう。
(what would, David, were to, become of, if, his wife) die ?

91 次の各文の(　　　)に適当な語句を補い英文を完成させよ。
(1) 彼が話すのを聞けば，あの人を日本人だと思うだろう。
(　　　) (　　　) (　　　) talk, you would take him for a Japanese.
(2) 水がなくては生きられない。
(　　　) it not for water, we couldn't live.
(3) 彼はいわば私の腹心の友だ。
He is, (　　　) (　　　) (　　　), my second self.
(4) 彼女はなんでも知っているような口ぶりだ。
She talks as if she (　　　) everything.

92 次の英文を和訳せよ。
(1) To speak more politely, you would do well.
(2) Provided that you are free, come to see me.
(3) We can begin to understand the importance of electricity by picturing what would happen if all electric current was shut off. Lights would go out; electric tools and machines would stop. Electric trains and streetcars would not run.
(4) An epidemic of yellow fever nearly prevented the building of the Panama Canal. If it hadn't been for three determined doctors, cargo ships might still have to sail all the way down around the tip of South America to get from the Atlantic to the Pacific Oceans.

93 次の日本文を英訳せよ。
(1) 彼らはまるで幽霊でも見たような顔をしていた。
(2) もし私に妹がいれば，とても幸せなのですが。
(3) 彼がまだ生きていればなあと思います。

第3章　構文

13　話　　法

A

94 次の各文の(　　　)に入る適当な語句を選び，記号で答えよ。

(1) John (　　　) he would come the next day.
ア said that　イ said me that　ウ told that　エ told to me that

(2) Mary said that (　　　) that movie three times.
ア I have seen　イ she has seen　ウ she saw　エ she had seen

(3) Mr. and Mrs. Smith got very upset when their daughter told them that she (　　　) drop out of school.
ア is going to　イ shall　ウ will　エ would

(4) My father told me that honesty (　　　) the best policy.
ア is　イ has been　ウ was　エ had been

95 次の各組の英文が同じ意味になるよう(　　　)に適する語句を入れよ。

(1) He said to me, “I will take you to the theater.”
He told me that (　　　) (　　　) take (　　　) to the theater.

(2) Ken said to me, “Do you know how far it is to the station ?”
Ken asked me (　　　) (　　　) (　　　) how far it was to the station.

(3) Nancy said to him, “Come and see me once in a while.”
Nancy told him (　　　) come and see (　　　) once in a while.

(4) She said to me, “I was going to visit you on that day.”
She told me that she (　　　) (　　　) going to visit me on that day.

(5) He said to me, “What time did you eat lunch ?”
He asked me what time (　　　) (　　　) (　　　) lunch.

(6) She said to me, “Don’t drink too much.”
She advised me (　　　) to drink too much.

(7) He said to me, “Did you watch the program on TV (　　　) ?”
He (　　　) me (　　　) I had watched the program on TV the previous day.

96 次の英文を下線部に注意して和訳せよ。

(1) He said that he would be sixteen the following year.

(2) Mike said that he had met her on the previous day.

(3) The teacher said that time flies like an arrow.

B

97 次の各文を間接話法に書き換えよ。

(1) Ken said, "I met this girl yesterday."

(2) He said to her, "May I use your camera ?"

(3) She said to me, "Where are you going ?"

(4) The doctor said to me, "Don't smoke too much."

98 次の各文を直接話法に書き換えよ。

(1) Today she said it would rain tomorrow.

(2) Jack told me that he had been to Europe five times.

(3) She asked me if I wanted that.

(4) I asked them to come at five o'clock.

99 次の英文の話法を変えよ。

(1) She said to him, "Will you have some coffee ?"

(2) I said to her, "Have you ever been abroad ?"

(3) I asked my brother what was the matter with him.

(4) He said to me, "Never forget that knowledge is power."

100 次の(　　　)内の語句を正しい順序に並べ換えよ。

(1) 彼は彼女がここにいてくれたらなあと言った。
He said (she, wished, that, there, were, he).

(2) He said to me, "God bless you !"
He prayed (bless, to, me, God).

(3) I said to him, "Work hard and you'll succeed."
I told him (work, and, to, would, succeed, he, hard).

(4) "Would you mind moving your car ?" said the lady.
The lady (me, move, asked, my car, to).

(5) He said, "Let's not say anything about it till we hear the facts."
He (not, suggested, anything, saying) about it till they heard the facts.

101 次の英文の話法を換え，和訳せよ。(2)は下線部のみ話法転換すること。

(1) He ordered them to go away and come back to him in an hour.

(2) I asked him how he liked it. “Terrible,” was his answer. “I couldn’t get a nice cup of tea anywhere. Thank goodness I’m back.” I asked him whether he hadn’t had any good food while he was there.

102 次の日本文を，直接話法を用いて英訳せよ。

(1) 「彼女の名前を知っていますか」と彼は私に言った。

(2) 「時間を浪費してはいけないよ」と父は私たちに言う。

103 **102** の日本文を，間接話法を用いて英訳せよ。

第3章　構文

14　特殊構文

A

104 次の各文の(　　)内から適する語句を選び，英文を完成させよ。

(1) He was too tired to go (any, more, still) farther.

(2) (None, Anyone, Everyone) but fools would believe such nonsense.

(3) "I can't use a computer." "(No, Both, Nor, Not) can I."

(4) Last Sunday Harry didn't go to church; nor (do, done, did, had, done) his sister.

(5) It was you who (are, is, was, were) wrong.

(6) I am (at, in, to, by) no means angry with you.

105 次の各文で省略できる部分を指摘せよ。

(1) The house was sold while it was being built.

(2) Correct the errors, if there are any errors.

(3) She is not so happy as she was happy.

(4) This is the reason why I came.

106 日本文に合うように，次の(　　)に適語を記入せよ。

(1) 彼は嘘をつくような人ではない。
He is the (　　) person to tell a lie.

(2) 「彼の病気はすぐ治りそうですか。」「そうはいかないようです。」
"Will he recover soon?" "I'm (　　) (　　)."

(3) 「映画を見に行きませんか。」「ぜひ行きたいです。」
"Would you like to go to the movies?" "I'd love (　　)."

(4) 私は彼女の兄弟をどちらも知っているわけではない。
I don't know (　　) of her brothers.

B

107 次の各組の英文が同じ意味になるよう(　　)に適する語句を入れよ。

(1) Whenever he went on a business trip, he took his wife with him.
He (　　) went on a business trip (　　) taking his wife with him.

(2) Everybody knows that.
(　　) does not know that?

(3) Why do you think so?
(　　) (　　) you think so?

(4) It's none of your business.
(　　) your own business.
It has (　　) (　　) (　　) with you.

(5) It snowed so much that the train couldn't leave the town.
The snow (　　) the train from leaving the town.

(6) We came to the museum after we walked for a few minutes.
A few minutes' walk (　　) us to the museum.

(7) Danny speaks French well.
Danny is a (　　) (　　) of French.

108 次の各文を，下線部を強調した文に書き換えよ。

(1) I had no doubt about it.
(2) John made the big kennel.
(3) Hiroko informed you of her arrival.

109 次の各文を，それぞれあとの指示に従って書き換えよ。

(1) As soon as he saw the policeman, he ran away. [Scarcely で始めて]
(2) Helen played the violin, so did Bob. [否定文に]
(3) I didn't know her name until yesterday. [下線部を強調して]

110 次の(　　)内の語句を日本文と同じ意味になるように並べ換えよ。ただし，文頭にくるものも小文字で示してある。

(1) 彼女が来ようとは夢にも思わなかった。
(I, did, imagine, little, that) she would come.

(2) 彼女は歳よりうんと若く見せようとした。
She (she, really, tried, much, to, younger, was, look, than).

(3) まもなくテッドは戻ってきます。
It (long, Ted, won't, before, back, be, comes).

(4) 彼は子供だが，その問題に答えることができる。
(he is, can, as, the question, he, child, answer, ,).

(5) 彼は病気のためにその会合に出席できませんでした。
(illness, his, him, the, prevented, meeting, attending, from).

(6) うちの子をかんだのはその犬です。
It is (my, the, that, bit, dog) child.

111 次の各文の間違いを訂正せよ。

(1) "I'm not good at playing music." "Nor do I."

(2) Her sad face made me feeling very unhappy.

(3) He doesn't work in this office no longer.

(4) Hardly he hung up when the door bell rang.

112 次の英文を和訳せよ。

(1) Great was Mother's joy when she saw me safely back.

(2) Not all Japanese are rich, however, and most of the middle-class people lead lives that are inferior in quality to those of well-off Americans and Europeans.

(3) You cannot locate the important words without trying to understand the sentences in which they appear.

(4) To her surprise, the boss accepted her offer.

113 次の日本文を英訳せよ。

(1) あんな話はほとんど信じられない。

(2) 一度も海外へ行ったことはない。［Never で始めて］

(3) 暗くなりかけていたし，さらに悪いことには，雨が降りだした。

第4章　品詞

15　前置詞

A

114　次の(　　)に適する語句をそれぞれあとの**ア**～**オ**，**カ**～**コ**から選び，記号で答えよ。なお，(1)～(5)は各組の英文に共通したものが入る。

(1) { One of my nephews came to my house and asked (　　) my advice.
　　His eldest son applied (　　) a position in the company.

(2) { He insists (　　) going there by himself.
　　(　　) an average I go to the movies once a month.

(3) { He was (　　) a hurry to let them know the accident.
　　She looks young for her age, but (　　) fact she is forty.

(4) { Nothing has resulted (　　) his efforts.
　　England is separated (　　) France by the sea.

(5) { The happy news filled my heart (　　) joy.
　　I am going to stay (　　) my aunt for a few days.

ア in　　**イ** on　　**ウ** for　　**エ** with　　**オ** from

(6) I had to drive very slowly (　　) the fog.

(7) I failed (　　) all my efforts.

(8) A car parked (　　) your house.

(9) He wants to go to Germany (　　) studying music.

(10) We use electricity for cooking (　　) gas.

カ in spite of　　**キ** instead of　　**ク** with a view to
ケ in front of　　**コ** because of

115 次の(　　)に適する語句を補い英文を完成させよ。

(1) Does the building belong (　　) your school?
(2) Life is compared (　　) a voyage.
(3) I go to school (　　) foot every day.
(4) He is older than you (　　) two years.
(5) She played the piano in the afternoon instead (　　) playing tennis.
(6) I happened to see him (　　) my way home.
(7) He spends a lot of money (　　) books.
(8) Something is wrong (　　) this telephone.
(9) I was absent from school (　　) account of illness.
(10) He went to school (　　) spite (　　) his illness.
(11) According (　　) today's newspaper, there was an accident in Kobe.
(12) Africa is suffering (　　) famine.
(13) He has a lot of friends to play (　　).
(14) Take an umbrella (　　) you in case it should rain.
(15) He graduated (　　) Tokyo University.
(16) Cows provide us (　　) milk.
(17) The work is (　　) much importance to them.
(18) Cherry blossoms are (　　) full bloom now.

116 次の各文の(　　)に入る最も適当な語をあとのア～コから選び，記号で答えよ。ただし，同じ語を何度使ってもよい。

(1) We left our children (　　) the charge of the nurse.
(2) Are you for or (　　) the plan?
(3) He is not content (　　) all his wealth.
(4) Do you think she broke the dish (　　) purpose?
(5) I don't know what has become (　　) the man.
(6) I am very anxious (　　) my son's health.
(7) He met (　　) a traffic accident on his way to the station.
(8) I prefer living in the country (　　) living in the city.
(9) Today we can't do (　　) television.
(10) She visited her husband in the hospital every day (　　) Sunday.

ア about	イ against	ウ for	エ in	オ of
カ but	キ on	ク to	ケ with	コ without

B

117 次の各文について，下線部が[　　　]内の語に最も近い意味を表すように，(　　　)に入れる最も適当な語をあとの**ア**～**サ**から選び，記号で答えよ。

(1) He answered the question (　　　) ease. [easily]

(2) He will go (　　　) speaking until tomorrow. [continue]

(3) Did you ask (　　　) an interview with Mr. Jones? [request]

(4) Some people are always finding fault (　　　) others. [criticize]

(5) His way of thinking is (　　　) date. [old-fashioned]

ア down　**イ** for　**ウ** in　**エ** off　**オ** on　**カ** out of
キ over　**ク** through　**ケ** to　**コ** up　**サ** with

118 次の各組の英文が同じ意味になるよう(　　　)に適する語句をあとの**ア**～**コ**から選び，それぞれ記号で答えよ。

(1) He is very honest, and so he wouldn't tell a lie.
He is (　　　) telling a lie.

(2) Please take care of my baby during my absence.
Please look (　　　) my baby during my absence.

(3) The boy kept holding a heavy stone.
The boy went (　　　) holding a heavy stone.

(4) We talked about it while we drank coffee.
We talked about it (　　　) a cup of coffee.

(5) He is happy to get married to an angelic wife.
He is happy to get married to an angel (　　　) a wife.

(6) The problem they are discussing now is very difficult.
The problem (　　　) discussion is very difficult.

(7) Twelve countries said 'Yes', but two said 'No'.
Twelve countries were (　　　) favor, but two were against.

(8) Her father persuaded her that she should accept the proposal.
Her father persuaded her (　　　) accepting the proposal.

(9) The work is rather easy, and I can do it.
The work is rather easy, and is (　　　) my power.

(10) As for me, that's all right.
(　　　) me, that's all right.

ア on　**イ** under　**ウ** above　**エ** in　**オ** with
カ into　**キ** after　**ク** over　**ケ** within　**コ** of

119 次の(　　　)に適切な語（前置詞など）を補い英文を完成させよ。

(1) マイクはオックスフォード大学の学生です。
Mike is a student (　　　) Oxford University.

(2) 正雄は，私の肩をポンとたたいた。
Masao patted me (　　　) the shoulder.

(3) シルヴィアと婚約中です。
I'm engaged (　　　) Silvia.

(4) 来月，医者と結婚することになっています。
I'm going to get married (　　　) a doctor next month.

(5) 私の部屋の鍵《かぎ》どこかしら。
Where's the key (　　　) my room, I wonder?

120 次の文中の(①)～(⑳)に適する語をそれぞれあとのア～シから選び，記号で答えよ。ただし，同じ語を2度以上使ってもよい。また，文頭にくるものも小文字で示してある。

This summer I went back (①) the United States to visit my family and friends. I flew (②) my wife and two children (③) Narita to Los Angeles (④) United Airlines. From L.A. we flew (⑤) Chicago. There we visited my mother and father. They live (⑥) a small apartment (⑦) 30 minutes (⑧) downtown Chicago. While we were there we went to the Lincoln Park Zoo and also went swimming (⑨) Lake Michigan.

(⑩) visiting my parents, we flew (⑪) Orlando, Florida and went (⑫) Disney World. We stayed there (⑬) three and a half days, (⑭) we couldn't see all that we wanted to see. There were (⑮) many things. We left Orlando (⑯) Thursday and flew to L.A. We went shopping and bought clothes (⑰) ourselves and souvenirs to take back to our friends (⑱) Japan. (⑲) we arrived in Narita, we were very tired (⑳) glad to be home.

ア about　イ after　ウ and　エ but　オ for　カ from
キ in　ク on　ケ to　コ too　サ when　シ with

121 次の日本文と同じ意味の英文となるように，文中の（ ① ）～（ ④ ）に適する語をあとのア～コから選び，記号で答えよ。

19世紀の中葉まで，徳川幕府による長い鎖国のために，日本は科学技術の面で西欧にずいぶん遅れをとっていた。

By the middle of the nineteenth century the long period of isolation (①) Tokugawa rule had (②) Japan technologically (③) (④) the West.

ア behind　イ very　ウ left　エ of　オ gave
カ back　キ late　ク far　ケ with　コ under

122 次の各文の下線部とほぼ同じ意味となるものを，あとのア～エから選び，記号で答えよ。

(1) We were having a pleasant conversation when Tom cut in.
ア interrupted　イ called　ウ appeared　エ disappointed

(2) The company has hard and fast rules against lateness.
ア many　イ difficult　ウ strict　エ flexible

(3) I wish you would make up your mind quickly.
ア decide　イ remember　ウ think
エ change your opinion

(4) Henry takes after his grandfather a lot.
ア follows　イ resembles　ウ misses　エ admires

(5) Please stand by me whenever I'm in trouble.
ア remember　イ rely on　ウ support　エ talk with

123 次の各文の下線部の意味として適切なものをあとのア～エより選び，記号で答えよ。

(1) The game was put off because of rain.
ア canceled　イ interrupted　ウ postponed　エ shortened

(2) It was out of the question for them to go against traditions.
ア brave　イ doubtful　ウ impossible　エ unusual

(3) The stars in the American flag stand for the states.
ア describe　イ display　ウ represent　エ reveal

(4) Honesty is the best policy in the long run.
ア certainly　イ eventually　ウ frequently　エ gradually

(5) She was asked to account for her conduct.
ア examine　イ excuse　ウ explain　エ express

(6) He promised to do it right away.
ア carefully　イ correctly　ウ immediately　エ successfully

124 次の各文の下線部とほぼ同じ意味となるものを，あとのア～エから選び，記号で答えよ。

(1) Don't be taken in by products claiming to help you lose weight in a week.

ア believed　イ deceived　ウ expected　エ pleased

(2) Kate used to get around Europe quite a lot when she was younger.

ア introduce　イ live in　ウ paint　エ travel in

(3) Once one has taken up the habit, smoking is very difficult to give up.

ア abandon　イ continue　ウ follow　エ treat

(4) On second thought, I've decided not to go with you.

ア After reconsideration　イ Under no obligation

ウ Upon receipt　エ Well in advance

(5) This table is really heavy. Can you give me a hand with it?

ア catch me　イ drive me　ウ help me　エ need me

第4章　品詞

16　形容詞

A

125 次の単語の形容詞を答えよ。

(1) anxiety　(2) strength　(3) maturity　(4) mystery
(5) importance　(6) hunger　(7) succeed

126 次の各文の(　　)に入る適当な語句を選び，記号で答えよ。

(1) A：What is your (　　) music?
B：I like rock'n'roll very much.
ア favorite　イ likely　ウ nice　エ exciting

(2) A：Hello. May I speak to Mr. Smith?
B：I'm afraid you have the (　　) number.
ア mistake　イ lost　ウ wrong　エ right

(3) A：I couldn't catch what he said.
B：Yes. He spoke too (　　).
ア quick　イ soon　ウ early　エ fast

(4) A：Oh no! It's already 8 o'clock. Why didn't you wake me up?
B：I woke you up (　　) times.
ア some　イ any　ウ many　エ no

(5) She looked quite (　　).
ア happy　イ happily　ウ happiness

(6) There aren't (　　) books on the shelf.
ア any　イ some　ウ no

(7) He also added a small moustache to look like a much (　　) man.
ア oldest　イ old　ウ older

(8) I feel very hot, so I want (　　).
ア cold something　イ something cold　ウ something to cold

(9) The camera was too (　　) for me to buy.
ア high　イ expensive　ウ cheap

B

127 意味の違いに気をつけて次の各語句および文を和訳せよ。

(1) the present mayor　　The mayor was present.
(2) a certain man　　It is certain that he will come.
(3) my late father　　My father was late.
(4) I have few friends in Japan.　　I have a few friends in Japan.

128 次の英文の(　　)の中から正しい語句を選べ。

(1) I have no bills, but I have (a few, few) coins.
(2) The sick boy looks very (good, well) today.
(3) Open your books to page (fifth, five).
(4) There were only a (small, little) number of students in the class.
(5) Take good care of (alive, living) things.

129 次の日本文と同じ意味の英文になるように，文中の(①)～(⑩)に適する語をあとの**ア**～**ス**から選び，記号で答えよ。

もしも諸君が百年前に歴史を学んでいたとすれば，古代エジプトについてはほとんど時間をかけないで終ったであろう。というのは，古代エジプト人があとに残した文字を解読できなかったので，歴史家たちが古代エジプトについてあまり知らなかったからである。エジプトはたいへん興味のある国であるから，大きな損をしたことになったであろう。巨大なピラミッド，不可思議なスフィンクス，そのほか古代エジプトにおける魅力ある生活の遺跡は語るべき物語をもっているからである。

If you (①) been studying history a century ago, you would (②) spent very little time (③) ancient Egypt, for historians (④) little about it (⑤) they could not read the writing that the ancient Egyptians (⑥) behind them. You would have (⑦) a great deal, for Egypt is a most interesting country. The (⑧) pyramids, the (⑨) sphinx, and other (⑩) remains of life in ancient Egypt have a story to tell.

ア knew　**イ** left　**ウ** large　**エ** had
オ mysterious　**カ** on　**キ** for　**ク** since
ケ have　**コ** huge　**サ** missed　**シ** in
ス fascinating

130 次の各文の下線部の語とほぼ同じ意味の語をあとのア～コから1つずつ選び，記号で答えよ。

(1) These dishes are quite fragile. Be careful with them!

(2) They eat a moderate amount of food.

(3) I heard a remarkable story yesterday.

(4) Mr. Brown is easily recognizable by his bald head.

(5) Jack has always remained loyal to his family.

ア clear　イ delicate　ウ faithful　エ identifiable
オ liberal　カ adequate　キ moral　ク weak
ケ surprising

131 次の英文の（ ① ）～（ ⑩ ）に入る最も適切なものをあとのア～コから選び，記号で答えよ。ただし，文頭にくるものも小文字で示してある。

The（ ① ）means of communication that humans have is words.（ ② ）animals are able to communicate with words, of course, but（ ③ ）animals are able to communicate with（ ④ ）another.

Bees have a fantastic ability to communicate. When they return to the hive, they do a dance that tells the（ ⑤ ）bees what kind of flowers they have found, how far away they are, and so on.

Many people believe that their pet dog can understand（ ⑥ ）language. Actually, what dogs learn is what certain tones of voice mean, not the（ ⑦ ）words. An interesting thing is that（ ⑧ ）animals, such as cats and dogs, have learned how to communicate with their masters. They beg for food, or mew until a door is opened. But（ ⑨ ）animals do not seem able to express their desires, such as begging for food from（ ⑩ ）other.

ア domestic　イ chief　ウ human　エ each
オ other　カ many　キ wild　ク actual
ケ no　コ one

132 次の日本文と同じ意味の英文となるように，文中の（ ① ）～（ ⑤ ）に適する語をあとの**ア**～**カ**から選び，記号で答えよ。

今日，環境破壊がたいへん速いペースで地球的な規模になっている。肥沃な土地が年間６万平方キロメートルの割合で不毛の砂漠に変わっている。破壊される熱帯林の面積は，毎年11万平方キロメートル以上に及ぶ。

Today environmental destruction is becoming（ ① ）at a very rapid pace.（ ② ）lands are（ ③ ）into barren deserts at the rate of sixty thousand square km per year. The area of（ ④ ）forests which is being（ ⑤ ）is more than one hundred and ten thousands square km per year.

ア destroyed　**イ** destructive　**ウ** fertile　**エ** global
オ tropical　**カ** turning

第4章　品詞

17　副　　詞

A

133 次の(　　)に適する語句を補い英文を完成させよ。

(1) あなたが行かないのなら僕も行かない。1人で出かけるほどバカじゃない。
If you do not go, I will not (　　). I know (　　) than to go alone.

(2) 第1案はあきらめねばならない。
The first plan must be given (　　).

(3) 彼女は教会へ行くことはめったにない。
She (　　) goes to church.

(4) 彼女には欠点があるからなおいっそう好きだ。
I love her (　　) the better for her faults.

134 次の各組の英文が同じ意味になるよう(　　)に適する語句を入れよ。

(1) Mr. Tanaka speaks German (　　).
Mr. Tanaka is a fluent (　　) of German.

(2) He is not too poor to own a car.
He is rich (　　) (　　) own a car.

135 次の各文の(　　)に入る適当な副詞をあとの**ア**～**キ**から選び，記号で答えよ。

(1) My aunt left hospital a few days (　　).
(2) It is (　　) interesting to read this book.
(3) He is (　　) obliged to you.
(4) It is (　　) seven o'clock, but Taro has not come (　　).
(5) My mother is (　　) working in the kitchen.
(6) I have heard it (　　).

ア very　　**イ** much　　**ウ** still　　**エ** already
オ yet　　**カ** ago　　**キ** before

136 次の各組の文を意味の違いがわかるように和訳せよ。

(1) ① She looks very well today.
　　② She sings very well today.

(2) ① I made it pretty well last night.
　　② Make yourself pretty.

(3) ① Has your father started yet?
　　② Has your father started already?

(4) ① She studies English hard.
　　② It is hard to study English.

B

137 次の(　①　)～(　⑤　)に適する語句をあとの**ア～エ**から選び，記号で答えよ。ただし，同じ語を2回以上使ってもよい。また，文頭にくるものも小文字で示してある。

London has one of the (　①　) efficient taxi services in the world —— 15,000 drivers operate 11,000 licensed cabs. (　②　) people than ever are using taxis at the moment, since the prices of other forms of public transport have risen (　③　) faster than those of taxis. Because of this, taxis make (　④　) use of taxi ranks than they did a few years ago, and are (　⑤　) frequently hailed in the street.

ア much　　**イ** more　　**ウ** most　　**エ** less

138 次の日本文を英訳せよ。

(1) 私はまだパンダを見たことがない。

(2) 幸運にも彼はその試験に合格することができた。

(3) 私はサッカーにはあまり興味がない。

C

139 次の英文を和訳せよ。

After many dangers, his ship ran aground and he had to leave his ship. But fortunately he could get to the shore of a small island.

140 次の英文の適当な位置に文末の[　　　]内の副詞を入れよ。

(1) All the boys were in the room. [almost]

(2) The boy knows the alphabet well. [enough]

(3) He spoke fast. [surprisingly]

(4) Will you go to see him this evening? [off]

(5) We spend our holidays at the seaside. [always]

(6) She was kind to show me the way to the school. [enough]

第4章　品詞

18 代名詞

A

141 次の各文の(　　　)に入る適当な語句を選び，記号で答えよ。

(1) All (　　　) who know her are very happy also.
　ア the　イ these　ウ those　エ they

(2) These twins are just alike. Nobody can tell one from (　　　).
　ア another　イ others　ウ the other　エ the others

(3) It was I that (　　　) wrong.
　ア are　イ am　ウ is　エ was

(4) I might as well die. (　　　) needs an old woman like me.
　ア Anybody　イ Everybody　ウ Nobody　エ Somebody

(5) (　　　) of us think that our country should be a democracy.
　ア No　イ Almost　ウ Every　エ Most

(6) (　　　) is more important than time.
　ア Nothing　イ Anything　ウ Everything　エ Something

142 次の英文の(　　　)の中から，正しい語句を選べ。

(1) Which skirt do you want? I want a larger (one, it).

(2) (All, Every) of the boys did (his, their) best.

(3) I am sure it is no fault of (you, yours, your's).

(4) Won't you have (some, any) more tea?

(5) "Which do you want, fame or money?" "I do not want (either, neither) of them."

(6) There were (no one, none) who bought an umbrella.

B

143 次の会話文の(　　　)内に適切な語をそれぞれ一語ずつ入れ，文を完成させよ。

(1) A：Oh, no! It's raining, and I forgot to bring an umbrella.
B：Don't worry. I have one. Maybe we can share (　　　).

(2) A：You must be very hungry after a long trip. (　　　) (　　　) to some sandwiches.
B：Oh, thank you. (　　　) look delicious.

(3) A：How do you like this sweater?
B：(　　　) is too bright. Please show me (　　　).

(4) A：Jack, what would you like to eat for dinner?
B：(　　　) will do. I'm very hungry.

144 次の日本文を参考にして，英文中の(　　　)内の単語のうち正しい方を答えよ。

私は時計をなくした。それを捜している。みつからなかったら新しいものを買わなければならない。時計は生活になくてはならないもののうちのひとつだ。

I have lost my watch. I'm looking for (1) (one, it). If (2) (one, it) isn't found out, I must buy a new (3) (one, it). (4) (One, It) is one of the most indispensable things in my life.

145 次の文中に誤りがあれば訂正せよ。

(1) Japanese deer are smaller than that in Europe.

(2) Tom drives well. ――So he is. (まったくだ)

(3) How much is that trousers?

(4) Such is the popularity of this novel that it will be a best seller before long.

146 次の英文を和訳せよ。

(1) You can argue about British food for a long time. Some people think it is awful; others think it is fantastic.

(2) What exactly is it that is passed from parents to children?

147 次の各組の英文が同じ意味になるよう(　　)に適する語句を入れよ。

(1) It has nothing to do with you.
It is (　　) of your business.

(2) There is no telling what will happen next.
It is (　　) (　　) tell what will happen next.

C

148 次の(　　)に適する代名詞を補い英文を完成させよ。

(1) My pajamas are here. Where are (　　), Ken?

(2) You should solve the problems for (　　), boys.

(3) I think (　　) strange that he is in his twenties.

(4) Do you know what (　　) sell at that shop?

(5) Take (　　) easy and help yourself to a drink.

(6) How long does (　　) take to drive to the supermarket?

149 次の日本文を参考に(　　)内の語句を並べ換え，1語補って英文を完成させよ。ただし，文頭にくるものも小文字で示してある。

(1) がっかりしたことに，私の英語は通じませんでした。
(make, English, I, to, in, could, disappointment, not, my, understood, ,).

(2) まもなくその患者は意識を取り戻した。
(before, not, it, himself, came, patient, long, was, the).

第4章　品詞

19　名　詞

A

150　次の単語の意味をあとのア～セから選び，それぞれ記号で答えよ。

(1) apartheid	(2) acid rain	(3) hostage
(4) non-smoker's right	(5) EC	(6) radioactive waste
(7) disarmament	(8) medical checkup	(9) Universiade
(10) WHO	(11) divorce rate	(12) solar battery
(13) atomic submarine	(14) environmental pollution	

ア　環境汚染	イ　人質	ウ　太陽電池	エ　健康診断
オ　酸性雨	カ　軍縮	キ　嫌煙権	ク　離婚率
ケ　放射性廃棄物	コ　原子力潜水艦	サ　（南アの）人種差別政策	
シ　国際学生競技大会	ス　世界保健機関	セ　ヨーロッパ共同体	

151　AとBの関係とCとDの関係が等しくなるように(　　　)に適する語を入れよ。

	A	B	C	D
(1)	brother	sister	father	(　　　)
(2)	grape	vine	apple	(　　　)
(3)	arm	hand	leg	(　　　)
(4)	chemistry	chemist	music	(　　　)
(5)	act	action	depart	(　　　)
(6)	datum	data	hypothesis	(　　　)

152　次の英文に相当する単語を書け。

(1) the month that comes between July and September

(2) the whole of people in a country

(3) a grown-up person

(4) a man who serves in an army

(5) a period of 100 years

153 次の各文の(　　)に入る適当な語句を選び，記号で答えよ。

(1) A (　　) is the part of a house where food is cooked.

ア kitchen　イ study　ウ bedroom　エ bathroom
オ living room

(2) Lunch is a meal served between (　　) and supper.

ア milk　イ dinner　ウ tea　エ breakfast
オ dessert

(3) A (An) (　　) is the brother of one's father or mother.

ア aunt　イ uncle　ウ grandfather　エ cousin
オ grandmother

(4) A place where many trees grow close together is called a (　　).

ア forest　イ mountain　ウ garden　エ field
オ farm

(5) The end of the day and the early part of the night is (　　).

ア morning　イ afternoon　ウ night　エ evening
オ midnight

154 次の英語が示す英単語をあとのア～オより選び，記号で答えよ。

(1) someone who is receiving medical treatment from a doctor or in a hospital

(2) someone who buys and uses products and services

(3) someone who is watching an event or game

(4) someone who is travelling in a vehicle, plane, boat etc, but is not driving it or working on it

(5) someone who is invited to an event or special occasion

ア passenger　イ spectator　ウ consumer
エ patient　オ guest

155 次の英文が示す英単語をあとのア～コより選び，記号で答えよ。

(1) a piece of land completely surrounded by water

(2) a place where many kinds of animals are kept so that people can go to look at them

(3) a situation that causes difficulties

(4) a tall narrow building

(5) an important city where the main government of a country, state etc. is located

(6) someone who teaches a particular subject, sport, or skill

(7) something you hope for and want to happen very much

(8) the number of years someone has lived or something has existed
(9) the organ inside your head that controls how you think, feel, and move
(10) what you earn by working and use in order to buy things, usually in the form of coins or pieces of paper with their value printed on them
ア age　イ brain　ウ capital　エ dream　オ instructor
カ island　キ money　ク problem　ケ tower　コ zoo

156 次の日本語に相当する英語の綴り字を書け。
(1) コーヒー　(2) ピアノ　(3) クリニック　(4) コンピュータ
(5) ウイルス　(6) プロテイン　(7) ハンカチ　(8) サッカー
(9) ナイフ　(10) ボランティア

B

157 次の各文の(　　)に適する語句を選び，記号で答えよ。
(1) Your suggestion that we take him back home is out of the (　　); he is too sick for that.
ア problem　イ medicine　ウ question　エ place
(2) (　　) is a person who travels in a bus, train, boat, airplane and so on.
ア A passenger　イ A passer-by　ウ A pedestrian
エ A customer
(3) We cannot repair this bicycle until tomorrow because the necessary parts are out of (　　).
ア sight　イ print　ウ stock　エ order
(4) The doctor took her temperature and felt her (　　).
ア blood　イ muscle　ウ nerve　エ pulse
(5) I moved my bags to make (　　) for the elderly gentleman to sit down.
ア room　イ lot　ウ seat　エ place
(6) The two organs in your body which you use when you breathe are called (　　).
ア lungs　イ bladders　ウ kidneys　エ brains

158 次の会話の(1)～(4)に入るべき語をそれぞれア～エから選び，記号で答えよ。

A：Can you tell me what time the doctor's (1) opens?
B：It's open now. The (2) will help you.
A：Excuse me. I just want to collect a (3).
B：Is it for some (4) for a headache?

(1) ア office イ surgery ウ hospital エ ward
(2) ア porter イ hostess ウ waitress エ receptionist
(3) ア prescription イ recipe ウ cure エ direction
(4) ア prevention イ liquid ウ medicine エ solution

159 次の英文の誤りを訂正せよ。

(1) She wants to be a child's doctor.
(2) All the furnitures in my room are old.
(3) I have done all of my homeworks.
(4) I bought two shoes yesterday.
(5) You have to change the train at Tokyo Station.

C

160 次の英語による説明に該当する英単語を記せ。

(1) a written account of a person's life
(2) a person living or located near one another
(3) liquid which comes out from the body through the skin to cool it
(4) a two-wheeled vehicle which one rides by pushing its pedals with the feet
(5) a small creature with no bones and a hard outer covering, six legs, and a body divided into three parts, such as an ladybug or kabutomushi

161 次の各文の下線部の表現に最も近い意味を持つものを，それぞれあとのア～エから選び，記号で答えよ。

(1) The elderly are beginning to demand rights for themselves.
ア aged イ brothers ウ children エ superiors
(2) He showed his disgust for the movie by leaving in the middle.
ア appreciation イ approval ウ dislike エ entertainment
(3) His work schedule determined the duration of their trip.
ア cost イ length ウ location エ pleasure
(4) This rule holds good at all times and places.
ア is made much of イ is practical
ウ is valid エ is worth obeying

第4章　品詞

20　冠　詞

A

162　次の各文の(　　　)に適する冠詞をあとのア～エから選び，記号で答えよ。ただし，文頭にくるものも小文字で示してある。

(1)　He must be (　　　) honest man.
(2)　A stone struck him on (　　　) head.
(3)　He usually goes to the movies once (　　　) month.
(4)　He was elected (　　　) chairman of the committee.
(5)　(　　　) Thames flows through London.
(6)　Birds of (　　　) feather flock together.
(7)　(　　　) English are fond of sports.
(8)　Children start (　　　) school at the age of six in Japan.
(9)　Will you close (　　　) door?
(10)　He is (　　　) only person for the job.
(11)　My neighbor has (　　　) very big house.
(12)　Where is Paul?　He went back to (　　　) hotel.
(13)　Can you play (　　　) tennis?
(14)　In this building, the restaurant is on (　　　) top floor.
(15)　My brother has (　　　) international driving permit.
(16)　(　　　) Canada is a large country.
(17)　(　　　) teacher's voice is too low.　I can't hear him.
(18)　Russia is (　　　) largest country in the world.
(19)　Can you speak (　　　) Japanese?
(20)　There are 50 stars on (　　　) American flag.

ア　the　　　イ　a　　　ウ　an　　　エ　不要

163 次の各文の(　　　)に適当な冠詞を入れ，不要なときは×印を入れよ。

(1) I spoke to (　　　) boy, but (　　　) boy ran away.

(2) This is (　　　) camera that I used when I took that picture.

(3) The postman comes twice (　　　) day.

(4) We have (　　　) lunch at (　　　) noon.

(5) We have (　　　) examination in (　　　) mathematics today.

B

164 次の英文の誤りを訂正せよ。

(1) He is still in the bed.

(2) I am younger of the two.

(3) I have never seen a such kind girl.

(4) In the most places in United States, children start school in September.

165 次の英文の誤っている単語を示し，訂正せよ。また，和訳せよ。

What is a most popular vegetable in the world?

166 次の英文を読んで和訳せよ。

I know why Mother decided to have a Halloween party for my sisters. She knew that she could keep an eye on them if they were at home.

167 必要な箇所に適当な冠詞を入れよ。

(1) I had big breakfast at nine.

(2) What difficult problem this is!

(3) That singer is loved by young.

(4) April is fourth month of year.

168 次の文を比較し，冠詞の用い方がどう違うのか述べよ。

(1) He is the principal of our school.

(2) He is a teacher of our school.

(3) They are the teachers of our school.

(4) They are teachers of our school.

第5章　発音，会話

21　発音・アクセント

A

169　次の各組の語のうち，下線部の発音がほかの3つと異なるものを選び，記号で答えよ。

(1)　ア　laughed　イ　stopped　ウ　finished　エ　omitted
(2)　ア　treat　イ　ready　ウ　reach　エ　speak
(3)　ア　grow　イ　blow　ウ　follow　エ　allow
(4)　ア　straight　イ　height　ウ　freight　エ　weight
(5)　ア　blood　イ　look　ウ　foot　エ　wood
(6)　ア　warm　イ　dark　ウ　farm　エ　large
(7)　ア　station　イ　planet　ウ　page　エ　later
(8)　ア　thumb　イ　northern　ウ　breath　エ　breadth
(9)　ア　telephone　イ　enough　ウ　ghost　エ　cough
(10)　ア　expression　イ　mansion　ウ　conclusion　エ　station

170　次の各組の語のうち，第1アクセントのある音節の位置がほかと異なるものを選び，記号で答えよ。

(1)　ア　bal-ance　イ　pat-tern　ウ　al-though
　　エ　dif-fer　オ　boy-cott
(2)　ア　mu-si-cian　イ　con-tin-ue　ウ　u-ni-verse
　　エ　suc-cess-ful　オ　phy-si-cian
(3)　ア　el-e-va-tor　イ　com-put-er　ウ　ad-ver-tise
　　エ　ed-u-cate　オ　com-fort-a-ble
(4)　ア　e-vent　イ　gui-tar　ウ　ho-tel
　　エ　fre-quent　オ　con-trol
(5)　ア　ad-vice　イ　air-mail　ウ　man-age
　　エ　or-ange　オ　pa-tient
(6)　ア　cer-e-mo-ny　イ　dif-fi-cul-ty　ウ　gen-er-al-ly
　　エ　in-tel-li-gent　オ　nec-es-sar-y
(7)　ア　ar-row　イ　fa-tigue　ウ　plat-form
　　エ　pref-ace　オ　fa-vor

(8) ア dec-o-rate　イ in-fa-mous　ウ pho-to-graph
エ tre-men-dous　オ an-ces-tor

(9) ア char-ac-ter　イ em-ploy-ee　ウ mi-cro-scope
エ rhet-o-ric　オ ca-pa-ble

(10) ア am-bas-sa-dor　イ har-mo-ni-ous　ウ hu-man-i-ty
エ lit-er-a-ture　オ me-trop-o-lis

171 次の単語の最も強く発音する部分を選び，記号で答えよ。

(1) knowl-edge
ア イ

(2) var-i-ous
ア イ ウ

(3) in-clude
ア イ

(4) dis-ease
ア イ

(5) at-ti-tude
ア イ ウ

(6) op-er-a-tion
ア イ ウ エ

(7) rec-og-nize
ア イ ウ

(8) ac-cu-rate-ly
ア イ ウ エ

(9) sci-en-tif-ic
ア イ ウ エ

(10) dis-com-fort
ア イ ウ

(11) tem-pe-ra-ture
ア イ ウ エ

(12) gov-ern-ment
ア イ ウ

(13) un-for-tu-nate-ly
ア イ ウ エ オ

(14) bac-te-ri-cid-al
ア イ ウ エ オ

(15) for-got-ten
ア イ ウ

(16) fif-ti-eth
ア イ ウ

(17) pro-nun-ci-a-tion
ア イ ウ エ オ

(18) su-per-mar-ket
ア イ ウ エ

(19) en-vi-ron-ment
ア イ ウ エ

(20) ac-ces-so-ry
ア イ ウ エ

(21) am-a-teur
ア イ ウ

(22) bal-co-ny
ア イ ウ

(23) pa-jam-as
ア イ ウ

(24) in-flu-en-za
ア イ ウ エ

(25) cur-ric-u-lum
ア イ ウ エ

(26) um-pire
ア イ

(27) sil-hou-ette
ア イ ウ

(28) vi-nyl
ア イ

172 次の単語の下線部と同じ発音をもつものを選び，記号で答えよ。

(1) allow　ア bowl　イ crown　ウ grow　エ knowledge
(2) rough　ア brought　イ tough　ウ doughnut　エ through
(3) moon　ア blood　イ bullet　ウ button　エ smooth
(4) chimney　ア mustache　イ chemistry　ウ church　エ scholar

173 次の単語のうち，最も強く読まれる部分の発音が，ほかと異なるものを選び，記号で答えよ。

(1) ア failure　イ satisfy　ウ state　エ aid

(2) ア indicate　イ drive　ウ apply　エ polite

(3) ア conductor　イ success　ウ introduction　エ judge

(4) ア value　イ atmosphere　ウ appear　エ examine

(5) ア blood　イ tool　ウ blue　エ suit

174 次の単語のうち，下線部が発音されないものを５つ選び，記号で答えよ。

ア enough　イ through　ウ laugh　エ high

オ house　カ woman　キ window　ク knife

ケ told　コ usually　サ climb　シ already

ス always　セ open　ソ tall　タ cold

チ island　ツ height　テ close　ト pencil

175 次の単語のうち，第３音節に最も強いアクセントのあるものを５つ選び，記号で答えよ。

ア op-por-tu-ni-ty　イ re-al-i-za-tion　ウ en-er-gy

エ in-di-vid-u-al　オ tech-ni-cian　カ au-then-tic

キ ma-chin-er-y　ク at-mos-phere　ケ math-e-mat-ics

コ in-ves-ti-gate　サ an-ces-tor　シ cir-cum-stance

ス cu-ri-os-i-ty　セ vol-un-teer　ソ man-ag-er

176 次の各組の語のうち，第２音節に最も強いアクセントのあるものを１つ選び，記号で答えよ。

(1) ア ho-tel　イ char-ac-ter
　ウ im-pulse　エ in-stru-ment

(2) ア dif-fer-ence　イ ig-no-rance
　ウ oc-ca-sion　エ en-ter-tain

(3) ア op-po-site　イ oc-cur
　ウ vol-un-teer　エ vol-ume

(4) ア per-son-al　イ di-rec-tion
　ウ gov-ern-ment　エ un-der-stand

(5) ア con-fer-ence　イ con-trar-y
　ウ in-vi-ta-tion　エ pre-cise

177 次の単語のうち，最も強く読まれる部分の発音が，ほかと異なるものを選び，記号で答えよ。

(1) ア success　イ infant　ウ report
エ unique　オ prefer

(2) ア photograph　イ manager　ウ opposite
エ dangerous　オ commercial

178 次の単語の下線部と同じ発音を含む語を，あとのア～オから選び，記号で答えよ。

(1) says
ア week　イ head　ウ heat　エ steak　オ danger

(2) muscle
ア tough　イ cough　ウ mouth　エ music　オ youth

179 次の単語の下線部と同じ発音のものを，あとのア～エから選び，記号で答えよ。

(1) recent　ア ancient　イ decorate　ウ financial　エ society
(2) country　ア although　イ doubt　ウ southern　エ thought
(3) imagine　ア capital　イ false　ウ major　エ sacred
(4) expand　ア exact　イ example　ウ exist　エ exhibition
(5) fear　ア bear　イ wear　ウ clear　エ earth

180 次の各組の単語の下線部の発音が3つとも同じ場合は○，2つ同じ場合は△，3つとも異なる場合は×で答えよ。

(1) healthy / thousand / thing
(2) cancer / major / hall
(3) discuss / muscle / unit
(4) enough / through / fight
(5) thirsty / dirty / July
(6) ground / could / cold

181 次の単語の第一アクセントのある音節を選び，記号で答えよ。

(1) news-paper
　　ア　イ
(2) ar-range
　　ア　イ
(3) in-ter-est-ing
　　ア　イ　ウ　エ
(4) a-gree-ment
　　ア　イ　ウ
(5) rec-re-a-tion
　　ア　イ　ウ　エ

182 次の各組の語のうち，最も強く発音する音節の位置がほかと異なるものを選び，記号で答えよ。

(1) ア be-gin　イ gui-tar　ウ vol-un-teer　エ e-nough
(2) ア note-book　イ po-lice-man　ウ yes-ter-day　エ In-ter-net
(3) ア sur-prise　イ air-port　ウ hos-pi-tal　エ ham-burg-er
(4) ア Ko-re-a　イ be-tween　ウ i-de-a　エ busi-ness
(5) ア for-eign　イ Eu-rope　ウ a-gree　エ sci-en-tist

183 次の各組の語のうち，下線部の発音がほかの３つと異なるものを選び，記号で答えよ。

(1) ア since　イ island　ウ white　エ climb
(2) ア example　イ excuse　ウ expensive　エ explain
(3) ア say　イ nature　ウ says　エ face
(4) ア dear　イ learn　ウ hear　エ clear
(5) ア missed　イ started　ウ liked　エ stopped

B

184 次の各組の単語の下線部の発音が３つとも同じの場合は○，２つ同じの場合は△，３つとも異なる場合は×で答えよ。

(1) { creature / create / health }
(2) { almost / swallow / bathroom }
(3) { shoulder / couple / could }
(4) { pain / face / way }

185 次の単語のうち，下線部が発音されないものを５つ選び，記号で答えよ。

ア doubt　イ receipt　ウ little　エ humble
オ palm　カ whistle　キ muscle　ク aisle
ケ hasten　コ castle　サ term　シ neighbor
ス salt　セ boyhood　ソ cupboard

186 次の各文の下線部と同じ発音を含む語を，あとのア～エから選び，記号で答えよ。

(1) Lead melts easily.
ア league　イ cleanse　ウ release　エ gleam
(2) He made a good academic record.
ア reference　イ prepare　ウ reserve　エ retire
(3) A tear rolled down her cheek.
ア bear　イ pear　ウ swear　エ fear

(4) He suffered a fatal wound.

ア group　イ round　ウ rough　エ surround

(5) He bowed to his teacher.

ア rainbow　イ arrow　ウ brow　エ blow

187 次の単語の最も強く発音する位置を選んだものとして間違っているものを選び，記号で答えよ。

ア pho-to-gra-phy　答—2
1 2 3 4

イ el-e-va-tor　答—1
1 2 3 4

ウ mos-qui-to　答—2
1 2 3

エ vol-ume　答—1
1 2

オ he-ro-ine　答—2
1 2 3

188 次の各組の語のうち，下線部の発音がほかの3つと異なるものを選び，記号で答えよ。

(1) ア head　イ heaven　ウ earth　エ health
(2) ア pillow　イ bright　ウ mine　エ idea
(3) ア houses　イ laughs　ウ says　エ toys
(4) ア coat　イ toast　ウ broad　エ goal
(5) ア throw　イ mouth　ウ thought　エ though

189 次の各組の語のうち，第1アクセントのある音節の位置がほかと異なるものを選び，記号で答えよ。

(1) ア for-get　イ mo-rale　ウ up-ward　エ ex-ist
(2) ア fur-ni-ture　イ he-ro-ic　ウ doc-u-ment　エ cat-a-logue
(3) ア in-ter-est　イ sig-na-ture　ウ vol-un-teer　エ sat-is-fy
(4) ア cor-rect　イ con-fine　ウ suc-cess　エ us-age
(5) ア vol-ume　イ trans-fer　ウ wor-ship　エ ter-ror

190 次の単語のうち，最も強く読まれる部分の発音が，ほかと異なるものを選び，記号で答えよ。

(1) ア advice　イ career　ウ mischief　エ occur
(2) ア pattern　イ product　ウ preface　エ prefer
(3) ア mechanism　イ calendar　ウ educate　エ entertain

(4) ア average イ develop ウ industry エ universe
(5) ア necessary イ mathematics ウ politician エ energetic
(6) ア accessory イ agriculture ウ democracy
エ photography

191 次の各組の語のうち，下線部の発音がほかの3つと異なるものを選び，記号で答えよ。

(1) ア repair イ prepare ウ weary エ swear
(2) ア patient イ favorite ウ bacon エ latter
(3) ア assembly イ distress ウ muscle エ scissors
(4) ア experiment イ complete ウ extremely エ immediate

192 次の各組の単語の下線部の発音が同じものを2つ選び，記号で答えよ。

ア { ball / take }
イ { sea / piece }
ウ { long / cup }
エ { tooth / bathe }
オ { zoo / noise }

193 次の各組のうち，第1アクセントのある音節の位置がほかと異なるものを選び，記号で答えよ。

(1) ア dam-age イ mis-take ウ oc-cur エ per-form
(2) ア en-er-gy イ ex-am-ine ウ hes-i-tate エ sat-is-fy
(3) ア mag-net-ic イ pol-i-tics ウ dra-mat-ic エ cli-mat-ic
(4) ア i-den-ti-ty イ a-bil-i-ty ウ tech-nol-o-gy
エ in-ter-est-ing
(5) ア char-ac-ter イ man-ag-er ウ car-pen-ter エ pio-neer

194 次の各組の左側に示された単語と第一アクセントのある音節の位置が異なるものを選び，記号で答えよ。

(1) pre-dict （ア con-struct イ dif-fer ウ con-front エ ap-plause）
(2) ex-e-cute （ア fas-ci-nate イ ded-i-cate ウ em-bar-rass
エ sep-a-rate）
(3) in-tel-lect （ア fac-ul-ty イ at-trib-ute ウ ig-no-rant
エ ad-e-quate）
(4) bi-og-ra-phy （ア an-tic-i-pate イ man-u-fac-ture ウ i-den-ti-fy
エ hy-poth-e-sis）
(5) phy-si-cian （ア dis-trib-ute イ en-deav-or ウ con-cen-trate
エ in-sur-ance）

第5章　発音，会話

22　会　　話

B

195 次の各会話の(　　　)に入る最も適切な表現をア～エから1つずつ選び，記号で答えよ。

(1) A：Do you know where my purse is?
B：(　　　)
ア No, I don't. Do you?　　イ Yes, I know it.
ウ It's on the table.　　エ I'd like to know it.

(2) A：Do you mind if I close this window?
B：(　　　)
ア Yes, of course.　　イ No, go ahead.
ウ Yes, you're welcome.　　エ No, please have it open.

(3) A：Why don't we go for a drive this afternoon?
B：(　　　)
ア Okay. Where shall we go?　　イ I accept your proposal.
ウ Because I am too busy.　　エ I'm sorry, but I can't drive.

(4) A：Thank you very much for a nice present.
B：(　　　)
ア Don't mention it.　　イ I'm sorry for that.
ウ The present was nice.　　エ You told me so.

(5) A：I feel sick today.
B：(　　　)
ア Are you?　　イ So am I.
ウ Oh, that's too bad.　　エ Why not?

(6) A：Lovely flower, isn't it?
B：(　　　) certainly is.
ア Yes　　イ It　　ウ No　　エ This

(7) A：Is there anything good on TV tonight?
B：(　　　)
ア Please clean up your TV set.
イ Look at the TV set.
ウ Yes. There's something with the TV set.
エ Yes. There's a new variety show starting tonight.

196 次の日本文と同じ意味の英文になるように，(　　　)に適する語句を入れよ。

(1) お風呂に入ってもいいですか。
Can I (　　　) a bath?

(2) 回復するのにどのくらいかかりますか。
How long will it (　　　) to recover?

(3) ひどい頭痛で困っています。
I'm (　　　) from a severe headache.

(4) 吐き気がひどいんです。
I (　　　) much like vomiting.

注 vomit 吐く

(5) すみませんが，トイレをお借りできますか。
Excuse me, but can I (　　　) your bathroom?

197 次の会話文の応答として適切なものを選び，記号で答えよ。

(1) A：Hello, doctor.
B：Hello, Mr. Sato. (　　　)
A：Nothing particular, but I haven't been feeling well.
ア Nice to meet you.　　イ What do you want?
ウ How are you doing?　　エ What brings you here today?

(2) A：May I ask you a favor?
B：Sure. What (　　　)?
A：Well, I need some money.
ア is the trouble　　イ are you doing
ウ is happening　　エ can you do

(3) A：Would you mind if I used your telephone?
B：(　　　). I'm waiting for an important call now.
A：O.K.
ア Of course　　イ I'd rather you didn't
ウ The line is busy　　エ Not at all

(4) A : I'd better be going.
B : So soon ? Why don't you stay a little longer ?
A : (　　), but I have to get up early tomorrow.

ア I think so　　**イ** I'd have to
ウ I will do it　　**エ** I'd love to

(5) A : Can you fix my alarm clock ? It doesn't ring.
B : Has it happened before ?
A : (　　).

ア It never happens any more　　**イ** That's the problem
ウ This is the first time　　**エ** It wouldn't happen before

198 次の会話文の(　　)に入る最も適切な文をそれぞれあとの**ア**～**コ**から選び，記号で答えよ。

(1) A : Did I keep you waiting ?
B : No, I just got here a couple of minutes ago.
A : It was easy to find this place, right ?
B : (　　)

(2) A : This is Tom Jackson. Can I speak to Mr. Williams, please ?
B : I'm sorry he's out now. (　　)
A : Umm, just tell him I called.

(3) A : We're open Tuesday through Friday.
B : (　　) you're closed on Monday ?
A : Yes, we're open just four days a week.

(4) A : Have you finished that assignment ?
B : Of course not. I need at least one more week.
A : I finished it last night.
B : (　　)

(5) A : What's your reservation number, sir ?
B : (　　) It's 090-397-220.
A : 090-397-220 ... Let me check.

ア Any time.　　**イ** Hold on, please.
ウ No problem.　　**エ** Who said
オ Would you like to leave a message ?
カ You mean　　**キ** Let's see ...
ク No kidding !　　**ケ** Sorry ?
コ That's too bad.

199 次の会話文の（　　）に入る最も適切な語句をあとの**ア**～**オ**から選び，記号で答えよ。ただし，それぞれの語は1回しか使用できない。

(1) A：If the festival lasts (　　) four weeks, that's four concerts, right?
B：Yes.

(2) A：Why are you giving the brochure to me?
B：This year, you are in charge (　　) picking the concerts.

(3) A：Nearly everything I know about baseball, I learned (　　) those cards.
B：I know. You are a walking baseball encyclopedia.

(4) A：This uniform is (　　) big for me.
B：We are playing softball. Who cares how you look?

(5) A：These trading cards are expensive.
B：How much did we spend (　　) that last set?

ア from　**イ** too　**ウ** for　**エ** on　**オ** of

200 次の各英文を，2人の会話としてまとまりができるように適切な順序に並べ換えたとき，1番目と3番目にくるものの記号を答えよ。

(1) **ア** Well, Dad let me have a puppy.
イ I like dogs very much, so I never mind.
ウ What's new with you?
エ It's a lot of work to take care of one.

(2) **ア** It is in front of the domestic airlines' ticket counter.
イ Excuse me, but are there any baggage lockers in this terminal building?
ウ Domestic departure.
エ Yes, there are. International or domestic?

(3) **ア** We came back last week.
イ I went there with my mother.
ウ We? Who did you go there with?
エ When did you come back from Korea?

201 次の会話文の(　　　)に入る最も適切な文をあとの**ア**～**キ**から選び，記号で答えよ。

エレン(E)が友人のアン(A)の家に飛び込んできて…

E：Ann, let me sit down for a minute. (　1　)

A：Sure. Do you feel sick? Did something happen?

E：I had an accident.

A：With your car?

E：Yes, in the parking lot over there. (　2　)

A：Was anyone hurt?

E：No, no one was hurt, but the car I hit has a big *dent in the side. I just backed out of the space without checking carefully. (　3　) I've never had an accident before. It was so stupid.

A：The other car was going too fast, wasn't it?

E：(　4　)

A：You look pale. Drink the water and take a deep breath. Did you call your insurance company?

E：Not yet. I will in a moment.

A：Whose car did you hit?

E：No one near here. A couple from Tokyo. They were coming to have lunch at the restaurant.

* dent　へこみ

ア　Call an ambulance right away.

イ　I don't think so.

ウ　It was all my fault.

エ　Did you hear the news?

オ　I was backing out and I hit a car.

カ　I didn't do anything wrong.

キ　Would you get me a glass of water?

C

202 次の日本文と同じ意味の英文になるように，(　　　)に適する語句を選び，記号で答えよ。

(1) 「どうぞ楽になさってください。」

"Please make yourself (　1　)."

ア easygoing　イ with us　ウ easily　エ at home

(2) A：ご親切にありがとうございます。

B：どういたしまして。

A：It's very kind of you.　Thank you.

B：My (　2　).

ア heart　イ pleasure　ウ happiness　エ joy

(3) 「どうしたらいいかさっぱりわかりません。」

"I'm all at (　3　)."

ア sea　イ air　ウ sky　エ fire

(4) 「お願いがあるんですが。」

"I have a (　4　) to ask of you."

ア matter　イ regard　ウ demand　エ favor

(5) A：彼女とは付き合わないほうがいいよ。

B：余計なお世話だ。

A：You should avoid keeping company with her.

B：(　5　).

ア Think of yourself　イ Out of your problem

ウ Don't discuss it　エ Mind your own business

203 次の各会話文の(　　　)に入る最も適切なものをあとの**ア**～**ク**からそれぞれ選び，記号で答えよ。ただし，文頭にくるものも小文字で示してある。

Lucy and Jake are agreeing to meet to study together.

Lucy : Hey Jake, (　1　) to study together this afternoon?

Jake : Absolutely. I really didn't (　2　) by Professor Williams.

Lucy : Really? I thought it was very clear. I enjoyed it.

Jake : You (　3　).

Lucy : Don't be so unkind to yourself. You're much better than me at history.

Jake : I like history. Anyway, where are we going to study?

Lucy : It's a really nice sunny day. (　4　) a place in the park and have a picnic while we study?

Jake : That sounds like a great idea. (　5　) if you buy something to drink.

Lucy : OK!

ア I'll buy some snacks　　**イ** the teacher is
ウ are you still OK　　**エ** are much smarter than I am
オ why don't we find　　**カ** will be difficult
キ like it very much　　**ク** understand that last lecture

Masataka is in an electronics store.

Clerk : (　6　) find something?

Masataka : Yes, I'm (　7　) a new MP3 player.

Clerk : I see. How about this one? It's the most popular brand.

Masataka : It's a little (　8　). Do you have anything cheaper?

Clerk : This one is cheaper, but it has (　9　) memory.

Masataka : That's all right. I (　10　) much memory. I'll take it.

ア looking for　　**イ** cheap for me　　**ウ** can I help you
エ much less　　**オ** too expensive　　**カ** don't need
キ do you need　　**ク** want to have

第6章　実践問題

23　空欄補充

A

204 次の(　　　)に適する語句をそれぞれあとから選び，記号で答えよ。

(1) What (　　　)in your house at the moment?

ア is happening　　イ does happen

ウ happens　　エ happening

(2) Did you (　　　) jeans to school when you were younger?

ア were wearing　　イ use wear

ウ use to wear　　エ have worn

(3) That bird (　　　) an eagle. It's much too small.

ア must not be　　イ can't be

ウ doesn't have to be　　エ was to be

(4) She likes (　　　) these paintings.

ア both　　イ neither

ウ either　　エ both of

(5) "You're not (　　　) to do the operation on your own," said the surgeon.

ア too experienced　　イ little experienced

ウ experienced enough　　エ full experienced

(6) Can you give me (　　　)?

ア any informations　　イ an information

ウ informations　　エ any information

205 次の(　　　)に適する語句をそれぞれあとから選び，記号で答えよ。

(1) What did you go to such a place (　　　)?

ア at　　イ to　　ウ for　　エ about

(2) You should not depend (　　　) your parents.

ア at　　イ in　　ウ of　　エ on

(3) Kate has heard nothing from Tom, (　　　) makes her uneasy.

ア that　　イ who　　ウ which　　エ where

(4) Steve hopes to finish (　　　) for his house.

ア pay　　イ paid　　ウ paying　　エ to pay

(5) (　　) you pay in cash or by credit card will make no difference.
ア How　イ Whether　ウ If　エ Although
(6) There (　　) no bus service, we had to take a taxi.
ア be　イ was　ウ been　エ being
(7) If I (　　) well last night, I would not feel so sleepy now.
ア sleep　イ slept　ウ have slept　エ had slept

206 次の(　　)に適する語句をそれぞれあとから選び，記号で答えよ。
(1) We shall write to him when he (　　) to his village.
ア will return　イ will have returned
ウ returned　エ returns
(2) Do it (　　) he tells you.
ア like as　イ as　ウ similar　エ as how
(3) He (　　) regularly, but now he never goes.
ア was used to go　イ use to go
ウ used to go　エ goes
(4) (　　) a sound could be heard.
ア No　イ Not any　ウ Not　エ Not of
(5) They told (　　) what had happened.
ア the officer　イ that the officer
ウ to the officer　エ of the officer
(6) (　　) go there in the summer.
ア Lot of people　イ A lots of people
ウ The lot of people　エ A lot of people
(7) Up to now, my sister (　　) there.
ア hasn't been　イ was not being
ウ isn't been　エ haven't been
(8) (　　) from him for a long time.
ア I not have heard　イ I have heard not
ウ Not I have heard　エ I have not heard
(9) I shall ask (　　) to help you.
ア of my father　イ to my father
ウ if my father　エ my father
(10) The man (　　) life was saved was my father.
ア whose　イ whom　ウ of whom　エ of which the

207 次の各文の(　　)に入る適当な語句を選び，記号で答えよ。

(1) I enjoy (　　) a walk every morning.

ア to go for　　イ going to　　ウ going for

(2) My father (　　) for ten years.

ア died　　イ is killed　　ウ has been dead

(3) He was (　　) by a young doctor.

ア taken good care of　　イ taken good care with

ウ taken good care

(4) You had better (　　) alone after dark.

ア not to go out　　イ not go out　　ウ not going out

(5) If I had a lot of money I (　　) abroad.

ア can go　　イ will go　　ウ could go

208 次の各組の英文がほぼ同じ意味になるよう(　　)に入る最も適当な語句をそれぞれあとのア～エから選び，記号で答えよ。

(1) There is no need for all of you to come on time.
Not all of you (　　) come on time.

ア are able to　　イ want to　　ウ have to　　エ don't to

(2) Our boss is good at pointing out our mistakes.
Our boss can find our mistakes quite (　　).

ア out　　イ good　　ウ well　　エ very

(3) Bill is the tallest student in his class.
Bill is taller than (　　) other student in his class.

ア the　　イ an　　ウ some　　エ any

(4) We should watch our baby very carefully.
Our baby should be (　　) very carefully.

ア watch　　イ watched　　ウ watching　　エ to watch

209 次の各組の英文がほぼ同じ意味になるよう(　　)内に適する語を入れよ。

(1) If you run every day, you will be stronger.
Running every day will (　　) (　　) stronger.

(2) As she is very sick, she cannot work.
She is (　　) sick (　　) she cannot work.

(3) Is Dean Smith a man with blue eyes?
Is Dean Smith a man (　　) (　　) are blue?

(4) We heard him call out for help.
He (　　) (　　) (　　) call out for help.

(5) He kindly lent me a lot of CDs.
It was very kind (　　)(　　)(　　)(　　) me a lot of CDs.

B

210 次の(　　)に適する語句を補い，英文を完成させよ。

(1) 何の用事でここに来たのですか。
(　　) brought you here?

(2) 毎日，日記をつけていますか。
Do you (　　) a diary everyday?

(3) 彼があなたのおじさんだとは少しも知らなかった。
I (　　) knew that he was your uncle.

(4) 今朝からずっと頭が痛い。
I've had a (　　) since this morning.

(5) 競争は本来悪いものではない。
Competition is not evil (　　) itself.

(6) 彼女は30代で結婚した。
She got married in her (　　).

(7) 何百万という人がベートーベンの音楽を愛好する。
(　　) of people enjoy Beethoven's music.

(8) 私が泊ったホテルは丘の上にあります。
The hotel (　　) I stayed is on the hill.

(9) 心配事のない人はほとんどいない。
Few people are (　　) from cares.

(10) 葉と植物の関係は肺と動物の関係と同じである。
Leaves are to the plant (　　) lungs are to the animal.

(11) 君はそこでいったい何をしたんだ。
What (　　)(　　) did you do there?

(12) 彼らの意見がいつでも正しいとは限らない。
Their opinions are (　　)(　　) right.

(13) 1匹の蝶がカーテンのうしろから飛び出してきた。
A butterfly flew out (　　)(　　) the curtain.

(14) いつ出発したらよいか教えてください。
Please tell us (　　)(　　) start.

(15) 彼女は幸福だったと言っていました。
She said that she (　　)(　　) happy.

(16) 生まれて初めてイギリスに来ました。
I have come to the U.K. (　　) the first time (　　) my (　　).

(17) 彼は貿易会社に勤務しています。

He (　　　) (　　　) a trading (　　　).

(18) 駅に着いたらすぐに電話をください。

Give me a (　　　) as (　　　) as you (　　　) to the station.

211 次の各文の(　　　)に適する語句をそれぞれあとから選び，記号で答えよ。

(1) できるだけ早く彼と連絡を取るようにします。

I'll (　　　) in touch with him as soon as possible.

ア take　　イ get　　ウ catch　　エ make

(2) あんなふるまいでは彼女の名声に傷がつくだろう。

Her reputation will suffer (　　　) such conduct.

ア from　　イ in　　ウ with　　エ for

(3) 今週の終わりまでに，この詩を暗記するように私たちは言われた。

We were told to learn this poem (　　　) by the end of this week.

ア by mind　　イ in heart　　ウ in mind　　エ by heart

(4) 彼らはその映画は退屈でつまらない，要するに，時間の無駄だと思った。

They found the movie boring and uninteresting, (　　　), a waste of time.

ア in slight　　イ in short　　ウ in small　　エ in little

212 次の(　　　)に適する語句をそれぞれあとから選び，記号で答えよ。

(1) The girl (　　　) the music room is a new student.

ア clean　　イ cleans　　ウ cleaning　　エ cleaned

(2) My mother asked me (　　　) some milk on my way home.

ア buys　　イ buy　　ウ to buy　　エ bought

(3) Mary keeps in good (　　　) by exercising for at least an hour everyday.

ア model　　イ measure　　ウ fashion　　エ shape

(4) We usually take our shoes (　　　) when we enter a Japanese house.

ア on　　イ in　　ウ out　　エ off

(5) Get up at once, (　　　) you will be late for school.

ア or　　イ lest　　ウ and　　エ as

(6) When you have a toothache, you usually go to see a (　　　).

ア carpenter　　イ dentist　　ウ farmer　　エ teacher

(7) It is (　　　) for children to play in busy streets.

ア dangerous　　イ famous　　ウ important　　エ safe

(8) The population of this city is not very (　　　).

ア many　　イ much　　ウ large　　エ lot

(9) Go up to the third (　　) on the escalator, please.
ア base　イ block　ウ ceiling　エ floor

(10) A person who lives next door is a (　　).
ア cousin　イ neighbor　ウ nephew　エ parent

(11) You'll never know (　　) you try.
ア since　イ after　ウ unless　エ however

(12) It's mean of you to take (　　) of my weak point.
ア care　イ advantage　ウ profit　エ home

213 次の(　　)に適する語句をそれぞれあとから選び，記号で答えよ。

(1) How (　　) has your aunt lived in New York?
ア far　イ late　ウ long　エ much

(2) When I entered the room, Toshio was (　　) soccer on TV.
ア finding　イ looking　ウ seeing　エ watching

(3) John and Patty enjoyed talking with (　　) other.
ア another　イ each　ウ one　エ person

(4) You must start (　　) once to get there in time.
ア at　イ by　ウ on　エ through

(5) My friend Noriko looks (　　) her mother.
ア as　イ by　ウ like　エ such

(6) I (　　) that spring were here.
ア desire　イ hope　ウ want　エ wish

(7) We had very (　　) rain last summer.
ア few　イ little　ウ lot　エ many

(8) The teacher (　　) Peter to do his best.
ア said　イ spoke　ウ talked　エ told

(9) I will see you (　　) three days.
ア in　イ on　ウ at　エ by

(10) Beth has three times (　　) books as I have.
ア more　イ few　ウ as many　エ as much

(11) It will (　　) you ten minutes to get to the station by bus.
ア make　イ drive　ウ take　エ cost

(12) Jack told you about the matter, (　　) he?
ア wasn't　イ doesn't　ウ did　エ didn't

(13) We trust Jane because she never (　　) her promises.
ア keeps　イ breaks　ウ throws　エ takes

⒁ "Lucy, you are (　　) on the phone." "I'll come over right away, thank you."

ア asked　イ spoken　ウ rung　エ wanted

⒂ It was careless of you to have the door (　　).

ア unlock　イ unlocked　ウ break　エ broke

⒃ The dog was nowhere (　　).

ア to find　イ being found　ウ to be found　エ finding

⒄ Jane was in the (　　) of drinking milk with all her meals.

ア habit　イ custom　ウ manner　エ trait

⒅ (　　) is often the case with Bob, he came late to school this morning.

ア Which　イ What　ウ As　エ Such

⒆ Since we (　　) turns driving, we didn't get too tired.

ア kept　イ took　ウ made　エ did

214 次の(　　)に適する語句をそれぞれあとのア～コから選び，記号で答えよ。

(1) Geography has played an important (　　) in Japanese history.

(2) Some of my (　　) live in the United States.

(3) In Japan, the percentage of (　　) families is increasing.

(4) My sister doesn't get (　　) with my brother.

(5) Many countries in Asia have high temperatures with high (　　).

(6) I have to go to Hokkaido, so I'd like to (　　) a flight from Tokyo to Sapporo.

(7) Is it possible to (　　) the reservation ?

(8) The journey to Hokkaido (　　) bus seemed endless.

(9) We usually (　　) out on Friday evenings.

⑽ Our faculty meeting will be (　　) on May 23.

ア relatives　イ divorced　ウ cancel　エ book

オ held　カ eat　キ humidity　ク along

ケ role　コ by

215 次の(　　)に適する語句をそれぞれあとから選び，記号で答えよ。

(1) Please remain (　　) for a while.

ア sat　イ seated　ウ seating　エ to seat

(2) Winter is just (　　) the corner.

ア at　イ on　ウ near　エ around

(3) I have to remember (　　　) the textbook tomorrow.
ア buying　　イ to buy　　ウ having bought
エ to have bought

(4) He kept his dog (　　　) to a tree in the garden.
ア tied　　イ tying　　ウ tie　　エ to tie

(5) If I were you, I (　　　) her.
ア help　　イ helped　　ウ had helped　　エ would help

216 次の各文の(　　　)に入る最も適切な語句をア～エから１つずつ選び，記号で答えよ。

(1) A : How (　　　) do you have?
B : I have a daughter and two sons.
ア family members　　イ many child　　ウ big family
エ many children

(2) A : Mr. Davis is (　　　) by many students, don't you think so?
B : I totally agree, and I like him, too.
ア like　　イ liking　　ウ liked　　エ likes

(3) A : (　　　) turn off the TV? I want to read this book.
B : But I'm watching!
ア Are you　　イ Did you　　ウ You are　　エ Will you

(4) Let's (　　　) our travel plan.
ア discuss on　　イ discuss of　　ウ discuss　　エ discuss about

(5) That's (　　　) I don't want to go to college.
ア because　　イ when　　ウ what　　エ why

217 AとBの関係とCとDの関係が等しくなるように(　　　)に適する語を入れよ。

	A	B	C	D
(1)	little	less	much	(　　　)
(2)	health	healthy	(　　　)	hungry
(3)	hot	cold	long	(　　　)
(4)	storm	calm	(　　　)	war
(5)	foot	feet	mouse	(　　　)
(6)	full	empty	(　　　)	private
(7)	buy	sell	fail	(　　　)

218 次の各文の(　　)に入る適当な語句を選び，記号で答えよ。

(1) My daughter likes (　　) history and math.

ア both　イ either　ウ neither　エ that

(2) The number of accidents (　　) steadily increasing in recent years.

ア are　イ has been　ウ have been　エ were

(3) How (　　) do you go to the hairdresser's?

ア far　イ long　ウ many　エ often

(4) The country is rich (　　) natural resources.

ア about　イ by　ウ in　エ to

(5) It's not my (　　) if the party is canceled.

ア blame　イ fault　ウ sin　エ wrong

(6) Mike always arrives on time. He's so (　　).

ア bored　イ industrial　ウ nervous　エ punctual

219 次の(　　)に適する語句をそれぞれあとから選び，記号で答えよ。

(1) I was not used to (　　) up till late at night.

ア sit　イ sitting　ウ sat　エ be sitting

(2) It's never too late (　　).

ア learning　イ be learned　ウ to learn　エ learned

(3) He has (　　) in bed these three days.

ア got ill　イ being ill　ウ was ill　エ been ill

(4) I feel much (　　) by your warm letter.

ア encourage　イ encouraging　ウ encouraged

エ be encouraged

(5) Who is the lady (　　) a long skirt?

ア wearing　イ wear　ウ wore　エ worn

(6) A full moon can (　　) tonight.

ア see　イ seeing　ウ saw　エ be seen

220 次の(　　)に適する語句をそれぞれあとから選び，記号で答えよ。

(1) Please let me (　　) when we will be able to get to USJ.

ア know　イ to know　ウ knowing

エ known　オ knew

(2) There are a few reasons (　　) we cannot agree to her plan.

ア which　イ when　ウ how

エ why　オ what

(3) The movie I watched the other day was very (　　).
ア excite　イ excited　ウ exciting
エ to excite　オ excitedly

(4) It will be dark by the time she (　　) to the hospital.
ア will get　イ gets　ウ got
エ have gotten　オ had gotten

(5) The doctor insisted that the patient (　　) in bed for a week.
ア remain　イ remains　ウ remained
エ would remain　オ has remained

221 次の各文の(　　)に入る適当な語句をそれぞれあとの**ア**～**ウ**より選び，記号で答えよ。

(1) The game has (　　) off due to the heavy rain.
ア to put　イ put　ウ been put

(2) It is impossible to make her (　　) the story.
ア understand　イ understood　ウ to understand

(3) Last night we enjoyed (　　) our high school days.
ア to talk about　イ talk for　ウ talking over

(4) It began to rain (　　) I arrived home.
ア when　イ just　ウ while

(5) Sometimes I (　　) up reading until three or four in the morning.
ア get　イ sit　ウ turn

(6) He is as great an artist as (　　) lived.
ア never　イ anyone　ウ ever

(7) (　　) he is quite old, Mr.Yamada plays tennis very well.
ア Though　イ In spite of　ウ Unless

(8) The (　　) of that bag was so high that I couldn't buy it.
ア money　イ price　ウ cost

222 次の各組の英文が同じ意味になるよう(　　)に適する語句を入れよ。

(1) It seems that he was rich.
He seems to (　　) (　　) rich.

(2) You have only to write your name and address.
(　　) you (　　) to do is to write your name and address.

(3) Would you mind if I watch TV?
Would you mind (　　) (　　) TV?

(4) If it were not for music, our life would be as dry as a desert.
(　　) (　　) music, our life would be as dry as a desert.

223 次の各文の(　　)に適する語句をそれぞれあとの**ア**～**エ**から選び，記号で答えよ。

(1) The traffic accident was caused by young man (　　) too fast.

ア drive　**イ** driving　**ウ** driven　**エ** to drive

(2) (　　) the rope, the climber would have fallen and been killed.

ア If it were not for　**イ** Were it not for

ウ If he were not　**エ** Had it not been for

(3) All of the members need to be back (　　) seven o'clock.

ア for　**イ** by the time　**ウ** by

エ until

(4) He went to see a doctor to have his stomach (　　).

ア examine　**イ** examining　**ウ** examined

エ to examine

(5) She is now quite different from (　　) she used to be ten years ago.

ア that　**イ** what　**ウ** where　**エ** which

224 次の各文の(　　)に入る最も適当な語句を選び，記号で答えよ。

(1) I am looking forward to (　　) you in the near future.

ア see　**イ** seeing　**ウ** seen　**エ** saw

(2) Will you tell me the reason (　　) you have come up with?

ア where　**イ** what　**ウ** why　**エ** which

(3) Dennis studies harder than (　　) student in his class.

ア any other　**イ** other any　**ウ** no other　**エ** other no

(4) This bridge has been (　　) construction for many years.

ア to　**イ** under　**ウ** for　**エ** with

(5) I saw a middle-aged man (　　) the house for sure.

ア to enter　**イ** to go　**ウ** enter　**エ** go

225 次の各文の(　　)に入る最も適切なものを，下の**ア**～**エ**より選び，記号で答えよ。

(1) When I went abroad, I had my wallet (　　) in the crowd.

ア steal　**イ** to steal　**ウ** stolen　**エ** stealing

(2) You didn't study hard. That's (　　) you failed the examination.

ア that　**イ** what　**ウ** when　**エ** why

(3) We want to go to the beach in his car on Saturday, because our car still won't (　　) yet.

ア have been repaired　**イ** have repaired

ウ repair　**エ** repaired

(4) Try to forget it; it isn't worth (　　) about.
ア worry　イ worrying　ウ to worry　エ worried

(5) She's very upset, so we had better (　　) her alone.
ア leave　イ take　ウ bring　エ have

C

226 次の各組の英文が同じ意味になるよう(　　)に適する語句を入れよ。

(1) Do you want me to carry your bags?
(　　) (　　) carry your bags?

(2) You shall have this fountain pen.
I (　　) (　　) you this fountain pen.

(3) Since it was Sunday, we had to go to church.
(　　) (　　) Sunday, we had to go to church.

(4) The policeman said to him, "Don't move."
The policeman (　　) him (　　) to move.

(5) I regret that I said such a thing.
I regret (　　) (　　) such a thing.

(6) There is little hope of his recovery.
There is little hope (　　) he will (　　).

(7) Whenever I go up to Nagano, I visit my grandfather.
I never go up to Nagano (　　) (　　) my grandfather.

(8) All you have to do is to study hard.
You (　　) (　　) to study hard.

(9) I saw him come in a hurry.
He was seen (　　) (　　) in a hurry.

(10) I know a girl with brown eyes.
I know a girl (　　) (　　) brown eyes.

(11) They told him to stay there until they came back.
They said to him, "Stay (　　) until (　　) (　　) back."

(12) My father neither drinks nor smokes.
My father does (　　) (　　) drink (　　) smoke.

(13) I was bored by the speech and I became sleepy.
The (　　) speech (　　) (　　) sleepy.

(14) I am sorry I could not speak French then.
I wish I (　　) (　　) (　　) French then.

(15) This fact shows that he is innocent.
(　　) (　　) this fact, he is innocent.

(16) You were stupid to make such a mistake.
It was (　　　) (　　　) (　　　) to make such a mistake.

(17) I have a lot of things to do.
I have a lot of things that (　　　) (　　　) (　　　).

(18) Our team consists of eleven girls.
Our team is (　　　) (　　　) (　　　) eleven girls.

227 次の各文の(　　　)に適する語句をそれぞれあとから選び，記号で答えよ。

(1) この穴を掘るのを私に手伝ってほしいのか。
Do you want me to help you (　　　) this hole?
ア dug　イ digging　ウ dugout
エ dig　オ digged

(2) 運命とは不思議な巡り合わせをもたらすものだ。
Fate has a strange way of (　　　) people meet.
ア getting　イ turning　ウ having
エ going　オ buying

(3) どうして私が君の父親だと思うのかね。
(　　　) makes you think I'm your father?
ア What　イ How　ウ When
エ Why　オ Where

(4) 建前以上にコネが重要なんだよ。
Connections (　　　) more than they should.
ア use　イ matter　ウ import
エ equal　オ value

(5) 住む家がない人が多い。
A lot of people have no houses (　　　).
ア for living　イ livable　ウ to be lived
エ to live in　オ to live

228 次の各文の(　　　)に適する語句をそれぞれあとの**ア**～**ト**から選び，記号で答えよ。ただし，同じ記号を２度以上用いてはならない。また，文頭にくるものも小文字で示してある。

(1) おつりはいらないよ。
(　　　) the change.

(2) この申込用紙に必要事項を記入して下さい。
Please (　　　) in this application form.

(3) ここで昔の恋人に会うなんて！
(　　　) meeting my old girlfriend here!

(4) このような事故はどのようにして起きたの？
How did such an accident (　　) about?

(5) そのようなことが二度と起こらないよう気をつけます。
I'll (　　) to it that it never happens again.

(6) 後ほど私に電話するよう彼に伝言をお願いできますか？
Can I (　　) a message for him to call me back?

(7) 急がないと，会議に間に合わないよ。
Hurry up, or you won't (　　) it to the meeting.

(8) ロンドンに行く前に忘れかけた英語を新しくやり直さなくちゃ。
I must (　　) up on my English before going to London.

(9) 友人が駅に着く時は，たいてい車で迎えに行きます。
I usually (　　) up my friends when they arrive at the station.

(10) 彼は約束を守る男だ；彼は決して君を失望させないだろう。
He is a man of his word; he'll never (　　) you down.

ア cut	イ let	ウ see	エ put
オ come	カ make	キ take	ク write
ケ fill	コ leave	サ keep	シ help
ス care	セ pick	ソ miss	タ brush
チ fancy	ツ guess	テ bring	ト mind

229 次の(　　)に適する語句をそれぞれあとのア～エから選び，記号で答えよ。

(1) Ideally, a living room should (　　) the southwest.
ア look at　イ face　ウ pull　エ bring

(2) I couldn't talk to her on the phone because the line was (　　).
ア out　イ up　ウ busy　エ over

(3) Our class (　　) the matter for a long time, but we didn't come to a conclusion.
ア discussed about　イ agreed
ウ talked to　エ discussed

(4) You should keep a close (　　) on small children playing outdoors.
ア tie　イ eye　ウ value　エ map

(5) She wasn't exactly a stranger. I'd met her once (　　).
ア old　イ past　ウ ago　エ before

(6) Hitomi needs to (　　) some money in order to be able to go on a trip to Kyoto during her spring vacation.
ア earn　イ create　ウ pay　エ catch

(7) His daughter (　　　) to him why she was late getting home.
ア suggested　イ explained　ウ taught　エ advised

(8) Look! There's a cat in the house. Someone must have left the door (　　　).
ア be opened　イ to open　ウ open　エ opening

(9) I could (　　　) sleep because of the noise last night.
ア few　イ seldom　ウ hard　エ hardly

(10) This job is so difficult that it is (　　　) my ability.
ア after　イ between　ウ beyond　エ upon

230 次の各文の(　　　)に入る最も適切なものを，あとの**ア**～**オ**より選び，記号で答えよ。そして，完成した文の下線部の意味として最も適切なものを，あとの①～⑤より選び，記号で答えよ。ただし，同じ語を2度以上用いてはならない。

(1) A："I have no idea."　B："The answer is right under your (　　　)."
(2) Linda has an (　　　) for beauty.
(3) "I don't want to do that," she said, wrinkling her (　　　).
(4) "I don't like science so his lecture is above my (　　　).
(5) A："Wish me luck."　B："I'll cross my (　　　) for you."

空所：ア brow　イ eye　ウ fingers　エ head　オ nose
意味：① have a sense of　② in front of you
　　③ wish well to you　④ show unpleasantness
　　⑤ too difficult

231 次の各文の空欄(　　　)に入る最も適当な語を下の**ア**～**オ**から選び，記号で答えよ。なお(1)については，英文の指示に従って答えよ。

(1) The group met secretly, because they didn't want to be influenced by any external factors.
In this sentence, what does 'ex' mean?
ア again　イ all / every　ウ big / large
エ many　オ outside

(2) These are some of the photos I took (　　　) we visited Rome.
ア when　イ where　ウ which
エ whom　オ why

(3) He's been coaching for many years now, so he's familiar (　　　) all the rules of the game.
ア at　イ by　ウ in
エ on　オ with

(4) I was (　　　) by the sound of a terrifying scream.

ア awake　　イ waked up　　ウ waking up

エ woke up　　オ woken up

(5) It's not my fault. The decision (　　　) before I started working there.

ア is taking　　イ had been taken　　ウ have taken

エ taken　　オ took

第6章　実践問題

24　語句の並べ換え

A

232　次の(　　　)内の語句を並べ換えて英文を完成させよ。ただし，不要な語が1語入っている。

(1)　こんなに興奮する映画は，今までに見たことがないよ。
I have (so, seen, never, exciting, movie, an, such) as this.

(2)　できるだけ早くこの件のお返事をいたします。
I will give you (as, as, possible, the answer, I, soon, this matter, can, about).

(3)　彼女はこのことについては何も知らなかったんだ。
She (nothing, know, about, not, anything, this, did).

(4)　言葉を使わずに他人に気持ちを伝えるのは難しいことだ。
It is difficult to (others, not, without, to, our feelings, communicate) using the language.

(5)　彼女はバレーをやっている最中にけがをした。
She (while, has, volleyball, was, playing, injured).

233　次の(　　　)内の語句を並べ換えたとき，2番目と5番目にくる語句を選び，記号で答えよ。ただし，文頭にくるものも小文字で示してある。

(1)　一日あたりどれくらいのお酒を飲みますか。
How (ア alcohol　イ do　ウ drink　エ day　オ per　カ much　キ you)?

(2)　お熱を計らせて下さい。
(ア me　イ check　ウ temperature　エ let　オ your).

(3)　間食をなさいますか。
Do (ア eat　イ you　ウ snacks　エ meals　オ between)?

(4)　姓はどのように書きますか。
(ア spell　イ how　ウ you　エ last　オ do　カ your　キ name)?

(5)　他に何か必要な情報はありますか。
(ア information　イ any　ウ that　エ need　オ is　カ other　キ there　ク you)?

(6) 彼女は，昨夜からずっとその小説を読んでいます。

She (ア been　イ the novel　ウ has　エ last night　オ reading　カ since).

(7) 向こうに立っている男の子は私の弟です。

(ア there　イ my brother　ウ over　エ the boy　オ is　カ standing).

(8) 誰もその問題の解き方が分からない。

(ア to　イ knows　ウ the problem　エ solve　オ how　カ nobody).

(9) どうやら傘を置いてきてしまったらしい。

I (ア have　イ to　ウ behind　エ my umbrella　オ seem　カ left).

(10) 間違いのことでくよくよしない方がよい。

You (ア better　イ your mistakes　ウ about　エ had　オ worry　カ not).

(11) 会に出ればよかった。

I (ア wish　イ the meeting　ウ been　エ I　オ at　カ had).

(12) 赤ん坊はおじの名を取ってロナルドと名づけられた。

(ア named　イ his uncle　ウ was　エ the baby　オ after　カ Ronald).

(13) 私はそんなに大きな動物を見たことがない。

(ア such　イ animal　ウ never　エ a　オ big　カ seen　キ I've).

234 次の(　　)内の語句を並べ換えたとき，２番目と４番目にくる語句を選び，記号で答えよ。ただし，文頭にくるものも小文字で示してある。

(1) 電話番号をお間違えでしょう。

I'm (ア the　イ have　ウ you　エ number　オ afraid　カ wrong).

(2) あなたのお母さんが先週作ったドレスを見せてください。

Please (ア the dress　イ made　ウ me　エ mother　オ show　カ your) last week.

(3) 時間より貴重なものは何もない，と言う人もいる。

Some people say that (ア is　イ than　ウ nothing　エ more　オ precious) time.

(4) 結婚相手を選ぶのにいくら注意してもしすぎることはない。

You（ア too　イ choosing　ウ be　エ careful　オ in　カ can't）your marriage partner.

(5) 天気予報によれば，あしたは10%の降水確率だ。

The（ア rain　イ a ten-percent　ウ will be　エ chance　オ says　カ there　キ of　ク weather report）tomorrow.

(6) お名前が呼ばれるまでしばらくここでお待ちください。

Please（ア here　イ a　ウ until　エ for　オ wait　カ while）your name is called.

(7) 神は自らを助ける者を助く。

（ア helps　イ God　ウ who　エ themselves　オ help　カ those）.

(8) いつまでここに滞在する予定ですか。

（ア you　イ long　ウ going　エ how　オ to　カ are）stay here?

(9) 私はたくさんの本を読もうと決心した。

I have（ア read　イ my　ウ to　エ made　オ mind　カ up）many books.

(10) 彼は食べるものを持ってくるのを忘れた。

He（ア forgotten　イ something　ウ to　エ has　オ to eat　カ bring）.

235 次の各文の(　　)内に適する語をそれぞれ選び英文を完成させるとき，(　*　)に入る語を記号で答えよ。

(1) I'm (　　) (　　) (　　) (　*　) (　　) (　　) gets dark.

ア finish　イ advised　ウ jogging　エ before
オ it　カ to

(2) I think (　　) (　　) (　　) (　　) (　*　) (　　) read this book.

ア too　イ to　ウ me　エ it's
オ difficult　カ for

(3) She was (　　) (　*　) (　　) (　　) (　　) (　　) to solve this math question.

ア was　イ she　ウ that　エ able
オ so　カ intelligent

B

236 次の(　　　)内の語句を並べ換えて英文を完成させよ。ただし，文頭にくるものも小文字で示してある。

(1) 君はぼくに何をしてほしいの。
(want, you, me, what, to, do, do)?

(2) 何でも自由に好きなものを取って食べてください。
(anything, help, to, like, yourself, you).

(3) それをもっと早く言ってくれよな。
You (me, told, earlier, should, that, have).

(4) これからさらにどれくらい日本に滞在なさいますか。
How (longer, are, much, to stay, going, you) in Japan?

(5) 落ち着いたらすぐ家に手紙を書いてよ。
Be sure to (as, as, settled, soon, you're, write home).

(6) 書くとき，Mr の後ろにピリオドは付けても付けなくてもいいのですか。
When we write, (a period after 'Mr', or not, the use, is, optional, of)?

(7) ホワイト先生の授業のお陰で英語の勉強に興味が出てきた。
(me, studying English, Ms. White's teaching, interested, has made, in).

(8) 政治のことで彼女と議論するのは無駄だと考えた。
I thought (about, argue, it, her, useless, to, with) politics.

(9) 君の選んだ題目は議論する価値があるかどうか疑問だね。
(you, the topics, discussing, I doubt, worth, whether, have chosen, are).

(10) この古い大邸宅には誰も住んでいないのですか。
I'm just (living, is, anybody, wondering, there, if, in) this old mansion.

(11) 彼は彼女の姿を見つけると，私の袖を引っ張った。
He (when, pulled, her, me, caught, by, of, the, sight, sleeve, he).

(12) アメリカでは夜間のクラスに参加する人がどんどん増えている。
(America, night, more, people, classes, more, are, and, attending, in).

(13) ジョンは目を閉じてベッドに寝ていた。
(closed, lying, on, with, his, the, John, was, bed, eyes).

(14) ビンの中にはお砂糖が残っているかしら。
(if, there, I, any, bottle, sugar, in, is, wonder, the, left).

(15) 医者は私に１日に三度服用する薬をくれた。
(doctor, three, gave, the, me, taken, be, a, to, some, day, medicine, times).

(16) 彼が退院したのは２日前のことだ。
(the hospital, he, two days ago, that, was, left, it).

⒄ 彼女は素晴らしい看護婦だったと考えられている。
(to, is, been, a fine nurse, have, thought, she).

⒅ 私は彼女が目に涙を浮かべて病室を出ていくのを見た。
(leaving the sick room, I, her, tears, her eyes, in, saw, with).

⒆ 日曜は休診日だ。
(no visitors, Sunday, when, the day, receive, is, we).

⒇ その検査はとてもつらいので，お年寄りには耐えられない。
(put up with, the examination, to, is, old people, too, hard, for).

237 次の(　　)内の語句を並べ換えたとき，4番目にくる語句を選び，記号で答えよ。ただし，不要なものが1つ含まれている。また，文頭にくるものも小文字で示してある。

⑴ これまでに地震にあった経験はありますか。
(ア an earthquake　イ you　ウ have　エ in
オ experienced　カ your life　キ even)?

⑵ フランスの首都はどこですか。
(ア is　イ what　ウ France　エ capital　オ which
カ of　キ the)?

⑶ 彼女のバースデー・パーティーには，たくさんの飲み物があった。
(ア birthday party　イ a lot of　ウ were　エ many
オ beverages　カ her　キ in　ク there).

⑷ あなたは，どんな種類の人を尊敬していますか。
(ア kind　イ of　ウ do　エ what　オ you　カ which
キ respect　ク person)?

⑸ ジョージは，試験に合格したらしい。
(ア I　イ George　ウ the test　エ that　オ hear
カ passed　キ over).

238 次の各文の(①)～(⑥)に適する語をア～キより選び，記号で答えよ。ただし，不要なものが1つ含まれている。また，文頭にくるものも小文字で示してある。

⑴ 彼は身体障害者の福祉のために少なからぬ貢献をした。
He (①) (②) (③) (④) (⑤) (⑥) of the handicapped.
ア the welfare　イ to　ウ much　エ made
オ contribution　カ a little　キ not

(2) 彼の病気は医者が最初に考えたよりも重症であった。

His illness was more serious (①) (②) first (③) (④) (⑤) (⑥).

ア was　イ the doctor　ウ be　エ thought
オ to　カ it　キ than

(3) ビルが飲んだ薬はとてもよく効いたので，一週間もしないうちに体調は元に戻った。

(①) (②) (③) worked (④) (⑤) (⑥) his condition returned to normal in less than a week.

ア which　イ that　ウ so　エ the medicine
オ took　カ well　キ Bill

(4) 他人の失敗のことを話しても何の役にも立ちません。

(①) (②) (③) (④) (⑤) (⑥) other people's failures.

ア about　イ it　ウ I　エ talking
オ is　カ use　キ no

239 次の(　　)内の語を並べ換えて英文を完成させるとき，不足するものが1語ある。その語句を選び，記号で答えよ。

(1) 彼はラジオをつけたまま寝た。

He (sleep, radio, the, to, on, went).

ア by　イ in　ウ for　エ with

(2) 二度とこんな間違いをしないように気をつけなさい。

Be (again, such, careful, mistake, not, a, to).

ア have　イ take　ウ make　エ run

(3) この本を読むには辞書なしでもすみますよ。

You (this, can, dictionary, read, book, a).

ア not　イ never　ウ with　エ without

(4) 銀行の前で，知らない人に声をかけられた。

I (a, in, of, spoken, stranger, front, was, bank, the).

ア to　イ of　ウ to by　エ of by

(5) 意味のはっきりしないことばを使わないようにしなさい。

Don't (you, meanings, clear, use, to, the words, not, are).

ア who　イ whose　ウ whom　エ which

240 次の(　　)内の語句を並べ換えたとき，２番目と４番目にくる語句を選び，記号で答えよ。

(1) 暗かったので，遊んでいる子どもたちは誰もいなかった。
There were (ア dark　イ it　ウ playing　エ no children　オ because　カ was).

(2) 私たちは美しい城で有名な町を訪れた。
We visited (ア its　イ famous　ウ castle　エ beautiful　オ the town　カ for).

(3) ミミは彼に何をあげたらいいのかわからなかった。
Mimi (ア give　イ did not　ウ to　エ what　オ him　カ know).

(4) マークは間もなく帰ってくるでしょう。
It will (ア long　イ comes back　ウ Mark　エ be　オ before　カ not).

(5) 彼は値段のついていない小さな絵を見た。
He saw (ア which　イ on it　ウ a small picture　エ have　オ did not　カ a price).

241 次の(　　)内の語句を並べ換えたとき，２番目と５番目にくる語句を選び，記号で答えよ。

(1) 彼は息子が彼女と結婚したことを誇りに思っている。
He's (ア his son　イ her　ウ having　エ of　オ married　カ proud).

(2) 君はもうその事実を知っても良い年ごろだ。
You (ア know　イ are　ウ the fact　エ enough　オ old　カ to).

(3) まるで空を飛んでいるような感じだ。
I (ア as　イ feel　ウ were　エ if　オ the air　カ I　キ in　ク flying).

(4) 言うまでもなく，僕たちはみんな君の主張を支持する。
It (ア that　イ saying　ウ support　エ we all　オ your claim　カ goes　キ without).

(5) 彼女が私たちの料理を気に入るかどうかは重要だ。
It (ア of　イ whether　ウ is　エ or not　オ importance　カ likes　キ she　ク to us　ケ our cooking).

242 次の日本文を英文にするとき，正しい語順のものをあとの**ア～オ**から選び，記号で答えよ。ただし，文頭にくるものも小文字で示してある。

「大災害の後には，からだの健康だけでなく，こころの健康にも細心の注意を払うべきです。」

① a	② after	③ as	④ as
⑤ attention	⑥ close	⑦ disaster	⑧ health
⑨ health	⑩ major	⑪ mental	⑫ pay
⑬ physical	⑭ should	⑮ to	⑯ we
⑰ well			

ア ②①⑥⑤⑯⑭⑫⑬⑦⑮⑩⑧③⑰④⑪⑨
イ ②①⑥⑤⑯⑭⑫⑩⑦⑮⑪⑧③⑰④⑬⑨
ウ ②①⑩⑦⑯⑭⑫⑥⑤⑮⑪⑧③⑰④⑬⑨
エ ②①⑩⑦⑯⑭⑫⑥⑤⑮⑬⑧③⑰④⑪⑨
オ ②①⑩⑤⑯⑭⑥⑮⑫⑦⑬⑨③⑰④⑪⑧

243 次の(　　　)内の語句を並べ換えて英文を完成させよ。ただし，文頭にくるものも小文字で示してある。

(1) うちの父は昨夜から寝込んでいます。
(my, been, has, father, sick, in) bed since last night.

(2) みなさんはここに来る必要はありません。
(do, here, come, have, you, not, to).

(3) この本はあなたのものですか？
(is, book, yours, this)?

(4) お互いに助け合うことほど大事なことはない。
Nothing (helping, other, important, more, is, each, than).

(5) その石はあまりに重くて，彼女には持ち上げることができなかった。
(was, the, lift, too, her, stone, to, for, heavy).

244 次の(　　　)内の語句を並べ換えたとき，３番目と５番目にくる語句を選び，記号で答えよ。ただし，文頭にくるものも小文字で示してある。

(1) 誰かが映画を見に行くことを提案したが，私は行きたくなかった。
(**ア** movies　**イ** going　**ウ** suggested　**エ** someone　**オ** the　**カ** to), but I never wanted to go.

(2) ストライクがとれないときはいつでも，彼女はボールのせいにする。
Whenever she doesn't get a strike, (**ア** ball　**イ** it　**ウ** the　**エ** she　**オ** on　**カ** blames).

(3) 彼女は失礼なことをすることがあるが，でもみな彼女が好きだ。

She can be rude; (ア everyone イ time ウ likes エ same オ the カ at) her.

(4) できるだけ強くロープをひっぱった。

I (ア the rope イ could ウ tight エ as オ drew カ as I).

(5) どれだけ年を取っても，私の気持ちは若い頃のままである。

(ア get イ matter ウ no エ how オ old カ I), I'm always young at heart.

(6) 何をするべきで何をするべきでないかを，自分の過ちから学べます。

You learn much about what to do and (ア your イ not ウ do エ from オ to カ what) mistakes.

245 次の各文の(　　)に適する語をア～オより選び英文を完成させるとき，(①)，(②)に入る語を記号で答えよ。ただし，文頭にくるものも小文字で示してある。

(1) この状況を何とかするにはこうしかない。

This is (　　) (①) (　　) (②) (　　) this situation.

ア deal　イ the only　ウ to　エ way　オ with

(2) 今夜はご親切にもお招きいただき，ありがとうございます。

It's very (　　) (①) (　　) (②) (　　) us this evening.

ア invite　イ kind　ウ of　エ to　オ you

(3) 約束を守らないなら友達の信用をなくすよ。

If you (　　) (①) (　　) (②) (　　) trust of your friends.

ア a promise　イ cannot　ウ keep

エ lose　オ you'll

(4) 他人がどのように感じているかを知る能力は仕事でも家庭でも大切である。

The (　　) (①) (　　) how (②) (　　) is important on the job and in the family.

ア others　イ capacity　ウ feel　エ know　オ to

(5) 最近子どもを背負っている女性を見ることが少なくなってきている。

(　　) (①) (　　) (②) (　　) on their backs these days.

ア carrying babies　イ fewer and fewer　ウ see

エ we　オ women

(6) 私がすぐ眠れるように，ラジオを消してくれませんか。

Please (　　)(　①　)(　　)(　②　)(　　) can get to sleep quickly.

ア I　イ so　ウ that　エ the radio　オ turn off

246 次の各文の(　　)内に適する語をそれぞれ選び英文を完成させるとき，(　＊　)に入る語を記号で答えよ。

(1) 口いっぱいに物をほおばって話してはいけません。

Don't (　　)(　＊　)(　　)(　　)(　　).

ア with　イ full　ウ mouth　エ speak　オ your

(2) この前お会いしてから随分背が高くなりましたね。

You (　　)(　　)(　＊　)(　　)(　　)(　　) you last.

ア have grown　イ taller　ウ since
エ saw　オ I　カ much

(3) この本は子供でも読めるくらい簡単だ。

This book is (　　)(　　)(　　)(　＊　)(　　)(　　).

ア easy　イ read　ウ young children
エ to　オ for　カ enough

247 次の各文の(　　)内に適する語をそれぞれ選び英文を完成させるとき，(　①　)(　②　)に入る語を記号で答えよ。ただし，文頭にくるものも小文字で示してある。

(1) これが私たちに残された，たった一つの方法だ。

This is (　　)(　　)(　①　)(　　)(　②　)(　　) for us.

ア left　イ only　ウ that　エ the
オ way　カ was

(2) だれがその小説を書いたと思いますか。

(　　)(　　)(　①　)(　　)(　②　)(　　) novel?

ア do　イ the　ウ think　エ who
オ wrote　カ you

(3) 彼はそのようなことをする男ではない。

He is the (　　)(　　)(　①　)(　　)(　②　)(　　) thing.

ア a　イ do　ウ last　エ man
オ such　カ to

(4) 右に曲がれば，大きなお寺が見えます。

Turning (　　) (　　) (①), (　　) (②) (　　) a large temple.

ア find　イ right　ウ the　エ to
オ will　カ you

(5) 十分なお金があったら，その本を買えたのに。

Had I had (　　) (　　), (①) (　　) (②) (　　) the book.

ア bought　イ could　ウ enough　エ have
オ I　カ money

248 次の(　　)内の語句を並べ換えたとき，3番目と5番目にくる語句の正しい組み合わせを選び，記号で答えよ。ただし，文頭にくるものも小文字で示してある。

(1) あなたの話をみんなが分かるように，わかりやすく説明してください。

Please explain clearly (① that　② you　③ everybody　④ can　⑤ so　⑥ understand).

ア ①－⑤　イ ③－②　ウ ③－⑥　エ ⑤－④

(2) そのセーターはどこで買ったのか教えてくれませんか。

Can you (① got　② the　③ you　④ where　⑤ me　⑥ tell) sweater?

ア ②－④　イ ④－①　ウ ⑤－③　エ ⑥－⑤

(3) できるだけ早く，ご返事をいただければ助かると思います。

I'm sure it will help me a lot if you (① as　② as　③ can　④ you　⑤ reply　⑥ soon).

ア ③－④　イ ③－⑥　ウ ⑤－⑥　エ ⑥－④

(4) ここはどこだか教えていただけませんか。

Will (① I　② me　③ tell　④ you　⑤ am　⑥ where)?

ア ①－②　イ ①－⑤　ウ ⑥－⑤　エ ②－①

(5) やりたいことをした方がいいですよ。

You should do (① would　② what　③ you　④ to　⑤ do　⑥ like).

ア ①－④　イ ③－⑤　ウ ②－③　エ ⑥－④

249 次の各文の(　　)内に適する語をそれぞれ選び英文を完成させるとき，(　①　)(　②　)に入る語を記号で答えよ。ただし，文頭にくるものも小文字で示してある。

(1) 帰りがけ，髪を切るため床屋に立ち寄った。

I dropped in at the barber's to (　①　) (　　) (　　) (　　) (　②　) my way home.

ア cut　イ hair　ウ have　エ on　オ my

(2) 精密な実験を行えば，どこが間違っているか分かるだろう。

Accurate (　①　) (　　) (　②　) (　　) (　　) find what is wrong.

ア enable　イ will　ウ you
エ to　オ experiments

(3) うぬぼれの強い人によくあるように，彼は自分が無作法であることに気づかない。

(　①　) (　　) (　　) (　②　) (　　) people who are proud, he is unaware of his rudeness.

ア the case　イ with　ウ as　エ often　オ is

(4) ちょっとそれを開けてくれませんか。

Perhaps you (　　) (　①　) (　　) (　②　) (　　) open it.

ア be　イ enough　ウ kind　エ to　オ would

250 次の(　　)内の語句を並べ換えたとき，3番目と5番目にくる語句の正しい組み合わせを選び，記号で答えよ。

(1) ご親切に，どうも。いくらお礼を申し上げても足りないぐらいです。

It's very kind of you. (① I　② too　③ thank　④ you　⑤ cannot　⑥ much).

ア ①−②　イ ①−⑤　ウ ⑥−⑤　エ ③−②

(2) もしも地球上に熱帯雨林がなかったとしたら，どうなるでしょうか。

What (① it　② were　③ for　④ rain forests　⑤ if　⑥ not) on the earth?

ア ①−③　イ ③−⑤　ウ ②−③　エ ⑥−④

C

251 次の各文の(　　)内に適する語をそれぞれ選び英文を完成させるとき，(　①　)(　②　)に入る語を記号で答えよ。ただし，文頭にくるものも小文字で示してある。

(1) Scarcely (　　) (　①　) (　　) (　　) (　②　) my cell phone started to ring.
ア got on　**イ** when　**ウ** I　**エ** the train　**オ** had

(2) In the past, (　　) (　　) (　①　) (　　) (　②　) an incurable disease and its victims were normally not to be told the name of their disease.
ア thought　**イ** as　**ウ** of　**エ** was　**オ** cancer

(3) (　①　) (　　) (　　) (　　) (　②　) her change her mind?
ア what　**イ** do　**ウ** think　**エ** you　**オ** made

(4) A well-balanced diet is essential for good health. It contains all the substances (　①　) (　　) (　②　) (　　) (　　) properly.
ア which　**イ** without　**ウ** function
エ our bodies　**オ** would not

(5) After the interview, he (　　) (　①　) (　　) (　　) (　②　) away.
ア given　**イ** the　**ウ** was　**エ** right　**オ** job

第 6 章　実践問題

25　文の書き換え

B

252 次の各文を(　　　)内の指示に従って書き換えよ。

(1) Bring me a cup of coffee. ［付加疑問文に］

(2) Jane sings very beautifully. ［感嘆文に］

(3) Because I didn't know what to do, I asked for his advice. ［分詞構文を用いて］

(4) I am sorry that you told him about the plan. ［I wish で始まる文に］

(5) Didn't they return those books to the library? ［態を変えて］

(6) Looking into the room, she saw her sister crying. ［接続詞を用いて］

(7) Clouds filled the sky. ［受動態に］

(8) Tell me the date and place of your birth. ［When and where で始まる疑問文に］

(9) It seems that she has been ill for a long time. ［She を主語にして始まる単文に］

(10) He is such a tall man that he can reach the ceiling. ［enough を用いた単文に］

(11) He was lying on his bed. His eyes were wide open. ［二文を一文に］

(12) I said to her, "Will you come in and take a seat?" ［間接話法を用いて］

(13) Nothing is as pleasant as traveling. ［最上級を用いて］

(14) He said that he had bought that book there the day before. ［直接話法を用いて］

(15) The house was built in 1964. ［能動態に］

(16) As soon as he opened the door, the telephone rang. ［Hardly で始まる文に］

(17) His name is known not only in Japan but also in foreign countries. ［as well as を用いて］

(18) I saw her in front of the church <u>last Sunday</u>. ［下線部を強調する文に］

(19) Please tell me. Where did you find the cat? ［二文を一文に］

第6章　実践問題

26　正誤問題

B

253 次の各文の下線部のうち，誤りのものが一箇所ずつある。誤りのものを選び，正しい語句にせよ。

(1) It has passed two years since my grandfather died.
ア イ ウ エ

(2) I wish I have more time to talk with you.
ア イ ウ エ

(3) How do you call this fish in English?
ア イ ウ エ

(4) All of us enjoyed to drive along the new expressway.
ア イ ウ エ

(5) Kate said that the movie is fun.
ア イ ウ エ

(6) The population of Japan is larger than this of London.
ア イ ウ エ

(7) Some like apples, other like oranges.
ア イ ウ エ

(8) I like a soccer best of all sports.
ア イ ウ エ

(9) It was very hot that I could hardly sleep.
ア イ ウ エ

(10) Mike talks as if he knows everything.
ア イ ウ エ

(11) Jeff was seen run up the stairs.
ア イ ウ エ

(12) I am knowing him very well since he was a child.
ア イ ウ エ

254 次の各文には，誤った語が一つずつ使われている。誤りの語を選び，正しい語にせよ。

(1) I didn't understand the lecture today. I was confusing.
(2) I'll never forget the day which I first met you.
(3) That's not that I meant.
(4) He couldn't speak, and he couldn't walk, too.
(5) I wish you can come with us.
(6) We are really looking forward to visit you during next summer vacation.
(7) He has many spare-time activity: he swims, paints, plays the violin and so on.
(8) She grew up being a nurse.
(9) I had my cell phone break by my dog.

C

255 次の各文の誤りをすべて訂正し，正しい英文に書き直せ。

(1) だれかがドアを閉めるのが聞こえました。
I heard that someone closed the door.
(2) 子供たちが鉄道線路の近くで遊ぶのは危険です。
Children are dangerous to play near the railroad.
(3) あなた私を愛していると言ってちょうだい。
Say that I love you.
(4) わたしは看護師になりたいです。
I want that I'll be a nurse.
(5) 彼女は卒業して以来，ずっと金沢にいます。
She is in Kanazawa since she has finished her school.
(6) ほとんどすべての母親が，子育てに悩みを抱えています。
Almost the mothers have trouble in raising their children.
(7) 看護学校の生徒らはみな，とても可愛く利口です。
Every students of the nursing school are so cute and smart.
(8) 205号室の患者がお金を盗まれました。
The patient in room 205 was stolen her money.
(9) 教師：アメリカと日本とではどちらが大きいですか。
生徒：アメリカです。
Teacher: Which is large, America or Japan?
Student : It's America, sir.

第6章　実践問題

27　会話問題

A

256 次の質問文に対する応答として最も適切なものを，あとの**ア**～**エ**から選び，記号で答えよ。

(1) Hello, Bill. It's been a long time, hasn't it?

ア Fine, thanks.　　**イ** How are you, too?

ウ It's very fine.　　**エ** It certainly has.

(2) Hi, Jane. How have you been?

ア Fine. And you?

イ Nice to meet you.

ウ I am taking a walk around here.

エ Please give my regards to your mother.

(3) Mr. Williams isn't here. May I take your message?

ア All right. I'll hand him a message.

イ No, thank you. I'll call back later.

ウ Thank you and the same to you.

エ This is Dr. Spencer speaking.

(4) When does Mr. Williams' flight leave?

ア The memo says it leaves at eleven thirty.

イ He's supposed to be in the airport at three o'clock.

ウ He left his office just a minute ago.

エ Then I'll go instead.

(5) Please pass me the salt.

ア You are here.　　**イ** Here you are.

ウ No thank you.　　**エ** Thank you very much.

257 次の質問文に対する応答として最も適切なものを，あとのア～ウより選び，記号で答えよ。

(1) Would you like a cup of coffee?

ア Here you are.　　イ Yes. Just let me know.

ウ Yes, please.

(2) Do you mind if I open the window?

ア No. Don't open the window.　　イ Of course not.

ウ Yes, as you like.

(3) Could you help me wash the dishes?

ア Certainly. I'd be happy to.　　イ I agree with you.

ウ Yes, I hope not.

(4) I've made an apple pie. Try some.

ア Here you are.　　イ How nice! Looks good.

ウ Oh, I'm glad I made it.

(5) Why don't we go to see a movie tonight?

ア Because I don't like it.　　イ Sounds good.

ウ That's true.

(6) I'm sorry to have kept you waiting so long.

ア No, thanks.　　イ That's all right.

ウ You're welcome.

258 次の各文を会話が成り立つように並べ換え，記号で答えよ。

(1) ア Certainly. Walk one block from here, and turn right. It is on your left.

イ You're welcome.

ウ Could you show me the way to the city hall?

エ Thank you very much.

(2) ア Yes. Who's calling, please?

イ One moment, please.

ウ Hello. Is this the Weston home?

エ This is George Brown. May I speak to Jane?

(3) ア All right. Then how about going dancing?

イ That's fine. Let's go.

ウ Well. I don't like movies very much.

エ How about going to the movie, Linda?

(4) ア I'd like to have this letter registered.
イ Yes. Thirty dollars.
ウ Can I help you?
エ All right, sir. Is cash enclosed?

(5) ア No. But is there a vacant room?
イ I'd like a room for tonight.
ウ Yes, sir. Would you like a single room or a double room?
エ Do you have a reservation, sir?

259 次の会話文の(　　　)に入る最も適切なものを，あとのア～エより選び，記号で答えよ。

(1) "How are you feeling today?"
"I feel better, but I still have a little headache."
"(　　　)"

ア I hope so.　　イ I hope you have.
ウ Take care of yourself.　　エ Fine, thank you.

(2) "Can I use your phone?"
"(　　　)"

ア Yes, you do.　　イ No, you need not.
ウ No, thank you.　　エ Sure.

(3) "Hello, this is Tom speaking. Can I talk to Mary?"
"(　　　)"

ア Yes, hold on a minute.　　イ I'm fine, thank you.
ウ No, I can't.　　エ See you again.

(4) "How's everything with you?"
"(　　　)"

ア I'll do it.　　イ All right.
ウ I'll do everything well.　　エ It's good for that.

(5) "Say hello to your parents for me."
"(　　　)"

ア Quite well.　　イ O.K., I will.
ウ Yes, let's.　　エ It's good for that.

260 次の会話文が成り立つように，(　　　)の中の綴り字で始まる英単語を答えよ。

(1) A：Aren't you coming with us?
B：If I could, I (w　　).

(2) A：Why don't you have some more?
B：No, (t　　).

(3) A：Will you go to the party?
B：Well, it (d　　).

(4) A：I missed her speech.　How was it?
B：It was well (d　　).

(5) A：May I help you?
B：I'm just (l　　), thank you.

261 次の会話を完成させるため，(　　　)に入る適切な文をあとの**ア**～**オ**から選び，記号で答えよ。

A：Hello.　May I help you?
B：My name is Eleanor Charles.　(　①　)
A：Just a minute ...　(　②　)
B：Thank you.
A：(　③　)
B：That's fine.　Ah, I asked for five people but there are only four of us this evening.
A：(　④　)
B：Right.
A：(　⑤　)
B：We don't drink.　We'll just have some soft drinks.
A：Sure.　What would you like?
B：A ginger ale, two Cokes and a glass of iced tea.
A：OK.　I'll be right back with them.

ア　How about this table over here?
イ　All right, so you're all here.
ウ　I have a reservation for five at seven o'clock.
エ　Would you like to have something to drink before your meal?
オ　Yes, Ms. Charles, this way, please.

262 次の会話を完成させるため，（　　　）に入る適切な文をあとの**ア**～**キ**から選び，記号で答えよ。

〈外出先から帰ってきた母親（M）と息子（S）の会話〉

M：Are you O.K？ What happened？

S：I fell out of the apple tree and broke my arm.

M：（ ① ）

S：Not anymore, but the doctor says I'll need a *cast for three weeks.

M：Three weeks！ How did it happen？

S：I was up in the apple tree and I slipped.

M：（ ② ）

S：No. Tom's father drove me in his car. He was washing his car in the yard, and heard my screaming.

M：（ ③ ）

S：I know, but I didn't climb that high. It was a little tree.

M：（ ④ ）

S：Yes, but I'll have to have a cast until October. I'll miss the beginning of soccer season.

M：There will be another soccer season.

＊ cast＝ギプス包帯

ア Does it hurt？

イ You're lucky it was just your arm.

ウ I told you not to climb trees.

エ No kidding.

オ How long have you been in hospital？

カ Did you call an ambulance？

キ You can't go to school for a while, can you？

263 次の会話を読んで，（　　　）に入る最も適切なものをそれぞれあとの**ア**～**エ**から選び，記号で答えよ。

(1) A：May I have your name, please？

B：（　　　）

A：Is that “Horne” ending with a letter ‘e’？

B：Correct.

ア I don't know.

イ Yes. It's Lina Horne.

ウ Who are you talking to？

エ I'm from Chicago.

(2) A：Nice to see you again. How have you been?
B：(　　　)
A：Pretty good. Thank you.
ア I'm doing fine. How about you?
イ It's too early to tell.
ウ I've been sick for a long time.
エ Me, too. Am I not?

(3) A：Excuse me, but is this the right bus for City Hall?
B：(　　　)
A：Thanks. You've been helpful.
ア Where can I take a bus for City Hall?
イ I'm afraid not. You should take a No. 6 bus.
ウ Good. You can come any time.
エ I don't know if this is the right bus or not.

(4) A：May I take your order, sir?
B：(　　　)
A：Yes. We have fish and chips with a green salad.
B：Good. I'll have that.
ア I'm still deciding. Will you come later?
イ Would you bring me a menu for vegetarians?
ウ I'd like to enjoy wine first. Could you name some?
エ Will you tell me what today's special is?

(5) A：First of all, let's discuss the schedule for next week.
B：OK. I can come Tuesday morning and Thursday afternoon.
A：(　　　)
B：Great! Then I don't think I'll have to be here Saturday morning.
A：No, you don't have to.
ア Sounds perfect. I'll be here on the same days.
イ I'm sure you should also come Saturday morning.
ウ I must ask you to come Saturday morning, too.
エ I'm sorry we are unable to decide on which day you should come.

B

264 次の会話文の(　　　)に入る最も適切なものを，あとの**ア**～**エ**より選び，記号で答えよ。

(1) A：I'm Mrs. Haurst. I'd like to make an appointment to see the dentist, please.
B：(　　　)
A：No, just a regular check-up.
ア When can you make it?
イ Shall I check for you?
ウ Could I have your name, please?
エ Is it urgent?

(2) A：What's your favorite sport, Ann?
B：(　　　)
ア It's to play mountain climbing.
イ Skiing is.
ウ I'm not good at swimming.
エ It's to do golf.

(3) A：Why don't we kill a little time playing pachinko?
B：(　　　)
A：Really? I love it. It's the best way I know to get rid of stress.
B：I would rather go to the dentist than play pachinko.
ア Yes, let's. I have nothing to do now.
イ That's too bad. You should play alone.
ウ Why not? Don't you like it?
エ No thanks. I can't stand pachinko.

(4) A：I got a flat tire on my way to work this morning.
B：(　　　)
ア I'm tired, too.
イ That's great. Can I have it?
ウ That's nice. But who's going to cook it?
エ That's too bad.

(5) A : How long have you been in Japan?
B : (　　　)
A : That's a long time.　You must have seen a lot.
B : Yes.　It's a fascinating place.

ア　Until next winter.
イ　It took me twenty years.
ウ　Off and on since 1976.
エ　Sometimes mainly in the summer.

265 次の会話の(　　　)に入る最も適切なものを，あとの**ア**〜**キ**より選び，記号で答えよ。

Robert : I'd like to have an appointment to see Mr. Brown.
Kate : All right.　(①)
Robert : Is he free any time tomorrow?
Kate : (②)　How about Thursday?
Robert : I'm busy then.　Friday would be better for me.
Kate : Well, he can see you at eleven on that day.
Robert : That's fine.　Could you give him these papers?
Kate : (③)　Would you like me to write down the appointment for you?
Robert : Yes, I'll be glad to.　I might forget it.
Kate : Very well.　Mr. Brown's office, eleven, Friday, January 19.　(④)
Robert : Thank you very much.
Kate : (⑤)

ア　Here you are.
イ　Maybe you'd better do it yourself.
ウ　May I help you?
エ　When would you like to see him?
オ　That's too bad.
カ　You're welcome.
キ　No, Mr. Brown will be out all day tomorrow.

266 次の看護師(N)と患者(P)の会話を読み，(　　　)に入る最も適切なものをあとの**ア**～**キ**より選び，記号で答えよ。ただし，同じ語を2度以上用いてはならない。また，文頭にくるものも小文字で示してある。

N：Let me (①) your temperature. (②) this until it beeps.

P：Okay. Oh, it's beeping.

N：37.5 degrees ℃. It's a little high. Don't you (③) a headache?

P：No, I don't. But I (④) a little tired.

N：How's your appetite?

P：I (⑤) all the dinner. That was very good. Is that my breakfast? What's that food like soup?

N：It is (⑥) kayu. Do you (⑦) it?

ア called　**イ** feel　**ウ** take　**エ** ate

オ have　**カ** keep　**キ** like

267 次の会話の(　　　)に入る最も適切なものを，あとの**ア**～**コ**より選び，記号で答えよ。

Taro：Hello, Yoko, long time no see.

Yoko：Hello, Taro, how have you been?

Taro：(①) Yoko, I'm thinking of having a party for John this weekend.

Yoko：(②)

Taro：Yes. (③)

Yoko：(④) It's a bit early in the year, but the weather is so great.

Taro：(⑤)

ア That's a good idea.

イ How about him?

ウ Do you mean a welcome party?

エ Who is John?

オ What about a barbecue?

カ I'm busy this weekend.

キ Have you thought of a dinner party?

ク Fine, thank you.

ケ Do you have any good ideas?

コ That is not a helpful suggestion.

268 次の看護師(N)と患者で大学生のグリーンさん(G)の会話の(　　　)に入る最も適切なものを，あとの**ア**～**オ**より選び，記号で答えよ。ただし，同じものを２度以上用いてはならない。

N：You're a member of the tennis club on the campus, right?

G：Yes, I am. I want to play tennis again after I get well.

N：You can. Do you think you could easily find a partner to play tennis with if you weren't a member of the club?

G：No, I don't think so. (①) It's difficult to find someone to play tennis with on the other days.

N：What do you do when you can't find a partner?

G：(②) I always want someone to enjoy it with.

N：It may be easy to find a partner while you are in school, but it will be difficult when you start working or have a family. (③)

G：Right. I'd like to go jogging with my wife when I get married.

N：That will help you to continue sports and to build family ties, too. (④).

G：I think so, too. (⑤)

ア Doing sports in a family helps to make exercise a lifelong habit.

イ So it may be a good idea to start some sport you can do alone.

ウ I hope my future wife will enjoy doing sports together.

エ I don't want to exercise alone.

オ We play tennis three times a week.

269 次の会話の(　　　)に入る最も適切なものを，あとの**ア～コ**より選び，記号で答えよ。

David wants to go to Tokyo Museum, but he seems to be lost. He meets Hanako and asks directions.

David　: I wonder where I am.
Hanako : (①)
David　: I lost my way.
Hanako : That's too bad. Where are you going?
David　: I want to go to Tokyo Museum. (②)
Hanako : Sure. Go straight ahead, then you'll see a post office on your left.
David　: Yes.
Hanako : Turn the corner to the left, and there's a department store on your right.
David　: (③)
Hanako : Well, it is about two hundred meters.
David　: I see. (④)
Hanako : Yes, it is. You can see it in front of City Hall.
David　: (⑤)
Hanako : About 5 minutes.
David　: Thank you very much for your help.
Hanako : Not at all.

ア Could you tell me the way?
イ How are you going?
ウ How long will it take to get there from here?
エ Will you take a map with you?
オ What do you like to do?
カ How far is the department store from the post office?
キ Do you have any friends in Japan?
ク Is Tokyo Museum near the department store?
ケ Have you ever lost your way?
コ What's the matter?

270 次の会話文を読んで，あとの問いに答えよ。

Alice : Hi, Cloe. I'm home. How was your day ?
Cloe : Oh...not so good.
Alice : What's the matter ? (①)
Cloe : I've been so sick all afternoon, with a very bad stomachache and a fever.
Alice : (②)
Cloe : Yes, but it didn't do any good. I feel worse.
Alice : What did you eat ?
Cloe : Not much. Just a hamburger for lunch.
Alice : (③)
Cloe : Rare.
Alice : Rare ?!
Cloe : I always eat my hamburgers rare.
Alice : Cloe, sounds like it might be food poisoning !
Cloe : Oh ! What do I do now ?
Alice : (④) Do you think you can make it ?
Cloe : Well, I'm pretty weak. I've been vomiting all afternoon.
Alice : Well, let's try. You really do need to see a doctor.

(1) 空欄(①)に入る最も適切なものを，下の**ア**～**エ**より選び，記号で答えよ。

ア That sounds good.
イ That's too bad.
ウ You look awful.
エ You look sad.

(2) 空欄(②)に入る最も適切なものを，下の**ア**～**エ**より選び，記号で答えよ。

ア Have you already seen a doctor ?
イ Have you ever had the same symptoms ?
ウ Did you have some trouble ?
エ Did you take any medicine ?

(3) 空欄(③)に入る最も適切なものを，下の**ア**～**エ**より選び，記号で答えよ。

ア How was it cooked ?
イ How often do you eat it ?
ウ When did you eat it ?
エ What ingredients did you use ?

(4) 空欄(④)に入る最も適切なものを，下の**ア**～**エ**より選び，記号で答えよ。

ア I'll buy you some medicine at the pharmacy.
イ Go outside for a bit of relaxation.
ウ I'll take you to the clinic.
エ You should stay in bed.

271 次の会話の( )に入る最も適切なものを，下の**ア**～**カ**より選び，記号で答えよ。

Janie : Who are you?
Ms.Wada : (①)
Janie : What are you going to do to me?
Ms.Wada : I want to show you how to clean your teeth.
Janie : (②)
Ms.Wada : Of course not. (③)
Janie : OK.
Ms.Wada : First brush the outside of the teeth like this. Please try it yourself.
Janie : OK. (④)
Ms.Wada : That's fine. Now go all the way around the outside of the teeth, brushing each tooth ten times like this.
Janie : (⑤)
Ms.Wada : Then brush the inside of the teeth the same way.
Janie : This is fun.
Ms.Wada : (⑥)
Janie : I enjoy this.
Ms.Wada : Then do all the top teeth the same way, and don't forget to brush your tongue.
Janie : OK.

ア Is it going to hurt?
イ Now brush the chewing surface.
ウ Is this good?
エ Please look at the mirror.
オ I am a dental nurse.
カ This tickles.

272 次の会話の(　　)に入る最も適切なものを，下の**ア**～**エ**より選び，記号で答えよ。

(1) A：Hello. (①) I speak to Sophia, please?
B：I'm (②), but she's not in right now.
(①) **ア** Can **イ** How **ウ** What **エ** When
(②) **ア** fine **イ** happy **ウ** sad **エ** sorry

(2) A：Would you tell Susie that Tony's having a party on Saturday?
B：(③).
A：And please ask her (④) she'd like to go with me.
B：All right, Peter. I'll give her the message.
(③) **ア** I hope so **イ** Never mind **ウ** Not at all **エ** Sure
(④) **ア** because **イ** if **ウ** where **エ** why

(3) A：I'm calling about the advertisement for a roommate. Are you (⑤) looking for someone?
B：Yes, I am.
A：Oh, good. I'm really (⑥) in it.
(⑤) **ア** almost **イ** since **ウ** still **エ** then
(⑥) **ア** excited **イ** interested **ウ** surprised **エ** wrong

(4) A：Look! Don't they (⑦) a perfect couple?
B：Yes, they really (⑧). I know them well. Both of them are so easygoing and sociable.
(⑦) **ア** get **イ** give **ウ** make **エ** take
(⑧) **ア** are **イ** do **ウ** have **エ** will

(5) A：Do you know (⑨) I can get a passport photo taken around here?
B：Well, (⑩) me think. Oh! There's a good place in the shopping center.
(⑨) **ア** what **イ** when **ウ** where **エ** why
(⑩) **ア** let **イ** make **ウ** put **エ** show

273 次の会話文を読んで，あとの問いに答えよ。

(1) Kae : Hi, Shun.

Shun : Hi, Kae. What's all this on your desk ?

Kae : I'm in the final planning stages of my study abroad and these are all the documents and details.

Shun : How exciting ! I forgot you were leaving so soon. You must really be looking forward to this. I see you are packing already.

Question : Where is this conversation most likely taking place ?

ア At a travel agency.
イ In Shun's room.
ウ In Kae's room.
エ At the host family's home.

(2) Kae : Yes. It's all a bit of a mess. I'm not really quite sure what to bring. Do you think this is too much ?

Shun : Kind of. What will the climate be like ?

Kae : Four seasons just like here, except generally warmer.

Shun : I see. Well, I think most people usually bring more than they need. You can always buy clothes cheaply there, or have some sent from home if you need them.

Question : Based on this part of the conversation, what is Shun suggesting ?

ア Kae should be careful of the weather at her travel destination.
イ Shun never brings enough clothes when he travels.
ウ Kae prefers to travel with inexpensive clothes.
エ Kae should take less with her.

274 次の会話文を読み，(　　　)に入る適切な文を以下から選び，記号で答えよ。

(1) A : Excuse me, where's the bus station ?

B : Sorry, I'm not sure. (　　　)

A : Thanks, anyway.

ア Go along this street, and you'll find it on the right.
イ I'll take you to the bus station.
ウ I'm a stranger here myself.
エ Turn left at the traffic lights.
オ You should take the subway.

(2) A：What seems to be the problem？
B：(　　　)
A：Sounds like you have the flu.
ア I don't have anything to worry about.
イ I have a high fever and a running nose.
ウ I seem to have left my wallet somewhere.
エ I'm so hungry that I could eat a horse.
オ I'm absolutely fine, thank you.

(3) A：Can I help you, sir？
B：Not right now, thanks. (　　　)
A：Well, if there's anything I can do for you, please let me know.
ア I'm just looking.
イ I've had enough.
ウ Keep the change.
エ My pockets are empty.
オ Show me another.

(4) A：When do you want to go to see a movie？
B：(　　　) It won't be crowded.
A：Sorry. I have a part-time job on weekday nights.
ア Actually, I don't feel like doing so.
イ Any time, day or night.
ウ Let's go to an all-night show next Sunday.
エ What about Monday night？
オ What's your favorite movie？

(5) A：Excuse me, don't you have any organic apples today？
B：I'm afraid we don't sell them.
A：(　　　) You had some yesterday. I saw them.
B：Oh, sorry. I'm new here.
ア Neither did I.
イ No, you don't.
ウ Nor do I.
エ So do I.
オ Yes, you do.

275 次は米国からの留学生 Tom とその友人 Kyoko の会話である。二人の会話が成り立つように空欄(①)~(⑤)に適当な語句をあとの**ア**~**コ**より選び，記号で答えよ。

Tom : You know, Kyoko, (①), I thought everyone here would look alike.

Kyoko : (笑いながら) That's funny because when I first went to the U.S., I thought everyone would look alike!

Tom : (②)! Everyone knows that the U.S. is a country of *immigrants, but I thought there weren't many foreigners in Japan.

Kyoko : There's more *diversity here than most people realize. There are (③) in Japan. Also, in recent years, Japan has *issued more work visas to people from a great number of countries than ever before.

Tom : Can you tell what country someone's from just by looking at them?

Kyoko : Well, actually, I always thought (④), but I've come to realize that it's often impossible to tell who's Japanese and who isn't.

Tom : In the U.S., you can't tell (⑤). I guess to some extent it's the same here in Japan.

* immigrant＝移民　diversity＝多様さ　issue＝発行する

ア if someone's an American by their looks
イ to be honest with you
ウ That's right
エ large Korean and Chinese populations
オ Japanese were different from other nationalities
カ few foreigners
キ I'm surprised to hear you say that
ク that I would like to go to the U.S.
ケ I'm so happy to be here
コ more Japanese

276 次の会話の(　　　)に入る最も適切なものを，それぞれあとの**ア**～**コ**より選び，記号で答えよ。

A：Hi, there.　Teddy!

B：Oh, hi.　What are you doing here, Chatty?

A：I came here to see my parents off.

B：Where are they going?

A：Hawaii.

B：What a coincidence!　I'm flying there too.

A：To Hawaii?　(　　①　　)　You had a terrible vacation there last summer.

B：That's right.　But I'm going again.

A：I remember your hotel was under repairs.
(　　②　　)　So you had to light candles in the room.　The restaurant in the hotel was closed because the kitchen was being renovated.　The White Dove was the name of the hotel, wasn't it?

B：Yeah.　That's right.　(　　③　　)
Yes.　My vacation was completely ruined last year.

A：Then you've chosen a different hotel, of course, haven't you?

B：Well, actually, I'm staying at the very hotel you have mentioned the White Dove.

A：No.　You're kidding.

B：No, I'm not.　(　　④　　)
If so, I'll be able to enjoy my vacation in pleasant surroundings this summer.

A：No way!　Good luck anyway.　And please call me when you get back.

B：OK.　I'll get you something nice from Hawaii.

ア　I can't guess how long the repairs will last.
イ　I'm sure they have completed the renovation by now.
ウ　But why do so many people go to Hawaii?
エ　There was construction noise everywhere.
オ　You had no electricity.
カ　I can't believe it.
キ　I don't care whether it is still noisy or not.
ク　I'm envious.
ケ　What a great memory you've got!
コ　How disappointing!

277 次の会話を読んで，(　　　)に入る最も適切なものを，あとの**ア**～**オ**から選び，記号で答えよ。

(1) Customer : Hi, I'd like to return this keyboard.
Shop : (　　　)
Customer : This is for PC, but I use a Mac. My wife bought me the wrong one by mistake.

ア Certainly sir. What seems to be the problem?
イ Did you pay by credit card?
ウ Have you used a Mac before?
エ I'm sorry sir. The shop will close in 5 minutes.
オ Would you like me to wrap it for you?

(2) Women : Marc? Marc Johnson?
Man : (　　　)
Woman : How've you been?

ア Are you working now?
イ It is me. Is it you?
ウ Maya! I haven't seen you for ages!
エ Susan, how've you been?
オ When did you graduate?

(3) Man : How about having the picnic down by the river?
Woman : (　　　)
Man : I could drive there, unload everything, then go back to park the car.

ア I went there last week. I really don't want to go again.
イ Is the park very far from here?
ウ It's too far from the car park.
エ Let's go to a barbecue instead.
オ The sandwiches and cakes won't take long to make.

278 次の会話文の(　①　)～(　⑤　)に入る最も適当なものをそれぞれあとのア～エから選び，記号で答えよ。

Nancy and Kiyoshi are talking about the plan of the summer vacation.

Nancy　: Just think, the summer vacation starts in a couple of weeks! The first semester's gone by in flash, hasn't it?　(　①　)

Kiyoshi : No, nothing definite, but I want to take off and go somewhere abroad for a change.

Nancy　: That sounds like a good idea.　(　②　)

Kiyoshi : I haven't decided for sure, but I was thinking of somewhere in Europe this time.

Nancy　: This time?　(　③　)

Kiyoshi : Yes, I went to America once, when I was in high school.　We had a great time, but well ...

Nancy　: You'd rather go somewhere different this time?

Kiyoshi : (　④　)　You see, I love classical music, and I've always had this dream of going to a concert in Europe.

Nancy　: (　⑤　)　I think you'd be *hard-pressed to find any good concerts in August.

Kiyoshi : Well, no.　My music teacher says that in Germany and Austria there's always a concert on somewhere, every day of the year!

*　hard-pressed＝困って

(　①　)

ア　Have you ever been to foreign countries?

イ　What are you going to do in the summer vacation?

ウ　Have you made any plans yet, Kiyoshi?

エ　When will you leave Japan?

(　②　)

ア　Where are you planning on going?

イ　I'm jealous of you.

ウ　What are you going to do in a foreign country?

エ　But is it very expensive?

(　③　)

ア　Is this your first time to Europe?

イ　Did you dislike going overseas, didn't you?

ウ　Then, you've never been abroad?

エ　So you've been abroad before?

(④)

ア Yes, I want to go to the jungles in the Amazon region.
イ Yes, but it's not just that.
ウ No, I'd rather go to America again.
エ No, I think America is the best country.

(⑤)

ア There are very famous orchestras in Europe, aren't there?
イ I wanted to be a conductor of an orchestra in my youth.
ウ But don't orchestras take the summer off?
エ What orchestra's music do you want to enjoy?

C

279 次の会話の(　　　)に入る最も適切なものを，あとの**ア**～**カ**より選び，記号で答えよ。

Mike : Hello, Judy. How nice to see you here! Do you come here often?
Judy : (①) In fact, it's exactly three years since we moved.
Mike : (②)
Judy : Last week my mother had an accident in her car. She was going along Oxford Street when it happened. Suddenly a motorcycle came out of another street and she had to stop very quickly, and she was hit by another car from behind. She banged her head on the car roof.
Mike : (③)
Judy : No, she never wears one. I don't think there were any in that car.
Mike : (④)
Judy : No, thank goodness, but the doctor said she should stay in hospital until she is completely better.
Mike : (⑤)
Judy : Yes, every day someone goes to the hospital to see her. She is a lot better now.
Mike : (⑥)

ア I hope your mother wasn't badly hurt.
イ And so you have just been to see her now?
ウ Well, tell me what you're doing here today, then.
エ I'm glad to hear that. Anyway let me pay for your coffee.
オ Did she have her safety belt on at that time?
カ Not as much as I'd like. I used to meet my friends here, but now I live a long way away.

280 次の会話の(　　)に入る最も適切なものを，あとのア～キより選び，記号で答えよ。

David and Mary are talking about their mobile phones.

David : Oh, hi Mary, look at this. It's my brand new mobile phone.
Mary : It looks very hi-tech. (①)
David : I know. They're getting smaller by the day.
Mary : Actually, in the past, I hated mobile phones. I know they're convenient, but they can be really irritating, too. They're everywhere. They're a form of noise pollution.
David : (②) The noise doesn't bother me.
Mary : Actually, for years I never had a mobile phone. I didn't want people to call me when I was in the street or having a nice meal in a restaurant. I wanted some peace and quiet.
David : But they're so handy.
Mary : (③) Nowadays you can play games on the phone, pay bills with it, or even use it like a subway ticket.
David : I know. (④)
Mary : Oh yes, and I love it, too!
David : Gosh, you've changed your opinion, haven't you? Actually I wanted to invite you to a party this weekend, so if you give me your number, I'll phone you. (⑤)
Mary : Oh, don't worry. I don't care anymore. I've become a very modern person ... at last!

ア By the way, do you have a mobile phone now?
イ Do you think I'm old-fashioned?
ウ I don't think I've ever seen one so small.
エ I'll try not to phone you when you're in a restaurant.
オ Maybe you can tell me how to handle my mobile phone.
カ No doubt about it.
キ Oh, I've got used to that.

281 次の(　　　)内の語句を並べ換えて会話を完成させたとき，1番目と4番目にくる語句を選び，記号で答えよ。

(1) Ken : Tom, you're late! What happened?
Tom : Sorry, I overslept! I set the alarm clock but it didn't go off. The (ア in my　イ must　ウ batteries　エ been　オ have　カ alarm clock) dead.

(2) Karen : I have a strong pain in my back.
Nancy : Let me see. Does it (ア when you lie　イ when you　ウ down or　エ hurt　オ get　カ more) up?
Karen : I'm not sure ... I don't think there's any difference.

282 本文中の日本語を参考に，下線部①④は英訳し，②③⑤は語句を並べ換えて英文を完成させよ。

A : Well, Ms. Jackson, thank you for going to the trouble to come here in the rain today.
B : Not at all. Thank you for this interview.
A : ①ご自身のことを話してください。
B : I was born in Kansas. ②My parents / they / there / farm / moved / wanted / because / to (両親は農業をしたいと思ってそこへ引っ越したのです。). But we had a bad fire on the farm, and the result was ... we were broke.
A : What did you do then?
B : Well, my parents had green thumbs. They worked so hard, and took over a garden supply store. They set aside enough money to ③I / me / college / business / send / majored / where / to / in / , (私を大学に行かせてくれて，私はそこで経営を専攻しました。).
A : ④他の会社で面接を受けたことはありますか。
B : Actually, no.
A : What are your career goals?
B : I think I'm an ambitious person, and ⑤I'd / somebody / be / like / really / to (ひとかどの人物になりたいと本気で思っています。) in the financial world.

第6章　実践問題

28　和訳・英訳

A

283 次の英文を日本語に訳せ。

(1) I couldn't help laughing at his funny story.

(2) I found the box empty.

(3) Generally speaking, if a man enjoys everything he eats, it shows that he is perfectly healthy.

284 次の英文を和訳せよ。

Yesterday, I met one of my old friends at a supermarket. He said that he was very busy every day taking care of his old mother then.

285 次の日本文を英文に訳せ。

(1) せきはどのくらい続いていますか。

(2) いつ足をケガしましたか。

(3) 血圧を計ります。

286 次の各文を(　　　)内の語を文頭にして，英語で表現せよ。

(1) この花は英語で何と呼ばれていますか。(What)

(2) 日本家屋の大半は木造です。(Most)

(3) 年をとればとるほど彼はますますいっしょうけんめいに勉強した。(The older)

(4) あなたがアメリカにやってきてからどのくらいになりますか。(How)

(5) 君か僕かどちらかが間違っている。(Either)

(6) 彼にはもう3年も会っていない。彼は今どこに住んでいるのだろう。(I)

287 次の各文の下線部の意味に最も近いものを，下の**ア**～**エ**から1つ選び，記号で答えよ。

(1) There is a fire in the building! You must leave <u>immediately</u>!

ア in a few minutes　　**イ** for a long time

ウ right now　　**エ** on time

(2) Have you ever seen a cherry tree full of little white blossoms?

ア birds　イ flowers　ウ insects　エ leaves

(3) Many people preserve fruits and vegetables for the winter.

ア buy in bulk　イ don't like

ウ eat quickly　エ keep in good condition

(4) Mary's ancestors first arrived in Canada in the 1500s from Europe.

ア friends in the neighborhood　イ brothers and sisters

ウ relatives from long ago　エ uncles and aunts

(5) My family lives in a distant suburb of Tokyo. We have to drive for a long time to reach the center of Tokyo.

ア far　イ foreign　ウ near　エ similar

B

288 次の英文は，どれも英語の格言かことわざである。日本語に訳せ。

(1) Time is money.

(2) A friend in need is a friend indeed.

(3) Health is better than wealth.

(4) A good medicine tastes bitter.

289 次の日本文を英文に訳せ。

(1) 医者は彼女の病気を治すためできるかぎりのことをした。

(2) コンピュータの発明で現代社会は大きく変わった。

290 次の会話を，下の語をすべて使用し英訳せよ。

A：わたし卒業したらいい仕事が見つかると思う？

B：どれだけ一生懸命に勉強するかによるよ。

［graduate, job, depend, hard］

291 次の英文を日本語のことわざで表す場合，最も適切なものをあとのア～オより選び，記号で答えよ。

(1) It is never too late to learn.

(2) A word is enough to the wise.

(3) Even Homer sometimes nods.

(4) Birds of a feather flock together.

(5) Two heads are better than one.

ア　猿も木から落ちる　　　　イ　類は友を呼ぶ
ウ　六十の手習い　　　　　　エ　一を聞いて十を知る
オ　三人寄れば文殊の知恵

C

292　次の会話文を，英訳せよ。

A：ついに21世紀になりましたね。
B：ええ，いいことが沢山あるといいわね。
A：うん。でも，グローバル化やＩＴ革命等の大変化が起こりそうだね。
B：教育も環境も難問を抱えているしね。
A：とにかく頑張るしかないよ。

第6章　実践問題

29　医療単語

A

293 次の英単語の意味を，あとのア～コより選び，記号で答えよ。

(1) cancer　(2) behavior　(3) dizziness　(4) function
(5) fatal　(6) muscle　(7) relax　(8) self-control
(9) vomit　(10) unconsciousness

ア　食べたものを吐く　イ　めまい　ウ　癌
エ　くつろぐ　オ　機能　カ　致命的な　キ　意識不明
ク　行動　ケ　筋肉　コ　自制

294 次の英語の意味を日本語で答えよ。

(1) aid(名詞)　(2) disease　(3) organic　(4) flood
(5) carrier　(6) prescription　(7) life-prolonging treatment
(8) superiority complex

295 次の各問いに答えよ。

(1) 次のうち，スペルミスのある単語はどれか，記号で答えよ。

ア　eyebrow(眉毛)　イ　sholder(肩)
ウ　throat(のど)　エ　thumb(親指)

(2) ホスピスと最も関係の深いものは次のうちのどれか，記号で答えよ。

ア　ambulance　イ　brain death
ウ　terminal care　エ　first aid

B

296 次の症状または兆候を英語で答えよ。

(1) 咳　(2) 頭痛　(3) 吐気　(4) 下痢
(5) 胃痛　(6) 便秘　(7) 歯痛　(8) 発熱

297 次の英語が示す英単語をあとのア～エより選び，記号で答えよ。

(1) sound physical or mental condition
ア health　イ diet　ウ fever　エ influenza

(2) a substance or preparation used in treating disease
ア poison　イ medicine　ウ blood　エ exercise

(3) a person under medical care
ア doctor　イ dentist　ウ patient　エ helper

(4) an unforeseen event or condition requiring prompt action
ア dream　イ recovery　ウ headache　エ emergency

(5) a place equipped for making scientific experiments or tests
ア hospital　イ restroom　ウ laboratory　エ clinic

(6) person, usually trained, who cares for people who are ill or injured
ア ecologist　イ nurse　ウ electrician　エ florist

(7) red liquid flowing throughout the body of man and the higher animals
ア blood　イ fuel　ウ atom　エ oxygen

(8) doctor who performs operations
ア psychiatrist　イ survivor　ウ surgeon　エ professor

(9) either of the two breathing organs in the chest of man and other animals
ア stomach　イ heart　ウ liver　エ lung

(10) the joint between your hand and the lower part of your arm
ア wrist　イ fingers　ウ ankle　エ elbow

298 次の英語による説明は何を指すか。(　　　)の中の綴り字で始まる英単語で答えよ。ただし，単数形で答えること。

(1) pressure caused by the problems of living, too much work, etc
→ (s　　)

(2) the organ inside your head that controls how you think, feel, and move
→ (b　　)

(3) the organ in your chest which pumps blood through your body
→ (h　　)

(4) liquid that comes out through your skin when you are hot, frightened, or doing exercise
→ (s　　)

(5) someone whose job is to treat people's teeth
→ (d　　)

(6) the organ on the side of your head that you hear with
→ (e　　)

(7) the cutting of the body in order to set right or remove a diseased part
→ (o　　)

(8) special selection of food for medical reasons or in order to lose weight
→ (d　　)

299 次の各文の最初の It は何を表すか。あとの**ア**～**オ**から選び，記号で答えよ。

(1) It is the means of causing air to flow into and from the lungs of a person who has stopped breathing. Oxygen is essential for life. A victim will not live more than a few minutes without an adequate supply of oxygen. Immediate action by the first aider is necessary if he is to save the victim from life. The mouth-to-mouth method is now regarded as the most practical because it promises more success for alone rescuer.

ア　酸素吸入　　**イ**　応急手当　　**ウ**　深呼吸
エ　人工呼吸　　**オ**　肺呼吸

(2) It is a disease in which some cells in the body begin to grow wildly, making a lump, or tumor. If the tumor can be cut out by a surgeon, the person may have many more years of normal life. If, however, tumor cells have spread to other parts of the body, they may start more tumors. When this happens, it might be impossible to save the person's life. Surgery is not the only treatment for this disease. Radioactive rays can control the growth of the tumors and so can some chemicals.

ア　がん　　**イ**　かいよう　　**ウ**　ＨＩＶ
エ　肥満　　**オ**　衰弱

第 6 章　実践問題

30　長文問題

B

300 次の英文を読んで，あとの問いに答えよ。

In reading for *self-improvement, you should cast a critical eye on what the author says. Unfortunately, however, too many readers read only at a *literal level. Too many, without knowing ①it, are slaves to other people's ideas. They tend to accept whatever is in print as truth. The trouble with this is that such people misread because they do not distinguish fact from opinion, *make inferences, or sense the author's bias.

To read critically, you need to be aware of your own bias or prejudice ②as well. We can be so biased about something that we do not allow ourselves to reason and think by ourselves. If we have heard someone repeat negative words about neighbors, politicians, other countries or the like, we tend to begin to believe those words ourselves, (③) even checking whether they are fact or mere opinion.

All of us have biases, even authors; so, as critical readers, we must be careful not to let our biases interfere (④) our comprehension. Similarly, we must be able to recognize an author's bias so that we may not be influenced until we have *investigated the facts.

＊ self-improvement＝教養　literal＝文字どおりの
make inferences＝推論する　investigate＝調べる

(1) 下線部①の it は何か。次のア～エから選び，記号で答えよ。

ア that you should cast a critical eye on what the author says
イ that they read only at a literal level
ウ that they are slaves to other people's ideas
エ that they tend to accept whatever is in print as truth

(2) 下線部②の as well のあとに補うとすればどれが適当か。次のア～エから選び，記号で答えよ。

ア as the author's　イ as what the author says
ウ as truth　エ as your own opinion

(3) 空欄(③)に入る適当な語を次のア～エから選び，記号で答えよ。

ア by　　イ for　　ウ with　　エ without

(4) 空欄(④)に入る適当な語を次のア～エから選び，記号で答えよ。

ア with　　イ against　　ウ in　　エ into

301 次の英文を読んで，(1)～(5)に入る適当な語をそれぞれあとのア～エから選び，記号で答えよ。

Researchers have long believed that an active life (1) people live longer. But new evidence suggests that at least for men it is marriage (2) provides *longevity benefits. Researchers also found that unmarried men between the ages of 45 and 64 were twice as likely to die within ten years (3) married men in that age range. What accounts (4) the healthful effect of marriage on men? Some researchers say that the poorer nutrition and greater amounts of smoking and drinking of unmarried men are related (5) their shortness of life.

＊ longevity benefit＝長寿という利益

(1) ア causes　　イ forces　　ウ helps　　エ urges

(2) ア but　　イ that　　ウ what　　エ who

(3) ア as　　イ for　　ウ not　　エ to

(4) ア for　　イ in　　ウ of　　エ to

(5) ア about　　イ not　　ウ of　　エ to

302 次の英文を読んで，あとの問いに答えよ。

Many Japanese who travel overseas bring back instant noodles (a) souvenirs. If you inspect the packages of noodles that they buy, though, you'll often find "made (b) Japan" ①print in tiny type.

Each year, some 13 billion servings of instant noodles are sold in ninety countries worldwide. Of the 8.4 billion servings consumed outside Japan, about 70 percent are either imported (c) Japan or sold (d). Japanese instant noodles are eaten around the world.

The reason Japanese companies have nearly conquered the world (e) their noodles is that they carefully study the tastes of the people in each country and sell noodles that match those tastes.

Noodles with a soy sauce flavor have been popular in other Asian countries, (f) course. One manufacturer, though, developed three flavors for the United States: beef, chicken, and pork. That company had learned that Americans care more about the flavor than the taste on the tongue, so they offered three varieties with flavors that Americans like.

Instant noodles are adapted to match local lifestyles. On the West Coast of the US, where the weather is good, noodles are mainly sold in cups so that they can be eaten outdoors. On the East Coast, they are mostly sold in packets so that they can be cooked at home.

The noodles marketed in America and Europe are shorter. This not only allows them to be eaten more easily with a fork, but also ②help to prevent slurping noises. And since many people there dislike hot water, the noodles are designed so they'll cook even in lukewarm water.

⑴ 下線部①，②を正しい形にせよ。

⑵ 空欄（ a ）～（ f ）に入る適当な語を次の**ア**～**カ**から選び，記号で答えよ。

ア of　**イ** by　**ウ** with　**エ** from　**オ** as　**カ** in

⑶ アメリカとヨーロッパで販売される即席めんの共通の工夫を２つ，日本語で答えよ。

⑷ 上の文を読んだ感想を，10語以上の英語を使って１文で表現せよ。

303 次の英文を読んで，あとの問いに答えよ。

Today in the world, it is getting more and more important （ ① ） people to understand each other. And English is a very useful language for them because it is ②speak by a lot of people all over the world. （ **ア** ） It is also taught at school as a foreign language in many countries.

And here are two very important things when you want to communicate with foreign people in English. （ **イ** ） First, try to prepare something to say before you start talking with them. （ **ウ** ） Communicating in English will be much easier （ ③ ） you are prepared. Next, try to use English as often as you can. At first you might make many mistakes, but you don't have to worry. （ **エ** ） ④Make mistakes is a very important step for you.

Remember these two things. If you can communicate, foreign people will understand you, and you will understand them, too.

⑴ 空欄（ ① ）に入る最も適当な語を答えよ。

⑵ 下線部②④の語を，それぞれ適する形に直して，１語で答えよ。

⑶ 空欄（ ③ ）に入る最も適当な語を次の**ア**～**エ**から選び，記号で答えよ。

ア but　**イ** and　**ウ** if　**エ** so

(4) 次の文は，（　ア　）～（　エ　）のどこへ入れるのが最も適切か，記号で答えよ。

Start the conversation with your favorite topics.

(5) 筆者が強調する，「英語でコミュニケーションするために大事な2つのこと」を日本語で説明せよ。

(6) 「外国人と友達になることはとても楽しいです」を，(make friends)の形を変えて使用し，英語に直せ。

304 Read the following, and answer the questions.

Americans tend to be health conscious and youth-oriented. There is no end to the number of fitness programs and the amount of equipment available to help people stay in shape — some of which is even advertised on TV in Japan! ①Americans place great emphasis on being youthful and see diet, fitness and health as paths to eternal youth. Americans, as a whole, however, are inclined to excessive eating and lack of exercise $_{\text{a}}$which make attaining this goal an ongoing struggle.

②While age certainly has its virtues in terms of experience, maturity and wisdom, it is not highly valued in the United States. The freedom, flexibility and vigor of youth are more attractive and highly sought after. Americans want to maintain their youthfulness, even while growing older. This contrasts with more traditional cultures, $_{\text{b}}$where age is highly revered and respected.

Americans are very sensitive about age, and often decline to answer when $_{\text{c}}$asked how old they are. People often respond to this question by saying, "What does age matter?", or "It's none of your business." Some people even answer by saying, "I am such and such years young" (as opposed to old). All of these responses point to the desire and the need to be, and to appear to be, youthful in the United States.

The whole outlook in America is youthful. People not only want to look young, they want to feel and act young, too. Americans generally do not subscribe to age-appropriate behavior very strictly. There are no magical ages that define middle old age. ③Americans are less likely than Japanese, for example, to feel middle-aged once they reach a certain age. Americans like to believe that they are as old as they feel. If you feel young, $_{\text{d}}$you are. Many Americans believe this and adopt and maintain a youthful outlook on life. ④This, coupled together with individualism and the high rate of divorce, makes it all the more necessary to maintain a youthful and attractive mind and body.

(1) 下線部①～④を和訳せよ。

(2) 二重線部 a ～ d について，次の問いに答えよ。

a 関係代名詞 “which” の先行詞に相当する部分を和訳せよ。

b 関係副詞 “where” に相当する内容を日本語で説明せよ。

c “asked” の前で省略されている２語は何か，文中の語句で答えよ。

d “you are” の後に省略されている語（句）は何か，文中の語（句）で答えよ。

305 次の英文を読んで，あとの問いに答えよ。

A fly settled one day upon a pot of honey, and finding it very much to his taste, began to eat it along the edge.

Little by little, however, he soon crept farther away from the edge, and into the pot, until at last he found himself (　a　) fast. ①His legs and wings had become so sticky with the honey that he could not use them.

Just then a moth flew by, and seeing him struggling there, said, “Oh, you foolish fly! ②Were you so greedy as to be caught like that? Your appetite was too much for you.”

The poor fly had nothing to say. But by and by, when evening came, he saw the moth flying round and round the lamp, each time a little closer to the flame, until at last he flew straight into ③it, and was burned to death.

“What!” said the fly, “are you foolish, too? You laughed (　b　) me for being too fond of honey; yet all your wisdom did not keep you from (　c　) with fire.”

④It is sometimes easier to see the fault of others than our own.

(1) 下線部①の文を，too～to を用いて単文で書き換えよ。

(2) 下線部②の文を日本語にせよ。

(3) 空欄(　a　)に入る適当な語を次のア～エから選び，記号で答えよ。

ア stick　　イ stuck　　ウ sticking　　エ to stick

(4) 空欄(　b　)に入る適当な語を次のア～エから選び，記号で答えよ。

ア on　　イ in　　ウ at　　エ to

(5) 空欄(　c　)に入る適当な語を次のア～エから選び，記号で答えよ。

ア play　　イ played　　ウ playing　　エ to play

(6) 下線部③の it は何をさしているか，本文中の語句で答えよ。

(7) 下線部④の It と同じ用法のものを，次のア～エから選び，記号で答えよ。

ア It is wrong to tell a lie.

イ It was last year that she passed the examination.

ウ How far is it from here to the hospital?

エ It is ten years since he died.

(8) 例にならって空所を埋めよ。

例： see — saw — seen

[①] — crept — [②]

[③] — [④] — become

keep — [⑤] — [⑥]

[⑦] — began — [⑧]

[⑨] — [⑩] — caught

306 次の英文を読んで，あとの問いに答えよ。

Mr. Jones is a very successful businessman. He works very hard, but he sleeps too little and worries too much. Last week he went to his doctor for a check-up. The doctor examined him carefully. "Well, doctor, what's the news?" He asked after the examination.

"The news isn't very good, I'm afraid," the doctor said. "My advice is: eat (a), drink (b), sleep (c), worry (d), work (e)."

"It's very kind of you to give me this advice," Mr. Jones said, "but ①it's impossible for me to follow it. I'm a busy man."

"If you don't follow my advice, you'll have ②a heart attack. It can easily happen. You must slow down and ③take it easy."

"How can I? I'm too busy."

"Would you describe yourself as a successful man?" the doctor asked.

"Yes, I think I would," Mr. Jones answered.

"Then let me ask you a question. What's the price of success?"

"Well, I don't really know."

"Then I'll tell you. It's (f)."

(1) (a)～(e)にそれぞれ "more" か "less" を入れよ。

(2) 下線部②の意味を日本語で答えよ。

(3) 下線部③の意味を日本語で答えよ。

(4) 空欄(f)に入る適当な語を次のア～エから選び，記号で答えよ。

ア money　　**イ** death　　**ウ** health　　**エ** a good life

(5) 下線部①を "it" の示す内容がわかるように和訳せよ。

307 次の英文を読んで，あとの問いに答えよ。

A neighbor ①told us about a trip he ②took with his two-and-a-half-year-old ③son. It was the ④first time the father and boy had been away by themselves.

The first ⑤night they ⑥spent in a hotel, the father moved his bed close to the boy's, and when they ⑦were both *tucked in, he ⑧turned out the light. After a few minutes, a little voice ⑨said, "It sure is ⑩dark, isn't it ?" "Yes," said the father, "it's ⑪pretty dark, but everything is all right." There was silence for a few more minutes, and then ⑫a small hand reached over and took the father's hand. "I'll just hold your hand," said the little boy, "in case you get frightened."

＊ tucked＝包み込む

(1) 下線部①②⑥⑦⑨の動詞の原形を英語で答えよ。

(2) 下線部③④⑤⑧⑩の語の意味と反対の意味合いを持つ語句を英語で答えよ。

(3) 下線部⑪の語の意味を日本語で答えよ。

(4) 下線部⑫のような行動を彼の息子が取ったのは何故か。次の**ア**～**オ**の中から正しいものを２つ選び，記号で答えよ。

ア 真っ暗なので怖かったから。

イ 怖い夢をみたから。

ウ 隣に寝ているのは母親だと勘違いしたから。

エ 初めて父親と二人だけで旅行したので，夜が不安だったから。

オ 毎晩こうして父親と寝ているから。

308 次の英文を読んで，あとの問いに答えよ。

Men can communicate; so can the other animals. But men can communicate across the barriers of time and space, while the other animals cannot, for man alone holds the secret of the greatest of all inventions; the written word. Beside ①this, the telephone, the radio, the television are the toys of children. ②Only recently, in fact, have men conquered, by means of the spoken word, any space larger than that over which the natural voice will carry, whereas down through the long course of history, writing has been of inestimable service in bringing men and nations closer together. We should know little enough, ③indeed, of that very history if we had to rely on oral tradition alone.

(1) 下線部①が示すものを，本文中から３語で抜き出して答えよ。

(2) 下線部②の内容の具体例を本文中から１つ抜き出して答えよ。

(3) 下線部③とほぼ同じ意味をもつ語句を，本文中から２語で抜き出して答えよ。

(4) 次のア～エのうち，本文の内容に合っているものには○，違っているものには×で答えよ。

ア 口伝えの歴史にのみ頼っていても，歴史自体について最低限の知識はもつことができる。

イ 話し言葉のみに頼らなければならないとしたら，そもそも歴史自体についてほとんど知識をもつことができないだろう。

ウ 話し言葉に比べたら，書き言葉は子どものおもちゃ程度の役にしか立たない。

エ 話し言葉にだけに頼るにせよ，本当の歴史についての最低限の知識はもつべきである。

309 次の英文を読んで，あとの問いに答えよ。

Many disabled people need help to overcome major difficulties that they face in everyday life. One of these is difficulty with reaching up high. Some manage with little problem. (①) need help. Recently, many mechanical and electronic aids are being used ②to help disabled people overcome their handicaps. Very small computers (③—1) microcomputers have been used for many years to control machinery in factories. Machines (③—2) this technology are now being made to help disabled people lead more normal lives.

Handicapped people often have trouble (④) about, both inside (⑤) outside their homes. While most cars can be adapted for use by partially-disabled drivers, automatic transmissions are easier for them to drive. Wheelchairs have made ⑥it relatively easy for many disabled people to travel short distances, but the more severely handicapped may need a special wheelchair that is power assisted. Lacking the strength to operate a normal wheelchair, ⑦they use special ones that can be operated by a single lever controlled by a finger, the movement of a toe, or even by breath. Powered wheelchairs can sometimes be folded up and carried in vehicles, but they are larger than hand-operated ones. So, ⑧some vehicles have been especially fitted with lifts that allow people to roll directly inside while still in their wheelchairs.

(1) 空欄(①)，(④)，(⑤)に入る適当な語句を，それぞれ次のア～エから選び，記号で答えよ。

①	ア Another	イ Other	ウ The others	エ Others
④	ア move	イ moved	ウ moving	エ on moving
⑤	ア but	イ and	ウ or	エ to

(2) 下線部②の不定詞の用法と同じ用法の不定詞が用いられている文を次のア～エから1つ選び，記号で答えよ。

ア He traveled around the world to find the treasure.

イ The little girl grew up to be a fine lady.

ウ She must be very rich to buy that necklace in cash.

エ He was very glad to see his old friend.

(3) 空欄(③—1)と(③—2)に入る語の適当な組み合わせを次のア～エから1つ選び，記号で答えよ。

ア (③—1) calling (③—2) used

イ (③—1) calling (③—2) using

ウ (③—1) called (③—2) used

エ (③—1) called (③—2) using

(4) 下線部⑥，⑦が指す内容を，本文中から抜き出して答えよ。

(5) 下線部⑧を和訳せよ。

310 次の英文を読んで，あとの問いに答えよ。

A gentleman entered a hospital in a small village. ①He came to visit his niece, Sue who had broken her leg in skiing. How glad Sue was when he gave her a box of ②her favorite candy! Her uncle suggested that she should open it. But ③she asked if she could save it for later. As soon as her uncle left she got her crutches and went down the hall. She went to the room of a 60-year-old woman suffering (a) cancer. She had been especially kind to Sue when Sue first came to the hospital. Now Sue wanted to repay her for her kindness. With a smile on her face she returned to her room.

A little while later, the lady left her room. She walked slowly to the room with the candy in her hand. Bob, a young boy (b) 14, was recovering from an operation. How pleased he would be (c) find the candy at his bedside! She, like Sue, returned to her room with a smile on her face.

(1) 下線部①の He came to visit his niece を次のように書き直した場合，(　　)に入る適当な語を答えよ。

He (　　) a visit to his niece

(2) 下線部②の her favorite candy を次のように書き直すと(　　)内にどんな語を入れたらよいか答えよ。

candy that she was most (　　) of

(3) 下線部③を次のように直接話法にする場合，(　　　)に入る適当な語を答えよ。

She said to him, “(　　　) (　　　) save it for later ?”

(4) (a) (b) (c) に適切な語を一語ずつ入れよ。

(5) 次の①，②の英文が示す意味の単語を，それぞれ英文中より抜き出して答えよ。英文中の単語が複数形の場合，複数形のまま答えよ。

① an act performed by a doctor upon any part of the body, often by cutting or removing the part having some disease

② a stick or support to help a patient or a lame person

311 次の英文を読んで，あとの問いに答えよ。

There are a variety of ways to move around in New York. As a matter of fact, I like walking best. You know why ? It is cheaper than other ways, for sure. In addition, ①it is almost always more exicting. You know there are a lot of things to see on the streets of New York City, such as street musicians, and street performers, and the people dressed in all kinds of interesting ways.

Although buses are not quite as popular as the subways for *visitors of New York, some local people like them better because they are cleaner. Probably ②the biggest reason local people prefer buses is that they are safer. So the buses are more popular among older people and people traveling late at night. A bad point about buses is that they are very slow during rush hours because they operate above ground.

The subway system in New York has both good and bad points. It is probably the only system in the world ③that operates 24 hours a day. That is convenient and causes a lot of problems at the same time. Since there is no regular cleaning time, subway trains and stations smell terrible.

* visitors of New York＝ニューヨークを訪れる観光客

(1) 下線部①の it は何をさしているか，次の**ア**～**エ**から選び，記号で答えよ。

ア ニューヨーク市内を移動すること

イ ニューヨーク市内を歩くこと

ウ ニューヨーク市内で面白いこと

エ ニューヨーク市内で安いもの

(2) 下線部②の内容として最も適当なものを，次の**ア**～**エ**から選び，記号で答えよ。

ア 地域の人がバスに乗りたがらないのは，運賃が高いからである。

イ 地域の人がバスを使うのを好む最大の理由は，より速いからである。

ウ ニューヨークの人がバスに乗りたがるのは，お金を貯められるからである。

エ ニューヨークの人がバスを好むのは，より安全であるからである。

(3) 下線部③の内容と一致するものを次の**ア**～**エ**から選び，記号で答えよ。

ア that lets trains run in the daytime but not at night

イ that does not stop trains even on rainy days

ウ that operates trains with their doors open all the time

エ that is never closed even at midnight

(4) 本文の内容と一致するものを次の**ア**～**エ**から選び，記号で答えよ。

ア 筆者は，お金がかからないのでニューヨークを移動するときは歩くことを好む。歩いていて面白いものを見るのも好きである。

イ ニューヨークの地下鉄は，清潔である所がよい。

ウ バスはニューヨークでは全くと言っていいほど人気がない。

エ ニューヨークのバスで困った所があるとしたら，老人が利用するのに不便であることである。

312 次の英文を読んで，あとの問いに答えよ。

Sometimes it seems as if no matter how much we have, we want more. But getting it isn't necessarily good for us — just look in the closet, the cupboard, or the garage. Or look at yourself in the mirror. In fact, let's start there, since cravings, a strong desire for food, can be especially bad for your health. (**ア**) Here's how to control them.

(**イ**) The next time you get a craving, ask yourself if you're stressed, sad, or bored. ①<u>If so</u>, you may be eating to fill emotional emptiness. Keep a "desire diary" for a week or more, and note your mood whenever you're hit by a strong desire to eat something. (**ウ**) If stress is your cause, exercise more to ease the pressure. If loneliness drives you to potato chips or ice cream, call your friend. (**エ**) Emotional hunger, on the other hand, often appears as desires for particular things like ice cream and fast food. (**オ**)

(1) 次の文が入る最も適当な箇所を，(**ア**)～(**オ**)から選び，記号で答えよ。

Remember that true hunger is easy to satisfy; any food will do.

(2) 下線部①の If so が指す内容を，日本語で答えよ。

(3) 急に食べたいという渇望に襲われたときはどうすればよいか。最も適当なものを，次の**ア**～**オ**から選び，記号で答えよ。

ア 食器棚や冷蔵庫の中を見ないようにするとよい。

イ ノートや日記に食べたいもののリストを書くとよい。

ウ 自分の気分をメモしておくとよい。

エ 気分転換にドライブに出かけるとよい。

オ 上記全て。

313 次の英文を読んで，あとの問いに答えよ。

① The Japanese tend to regard themselves not so much as individuals, but as members of a group —— the family, the company, the nation. The family is the basic group, followed by the class-mate group at high school and university, then the company group and then the regional group —— village, town or city. The consciousness of the national group is now reviving again.

The family group consists of the parents and children, plus the grandparents if they live in the house or nearby. ② In fact, over the past fifteen years the formation of the Japanese household has gradually changed from the three-generation to the western type two-generation unit; grandparents are not living with their married children and grandchildren as much as they used to do.

(1) 下線部①，②を和訳せよ。

(2) 本文中に，日本人は成長していく過程で四種の集団に属すると述べられている。それらを日本語で列挙せよ。

314 次の英文を読んで，あとの問いに答えよ。

① Blood doesn't flow through the human body the way water flows through a regular series of pipes. The *vessels through which blood is pumped out of the heart to all parts of the body are the arteries. But the arteries that are some distance from the heart keep on dividing and dividing until they become tiny vessels called capillaries. And the blood flows much more slowly through these vessels than it does through arteries.

Capillaries are fifty times thinner than a human hair, so that the blood *corpuscles pass through them in single file. It takes a quantity of blood about one second to flow through a capillary.

Blood is constantly flowing through the heart. It takes about 1.5

seconds for a given quantity of blood to pass through the heart. Blood flows from the heart to the lung and back to the heart. This takes about 5 to 7 seconds.

Blood also flows from the heart to the brain and back to the heart. This takes about eight seconds. The longest trip the blood has to make is from the heart through the trunk and the (②) to the toes and then back to the heart. This takes about 18 seconds.

The (③) required for the blood to circulate through the entire body —— that is, from the heart to the lung to the heart to the body to the heart —— is about 23 seconds.

But the condition of the body has an effect on how fast the blood flows. For example, fever or work can increase the number of heartbeats and make blood flow twice as fast. A single blood cell makes about three thousand round trips through the body in one day.

＊ vessel＝管　corpuscle＝血球

(1) 下線部①の内容として最も適当なものを，次の**ア**～**エ**から選び，記号で答えよ。

ア 血液の流れ方は，ちょうど水が水道管の中を流れるのと似ている。

イ 血液の流れは，水道管を水が流れるのとは，異なっている。

ウ 血液は，体の中にある水道管のようなものを通って流れている。

エ 水が水道管の中を流れるように，血液は血管を通って流れている。

(2) 空欄(②)に入る適当な語を次の**ア**～**エ**から選び，記号で答えよ。

ア brain　**イ** heart　**ウ** legs　**エ** lungs

(3) 空欄(③)に入る適当な語を次の**ア**～**エ**から選び，記号で答えよ。

ア time　**イ** trip　**ウ** brain　**エ** heart

(4) 本文の内容に合うように，次の英文の下線部に入る最も適当なものを，次の**ア**～**エ**から選び記号で答えよ。

Capillaries are ________.

ア much bigger than arteries

イ much bigger than a human hair

ウ too narrow for blood to pass

エ distant from the heart

(5) 本文の内容に合うように，次の英文の下線部に入る最も適当なものを，次の**ア**～**エ**から選び記号で答えよ。

The blood flow takes ________ to make a circuit through the brain from the heart.

ア much less than eight seconds
イ for more than eight secouds
ウ almost eight seconds
エ about 5 to 7 seconds

(6) 本文の内容と一致するものを次のア～エから選び，記号で答えよ。

ア Fever can make the blood flow faster than usual.
イ It takes a day for blood to flow through the entire body.
ウ The blood flow between the heart and the brain takes shorter than the one between the heart and the lung.
エ The quantity of blood flows faster when it passes through capillaries.

315 次の英文を読んで，あとの問いに答えよ。

Most of the earth's surface is covered with water. The waters may be deep or (a), (b) or light, cold or (c), clear or (d), calm or stormy. They may be salt or (e).

Land covers less than a third of the earth's surface. [A] It may be ①open grassy plains, ②deep forest, ③deserts, or ④snow-covered mountains. Life in some form is found almost everywhere. However, for life to exist, certain conditions must be present.

(1) (a)～(e)に入る適当な語を次のア～クから選び，記号で答えよ。

ア dry	イ fresh	ウ low	エ muddy
オ shallow	カ dark	キ high	ク warm

(2) [A]の英文中の①～④が表す具体的な場所は下記のどれであるか，次のア～オから選び，記号で答えよ。

ア ナイアガラの滝	イ アマゾン	ウ ヒマラヤ山脈
エ サハラ砂漠	オ モンゴル草原	

316 次の英文を読んで，あとの問いに答えよ。

It was many years (A) Columbus discovered America (B) people had the courage to come to this continent to live. ①A few came for adventure, but many who chose to come were not happy in Europe. Some of them did not like the way their country was ruled. Others did not want to follow their King's religion $_{a}$as the law demanded.

Many dreamed (C) riches and land (D) their own. Everything they had heard about the New World $_{b}$seemed a promise of a better world.

How strange and frightening it must have been for the first people who finally reached our shores and saw nothing (E) lonely wilderness

—— no houses, no schools, nothing that resembled the civilization c they had left behind them, and d which they had always known.

(1) 空欄(A), (B)には，正反対の意味の接続詞が入る。適切なものは何か答えよ。

(2) 空欄(C), (D), (E)に入る適当な前置詞を，次のア～エから選び，記号で答えよ。

ア of　　イ but　　ウ about　　エ on

(3) 下線部 a ～ d について，次の問いに答えよ。

a この as の意味は，次のア～エのうちどの as と等しいか，記号で答えよ。

ア Do as you are told.

イ Rich as he is, he is not happy.

ウ He came into the room as I was sleeping.

エ He treated me as a child.

b この seemed の主語は次のア～エのうちのどれか，記号で答えよ。

ア the New World　　イ a promise　　ウ Everything

エ they

c この they は次のア～エのうちのどれを受けるか，記号で答えよ。

ア churches　　イ shores　　ウ wilderness

エ the first people

d この which の先行詞は次のア～エのうちのどれか，記号で答えよ。

ア them　　イ civilization　　ウ nothing

エ churches

(4) 下線部①を和訳せよ。

317 次の英文を読んで，あとの問いに答えよ。

① Age is catching up with the baby boomers —— one third of the population born between 1946 and 1964 —— but many aren't ready to admit it.

A survey of more than 1,200 30-to-50-year-olds finds that most (76%) are convinced that they look (②) than their actual age. Most (73%) also believe that people who were 50 a generation ago looked a lot (③) than today's 50-year-olds do.

As boomers get older, 66% worry about gaining (④), 30% worry about losing (⑤), 28% worry about getting facial (⑥) and 24% worry about getting (⑦) hair.

When judging people's age, most boomers (58%) are influenced by facial (⑥) or ⑧ brown spots. Lesser numbers are influenced by (⑦) hair (46%), excess weight (37%) and hair loss (34%).

More than (　⑨　) (37%) of boomers think men age more gracefully than women; 22% say women age more gracefully. Most (77%) think women worry more than men about an aging facial appearance.

(1) 下線部①の Age の意味として適当な語を，次のア～エから選び記号で答えよ。

ア 老齢　　**イ** 年齢　　**ウ** 時代　　**エ** 生涯

(2) 空欄(　②　)，(　③　)には反意語関係にある語の形容詞の比較級が入る。適切なものは何か答えよ。

(3) 空欄(　④　)～(　⑦　)に入る適当な語を次のア～エから選び，記号で答えよ。

ア gray　　**イ** weight　　**ウ** wrinkles　　**エ** hair

(4) 下線部⑧の意味を日本語で答えよ。

(5) 空欄(　⑨　)に1/3（3分の1）を表す英語を2語で答えよ。

318 次の英文中の空欄(　①　)～(　③　)には，下に示された文が入る。それぞれの日本文を英訳せよ。

British movie director Alex Cox is making a television documentary introducing *Kurosawa and his works. He first *hatched the documentary idea more than a decade ago, but it was only after Kurosawa's death that the plan *became financially viable.

Cox says, "(　①　)."

Cox plans to interview various world class directors who have been influenced by Kurosawa, including *Steven Spielberg, Francis Coppola, Martin Scorsese and *Bernardo Bertolucci.

"(　②　) but (　③　)," Cox says, adding that he hopes the documentary would help elevate Kurosawa's *stature internationally.

* Kurosawa＝日本の映画監督，黒沢明のこと　　hatch＝企画する
become financially viable＝予算のめどがついて実行可能になる
Steven Spielberg, Francis Coppola, Martin Scorsese＝3人とも米国の映画監督
Bernardo Bertolucci＝イタリアの映画監督　　stature＝名声

① 「本当に彼がまだ生きていればなあと思います」

② 「黒沢という名前は，欧米でよく知られています」

③ 「一般の人々は，彼の作品を実際に見る機会がほとんどないのです」

319 次の英文を読んで，あとの問いに答えよ。

Many of us can remember receiving chemistry sets as presents when we were children. Even though they were small, these were still serious toys and had to be used carefully. Even though it was on a very small scale, this was still an (　　　) to the world of chemistry and to the scientist called a chemist. Now what is the difference between a chemist and a chemical engineer? In other words, what is chemical engineering and how is it different from chemistry?

A chemical engineer is a ①cross between a scientist and an engineer. He must have a thorough knowledge of chemistry but he must also have something else. He must know how to apply his knowledge outside his own laboratory. He must be able to manufacture important and widely used chemicals in large quantities. Thus the main purpose of the chemical engineer has been to design and operate large factories so that he or she could make chemicals in large amounts, over a long period of time. Money was also a factor, so it was important to manufacture such chemicals as cheaply as possible. Finding cheaper and better ways to use old sources of energy was also part of the chemical engineer's job.

Chemical engineering sounds new, but it is actually very old. People in early civilizations who took the process of *fermentation and used it to make alcoholic beverages in quantity were actually chemical engineers. No one called them ②that because the word had not been ③invented yet. In fact, the word itself did not begin to be used until around the beginning of this century. Still, that is what they were.

It was during the nineteenth century, during the Industrial Revolution, that a demand for better manufacturing processes began. Therefore there was a greater demand for chemists who understood about manufacturing. ④Not long afterwards the automobile was invented and since it used gasoline, the oil industry became much more important than it had ever been before. It was because of the growth of the oil industry that chemical engineers really became important, because there was much competition among the various companies for better and cheaper methods of making gasoline from oil.

In today's modern age, ⑤the use of computers has greatly improved the work of the chemical engineer. Differences in factory design, climate, energy sources, and other things can be given to the computer so that the best methods can be chosen for manufacturing.

What other examples of a chemical engineer's work can you think of?

Can you explain in your own words the difference between a chemist and a chemical engineer?

＊ fermentation＝発酵

(1) 空欄(　　　)に入る適当な語を次の**ア**～**オ**から選び，記号で答えよ。

ア institution　**イ** exit　**ウ** authority
エ invention　**オ** introduction

(2) 下線部①の cross のここでの意味として最も適当なものを次の**ア**～**オ**から選び，記号で答えよ。

ア 南十字星　**イ** 中間的な人　**ウ** 布
エ 十字の形　**オ** 試練

(3) 下線部②の that がさすものを次の**ア**～**オ**から選び，記号で答えよ。

ア chemistry　**イ** people in early civilization
ウ the process of fermentation　**エ** chemical engineering
オ chemical engineers

(4) 下線部③の invented と置き換えた場合に全く別の意味になるものを次の**ア**～**オ**から選び，記号で答えよ。

ア produced　**イ** known　**ウ** demanded
エ made　**オ** used

(5) 下線部④の Not long afterwards と置き換えてもほぼ同じ意味になる表現を次の**ア**～**オ**から選び，記号で答えよ。

ア Not very late　**イ** Soon　**ウ** Until now
エ Lately　**オ** Recently

(6) 下線部⑤の the use of computers の言い換えとして最も適当なものを次の**ア**～**オ**から選び，記号で答えよ。

ア using computers　**イ** whether to use computers
ウ the way to use computers　**エ** which computers to use
オ how many computers to use

320 次の英文を読んで，あとの問いに答えよ。

When they were young boys, Orville and Wilbur Wright received an inexpensive toy from their father. It was a flying toy made (　a　) cork and bamboo. The body was made (　a　) paper and the power was supplied by a rubber band. The toy was able to fly across the living room using its own power.

The boys were fascinated. Older brother Wilbur began reading every book and newspaper article he could find about wings and flying machines. Orville later ①write, "We were lucky enough (　b　) grow up in an environment (　c　) there was always much encouragement to children to pursue intellectual interests; to investigate whatever aroused ②curiosity." From what he read, he became convinced that it was possible to build an aircraft that would carry a man through the air.

To support themselves, in 1892 the two brothers started a bicycle business in Drayton, Ohio. The selling and repair of bicycles provided a basic living, but their devotion was to something else. In a workshop behind their bike shop, they produced not only bicycles (d) also gliders and kites. These gliders and kites were essential for finding out the effect of wind on wings.

In 1900 the brothers set up tents near Kitty Hawk. They ③build a huge glider and began testing it in the strong winds from ④the (A) Ocean. Sometimes one brother would ride in the glider like a kite with a man on board. The "pilot" manipulated the controls to learn how the wings would move in the wind. They succeeded (e) keeping their craft aloft for several hundred meters.

(1) 空欄(a)～(e)に入る適当な語を次の**ア**～**ク**から選び，記号で答えよ。

ア of　**イ** in　**ウ** at　**エ** from
オ to　**カ** but　**キ** with　**ク** where

(2) 下線部①③を文法的に正しく書き換えよ。

(3) 下線部②の形容詞形を答えよ。

(4) 下線部④が「大西洋」という意味になるように，空欄(A)に入る適当な語を次の**ア**～**ウ**から選び，記号で答えよ。

ア Arctic　**イ** Atlantic　**ウ** Pacific

(5) ライト兄弟が育った環境について，弟のオーヴィルは何を追い求める刺激があったと書いているか，日本語で6字以内で答えよ。

(6) ライト兄弟が作ったグライダーや凧《たこ》は，何をするのに重要であったか，日本語で20字以内で答えよ。

(7) 次の①～③のうち，本文の内容に合っているものには○，違っているものには×で答えよ。

① ライト兄弟が子どもの頃父親からもらったおもちゃの動力は輪ゴムだった。

② 生計を立てるためにライト兄弟が始めた商売は自動車販売だった。

③ 1900年にライト兄弟はゲティズバーグの近くにテントを立てた。

321 次の英文を読んで，あとの問いに答えよ。

"Other countries have a climate; in England we have weather." This statement, often made by Englishmen to describe the peculiar meteorological conditions of their country, is (a) right to the point and true. It is well expressed (b) in it we see the Englishman insisting that what happens in England is not the same as what happens elsewhere; its truth can be ascertained by any foreigner who stays in the country for longer than a few days.

In no country other than England, it has been said, can one experience four seasons in the course of a single day! Day may break as a gentle spring morning; an hour or so later black clouds may have appeared from (c) and the rain may be pouring down. At midday conditions may be really wintry with the temperature down by about eight degrees or more centigrade. And then, in the late afternoon the sky will clear, the sun will begin to shine, and for an hour or two before darkness falls, it will be summer.

①In England one can experience almost every kind of weather except the most extreme. (Some foreigners seem to be under the impression that for ten months of the year the country is covered by a dense blanket of fog; this is not true.) The problem is that we never can be sure when the different types of weather will occur. Not (d) do we get several different sorts of weather in one day, but we may very well get a spell of winter in summer and vice-versa.

This uncertainty about the weather has had a definite effect upon the Englishman's character; it tends to make him cautious, for example. The foreigner may laugh when he sees the Englishman setting forth on a brilliantly sunny morning wearing a raincoat and carrying an umbrella, but ②he (A) (B) regret his (C) later in the day! The English weather has also helped to make the Englishman adaptable.

It has been said that one of the reasons why the English colonized so much of the world was that, (e) the weather conditions they met abroad, they had already experienced something like them at home!

And, of course, the weather's variety provides a constant topic of conversation. Even the most taciturn of Englishmen is always prepared to discuss the weather. And, though he sometimes complains bitterly of it, he would not, even if he could, exchange it for the more predictable climate of other lands.

(1) 空欄(　a　)に入る適当な語を次の**ア**〜**エ**から選び，記号で答えよ。

ア between　**イ** both　**ウ** by　**エ** either

(2) 空欄(　b　)に入る適当な語を次の**ア**〜**エ**から選び，記号で答えよ。

ア that　**イ** because　**ウ** if　**エ** whether

(3) 空欄(　c　)に入る適当な語を次の**ア**〜**エ**から選び，記号で答えよ。

ア there　**イ** anywhere　**ウ** here　**エ** nowhere

(4) 空欄(　d　)に入る適当な語を次の**ア**〜**エ**から選び，記号で答えよ。

ア but　**イ** because　**ウ** only　**エ** that

(5) 空欄(　e　)に入る適当な語を次の**ア**〜**エ**から選び，記号で答えよ。

ア whatever　**イ** whenever　**ウ** whichever　**エ** however

(6) 下線部①の内容として最も適当なものを，次の**ア**〜**エ**から選び，記号で答えよ。

ア　イギリスでは，ほとんどあらゆる種類の天候を最低1回は経験できる。

イ　イギリスでは，最も極端な天候を除けば，ほとんどあらゆる種類の天候を経験することができる。

ウ　イギリスでは，急激な天候の変化をいつでも経験できる。

エ　イギリスでは天候が変わりやすいので，イギリス人は常に急激な天気の変化に備えている。

(7) 下線部②が「自分が笑ったことを後悔するのも無理はない」という意味になるように，空欄(　A　)〜(　C　)に入る語の適当な組み合わせを次の**ア**〜**エ**から1つ選び，記号で答えよ。

	(A)	(B)	(C)
ア	cannot	be	laughing
イ	may	well	laughing
ウ	must	do	laugh
エ	should	make	laugh

(8) 本文の内容と一致するものを次の**ア**〜**エ**から選び，記号で答えよ。

ア　イギリスを訪れると，イギリスの気候が，他の多くの国々の気候とだいたい同じであることが分かる。

イ　イギリスの天気を予測するのは難しくない。

ウ　イギリスの天気が変わりやすいことは，イギリス人が用心深い理由の一つになっている。

エ　イギリスの天候は，順応性を持ったイギリス人の気質に，ほとんど影響を与えていない。

322 次の英文を読んで，あとの問いに答えよ。

① 'Brisk walks' to prevent cancers

About 10,000 cases of breast and *bowel cancer could be prevented each year in the UK if people did more brisk walking, claim ② experts. The World Cancer Research Fund scientists say any ③ moderate activity that makes the heart beat faster should achieve the same. For example, data suggest 45 minutes a day of moderate exercise could prevent about 5,500 cases of breast cancer. ④ Physical exercise helps prevent *obesity, (a) is a cancer risk factor.

The WCRF team ⑤ stress in their report that it is the total time a spend being active that is important. You do not need to set (b) half an hour each day to exercise. Shorter *bouts of activity will be just as beneficial as long as they add up to the same, the *charity says. Alongside brisk walking, other activities that would count include cycling or swimming at a leisurely pace, dancing, gardening and vacuuming combined with other housework, says the WCRF.

Their head of science, Dr. Rachel Thompson, said by making small changes to their daily routine people could achieve significant health ⑥ gains. "There is now very strong evidence that being physically active is important for cancer prevention. Even relatively modest increases in activity levels could prevent thousands of cancer cases in the UK every year. These ⑦ figures also show you do not have to go to the gym every day to benefit. ⑧ You can reduce your cancer risk just by making small changes and this is highlighted by the fact (c) so many cancer cases could be prevented through something as simple as brisk walking. By taking up walking as a hobby or even walking to the shops instead of b take the bus or car, people can make a real difference to their health."

Henry Scowcroft, science information manager at Cancer Research UK, said: "You don't have to be an athlete to reduce your cancer risk. There's solid evidence that certain cancers - including breast and bowel cancer - are (d) common in people who do regular, moderate exercise such as brisk walking." (*BBC News*, August 31, 2010)

＊ bowel＝腸　obesity＝肥満　bout＝一期間　charity＝慈善団体

(1) 下線部②③④⑤⑥⑦の語の意味と近い意味合いを持つ語をそれぞれ次のア～コから選び，記号で答えよ。

ア bodily　イ intense　ウ appropriate　エ imply
オ number　カ specialist　キ emphasize　ク valid
ケ period　コ improvement

(2) 空欄(a)～(d)に入る適当な語をそれぞれ次の**ア**～**エ**から選び，記号で答えよ。

(a)	ア that	イ it	ウ what	エ which
(b)	ア down	イ off	ウ aside	エ back
(c)	ア which	イ that	ウ where	エ why
(d)	ア so	イ less	ウ very	エ more

(3) 二重下線部 a b の動詞を適当な形に直せ。

(4) 下線部①⑧を和訳せよ。

(5) brisk walking 以外の有効な活動を本文から５つ探し，日本語で答えよ。

323 次の英文を読んで，あとの問いに答えよ。

Do you know that we need seven thousand cups of water to change one cup of *misoshiru* into clean water? Do you know that out of a fifteen-year-old big tree we can only get about seven hundred paper bags? Aika Tsubota thought about these things and worried about the future of the earth. She died in 1991, when she was only twelve years old, but she had found a very important fact.

Our earth has a long history, but many people say that ①it is in danger now. We have polluted the air, sea, and land. We have killed too many kinds of animals, birds, and plants. These are our problems, not other people's problems. "Isn't there anything we can do?" Aika thought.

She found that there are many things we can do to save the earth. For example, we can stop using *waribashi*. If we carry our ②own chopsticks with us, we can use them when we eat out. ③That means we don't have to cut down so many trees. When we go shopping, we can use our own bags instead of receiving paper or plastic bags at stores. Or we can collect used cans for recycling. ④If you look around, you'll find many other things that are good for the earth.

We have only one earth. We can't make ⑤another. All the countries should work together for a clean earth. We must do everything we can to save the earth before it is too late. We must not forget Aika's dream for a beautiful earth.

(1) 下線部①に関して，本文の内容に合うように，次の文の(　　)に入る適当な語を日本語で答えよ。

人間はこれまで(a)や(b)や(c)を汚染してきたり，あまりにも多くの種類の動物や(d)や(e)の命を奪ってきたので，地球は今危険な状態になっている。

(2) 下線部②の意味として適切なものを，次の**ア**～**エ**から選び，記号で答えよ。

ア 特別の　　**イ** ～だけ　　**ウ** ～自身の　　**エ** それぞれの

(3) 下線部③の That は何を指しているか。次の**ア**～**エ**から選び，記号で答えよ。

ア 外食をするときに割り箸を使うことをやめ，自分の箸を持参して使うこと。

イ 地球を守るために私たちができること。

ウ 店でビニール袋に入れてもらわないで済むように，マイバッグを持ち歩くこと。

エ 家を建てるときに新しく切った木ではなく廃材を使うこと。

(4) 下線部④の意味として最も適切なものを，次の**ア**～**エ**から選び，記号で答えよ。

ア 周りを見てみればたくさんのことが分かり，それらは地球のためにいいことなのである。

イ あなたが家の周りを周ってみると，地球のために他にたくさんのいいことがあると分かるだろう。

ウ 周りを見回してみれば，地球のために良いことは他にもたくさん見つかるだろう。

エ 周りを見回してみたとしたら，あなたは今やっていることとは別のことが地球のために良いと分かるだろう。

(5) 下線部⑤の示すものとして最も適切なものを，次の**ア**～**エ**から選び，記号で答えよ。

ア もうひとつのこと　　**イ** もうひとつの地球

ウ もうひとつの国　　**エ** もうひとつの夢

(6) 本文の内容と一致しないものを次の**ア**～**エ**から選び，記号で答えよ。

ア 坪田愛華は，地球の将来のことを心配し，長年活動を続けている。

イ 私たちの地球は危険な状態にあるといわれ，その中で起こっている問題は他人事ではない。

ウ 私たちは，買い物に行くときには，ビニール袋を受け取る代わりにマイバッグを使うことができる。

エ きれいな私たちの地球を救っていくために，私たちができる全てのことをしなくてはならない。

324 次の英文を読んで，あとの問いに答えよ。

One of the most interesting of all studies is the study of words and word origins. Each language is composed of several earlier languages, and the words of a language can sometimes be traced back through two or three different languages to their origins. Again, a word from one language may pass into other languages and develop a new meaning. The word "etiquette," which is of French origin and originally meant a label or a sign, passed into Spanish and kept its original meaning. So in Spanish the word "etiquette" today is used to indicate the small tags which a store attaches to a suit, a dress, or a bottle. The word "etiquette" in French, however, gradually developed a different meaning. It later became the custom to write directions on small cards or "etiquettes" as to how visitors should dress for and act during an important ceremony at the royal court. Thus, the word "etiquette" began to indicate a system of correct manners for people to follow. With this meaning, the word passed into English.

Consider the word "breakfast." "To fast" is to go for some period of time without eating. Thus, in the morning, after many hours during the night without food, one "①breaks his fast."

Consider the everyday English expression "Good-bye." Many, many years ago, people would say to each other on parting; "②God be with you." As this expression was repeated over and over million of times, it gradually became shortened to "good-bye."

(1) 次の文が本文の内容に合うように，(　　　)に入るものをあとの**ア**〜**エ**より選び，記号で答えよ。

① どの言語も(　　　)。

ア それぞれ各民族の精神の象徴である
イ 各地の文化の中心的な役割を果たしている
ウ いくつかの古い言語から成り立っている
エ 支配権をめぐって熾烈な戦いをしてきた

② 単語のなかには，(　　　)ものもある。

ア 言語の象徴的特徴を示す
イ 言語学的に意味を解明できない
ウ 言語の魂とも言える
エ 他言語に語源を持つ

③ 単語のなかには，(　　　)ものもある。

ア 他言語の発展に大きな影響を与えた
イ 他言語の中にはいって元の意味を保った
ウ 他言語に圧倒されて消滅した
エ 他言語の影響を受けて音声的に変化した

④ "etiquette" の語源は(　　　)であり，その意味は標札とか標識という意味である。

ア スペイン語　　　**イ** フランス語
ウ イタリア語　　　**エ** 英語

⑤ “etiquette”の語源学的意味を残しているのは(　　　)である。

ア　スペイン語　　　　イ　フランス語

ウ　イタリア語　　　　エ　英語

⑥ フランスでは，“etiquette”と呼ばれる小さな紙片に(　　　)。

ア　商品ではなく展示品だから悪しからずという意味が込められていた

イ　宮廷の式典に出席する各界の紳士淑女の名前を書いた招待状が送られた

ウ　宮廷の重要な式典で国王に謁見する出席者の順番が仰々しく書かれた

エ　宮廷の重要な式典の出席者の服装や振舞についての指示が書き込まれた

⑦ 英語の“etiquette”という単語は，(　　　)という意味である。

ア　紳士淑女の修めるべき基本的教養

イ　遵守すべき形式美の枠

ウ　伝統を重んじる洗練された立居振舞

エ　人々が守るべき一連の礼儀作法

⑧ 単語や語源の研究は(　　　)の一つである。

ア　最も困難な研究　　　　イ　最も楽しい研究

ウ　最も重要な研究　　　　エ　最も期待される研究

(2) 下線部①②を和訳せよ。

325 次の英文を読んで，あとの問いに答えよ。

Some people become *harsh critics the (　a　) they suspect they are not going to get exactly what they want exactly when they want it. They seem to have no end of feelings to *vent. They tend to be spoiled, *intolerant people who believe they are *entitled to have everything their way.

Sarah realized that she and her children were constantly tiptoeing around her husband, Larry. ①He didn't want the children to have their friends around because it disturbed him. His friends, of course, could come over (　b　) he wanted them to. He didn't allow the kids to play the music they liked, but he could play his music as loud as he wanted it. He demanded a quiet, orderly household and if he didn't get it, he criticized Sarah and the children *unmercifully.

Sarah examined the intent behind Larry's criticism and decided that Larry's behavior was due (　c　) his being spoiled and having an *exaggerated sense of entitlement. His *outbursts were frequent, but he wasn't just venting anger or frustrations with them. He was really demanding his own way.

When Larry was growing up his mother had solved every problem, large or small, in her son's life. She had taught him that he was so wonderful and so special he did not have to put (d) with the same frustrations and *discomforts as ordinary *mortals. (② Larry, view, the, learned, world, to, According), he *deserves his way no matter what, and the person who tries to *thwart him must be punished and learn to *toe the line.

Sarah had a long struggle to change ③ Larry's pattern of behavior, but the *coping techniques helped her and the children (e) up for their right to enjoy their own home.

＊ harsh＝手厳しい　vent＝ぶつける
intolerant＝不寛容な　entitled＝資格がある
unmercifully＝情け容赦なく　exaggerated＝過度の
outburst＝(感情の) 爆発　discomfort＝不快
mortal＝人間　deserve＝～に値する
thwart＝妨げる　toe the line＝上からの命令に従う
coping techniques＝能動的対処方法

(1) 空欄(a)～(e)に入る適当な語をそれぞれ次の**ア**～**オ**から選び，記号で答えよ。

ア stand　**イ** second　**ウ** up　**エ** whenever　**オ** to

(2) 下線部①を和訳せよ。

(3) 下線部②の語句を並び換えて「ラリーが身につけた世界観によれば」という意味の英文を完成させよ。

(4) 下線部③が生じた原因は何か，本文に即して日本語で答えよ。

326 次の英文を読んで，あとの問いに答えよ。

Edgar Poe was born in eighteen-oh-nine in Boston, Massachusetts. His parents were actors. At that time, actors were not accepted by the best society. Edgar was a baby when his father left the family. He was two years old when his mother died. He was taken into the home of a wealthy businessman, John Allan. He then received his new name — Edgar Allan Poe.

Edgar attended schools in England and in Richmond, Virginia. As a young man, he attended the University of Virginia in Charlottesville. He was a good student. He was a member of the Jefferson Literary Society. And then, Edgar went to Boston and began working as a writer and editor for monthly magazines. He also served in the army for two years. Edgar Allan Poe worked hard. He became a successful editor. He published three books of poetry. He also began writing stories. Five of his stories were printed in a publication in Philadelphia, Pennsylvania in eighteen thirty-two. Yet he was not well paid. His life was difficult. He was poor, and he was troubled by sicknesses of the body and mind. Poe *suffered from depression. He drank alcohol to escape his fears. The alcohol had a very bad effect on him.

Through all his crises, Edgar Allan Poe produced many stories, poems, and works of criticism. Some of his stories won prizes. Yet he did not become famous until eighteen forty-five. That was when his poem "The Raven" was published. Most American writing is *realistic. But Poe's interests and way of writing were not realistic at all. Poe's work has been praised most in France. He had a great influence on many French writers. Poe's best-known poem is "The Raven." Some people love it. They say it is like music. Others hate it. They say it sounds forced and unnatural — like bad music.

＊ suffer from depression＝うつ病になる
realistic＝現実主義の，写実派の

(1) 主人公が生まれた西暦年を算用数字で答え，生まれ故郷をできるだけ詳しく日本語で答えよ。

(2) 主人公は両親とは結局一緒には暮らせなくなったが，父親および母親と別れたのはそれぞれ彼のいつ頃だったか，日本語で答えよ。

(3) 彼は成人の頃，正式にはどんな名前で呼ばれていたか，英語で答えよ。

(4) 次の**ア**～**オ**のうち，本文中の内容に合うものを２つ選び，記号で答えよ。

ア 彼は他の国には出て行ったことがなく，アメリカだけで生涯をすごした。

イ 彼はヴァージニア大学には通ったことがあり，とても善良な学生であった。

ウ 彼は軍隊で兵役についたことはなく，すぐに仕事についた。

エ 彼は月刊雑誌編集者として働いている間にも，詩や小説も書き，それに相応して収入も増えた。

オ 彼は病気の恐怖から逃れるために，身体に悪いのにお酒を飲みすぎることもあった。

(5) 下線部は「それは『大鴉(おおからす)』という詩が出版された時であった」といっているが，それとは西暦何年で，彼がどうなった時であるか，日本語で説明せよ。

(6) 主人公はアメリカよりもフランスの作家に影響を与えたとあるが，その理由を簡単に述べよ。

(7) ところで，この主人公の名前は日本でもよく知られていて，この人の名前から日本名を作り，自分の名前にしてしまった作家がいる。作品には「怪人二十面相」がある。その作家の名前を漢字5文字で書け。

327 次の英文を読んで，あとの問いに答えよ。

*Cell phones are very popular today. The basic idea of cell phones begins in 1947, with the use of cell phone communication in police cars in the United States. However, the first call on a portable cell phone was not made until 1973. By 1987, more than one million Americans were using cell phones. Today, more than 69 million Americans, 65 million Chinese, 63 million Japanese, 55 million Germans, and 43 million *Britons use them.

Cell phones seem to be especially popular in Japan. ①Japan is one of the few countries in the world in which there are more cell phones than regular telephones. Wherever you go in Japan, you can see someone using a cell phone. Japanese use cell phones to send and receive e-mail and *text messages, to *browse the web, play games, and shop.

Japan has some of the best cell phones systems and services in the world. The phones are very lightweight, and can display full color images on their *LCD screens. They also have built-in cameras so that the user can take snapshots or even short videos and send them to friends. Japanese cell phones are *user-friendly and convenient.

Service is very good, and unlike in many other countries, ②it seems that there is no place in Japan, including tunnels and underground shopping malls, where you cannot use a cell phone.

Yes, cell phones are wonderful; however, there is one problem. Many Japanese feel very isolated nowadays. One of the reasons for this is the use of cell phones to exchange information.

Communication is an art, and like any art it takes practice. Cell phones will never replace face-to-face communication. Humans will always feel isolated if they do not talk to other people in person.

* cell phone(s)＝携帯電話　Britons＝英国人
text messages＝テキスト・メッセージ　browse＝拾い読みする
LCD(Liquid Crystal Display)＝液晶表示
user-friendly＝使いやすい

(1) 下線部①，②を和訳せよ。

(2) 次のア～エのうち，本文の内容に合っているものには○，違っているものには×で答えよ。

ア Cell phone communication began in the United States.

イ Japan has the highest number of cell phone users in the world.

ウ People only use cell phones to make phone calls.

エ Japanese cell phones do not weigh very much.

(3) 次のア～エの語に第1アクセントをつけ，その語の意味を答えよ。

(例) Japanése（日本人）

ア images　イ convenient　ウ isolated

エ nowadays

(4) 本文で筆者が一番言いたいことは何か，文中より抜き出して答えよ。

328 次の英文を読んで，あとの問いに答えよ。

Don't miss out!

The world's best known shirts are now on sale at this shop!

A wide range of colors, sizes, and styles are available!

Machine washable, no need to iron.

Best gifts for your parents, friends, and someone you love.

(1) Where is this advertisement from?

ア A clothing store　イ A hair salon

ウ A dry cleaner　エ A gift shop

(2) Which is NOT true about the items on sale at this shop?

ア They are famous brands.　イ They have many different colors.

ウ They can be washed.　エ They must be ironed.

MEMO FOR: *Jonathan Edwards*

DATE: *August 31*

TIME: *12:30 p.m.*

While you were at lunch break:

Ms.Mary Kay of Info Tech called

PHONE: *713-5506* EXT. *22*

MESSAGE:

She wants to have the estimate for the car by next week.

She expects a call from you.

Taken BY: *Joe Smith*

(3) Who wrote down this memo?

ア Jonathan Edwards　　イ Mary Kay

ウ Info Tech　　エ Joe Smith

(4) When was the message taken?

ア In the morning　　イ Around noon

ウ At coffee break　　エ In the evening

(5) Who expects a call?

ア Jonathan Edwards　　イ Mary Kay

ウ Info Tech　　エ Joe Smith

329 次の英文を読んで，あとの問いに答えよ。

In Japan traffic keeps to the left, but in the U.S., Canada and all the countries on the mainland in Europe they drive on the right. Only Britain and Ireland do the same as Japan. This causes great confusion.

American drivers in Japan are doubly shocked, because they also have to adapt their driving to narrower roads. European motorisis in Britain often bring their own cars, with the *steering wheel on the left. On roads near the coast there are "Keep Left" signs in many languages.

①They are useful as a reminder, but they can't do anything about the obvious difficulty of driving a car with the steering wheel on the wrong side.

If the driver wanted to overtake another *vehicle, he would not be able to see very far ahead. Either he would have to (②) and stay behind, or he might take a risk and have an accident. There might be (③) accidents involving foreign drivers if they left their cars at home and hired ones with right-hand drive in Britain or Ireland. That is what the British and the Irish say, but Europeans say ④the opposite.

They think it would be more sensible if those two countries changed over to driving on the right. Then there would be a single, simple European and American standard.

Until the early 1960's Sweden drove on the left, too. Cars at the borders with Norway and Finland would change sides. That the Swedish government decided that Sweden would adopt the European standard, and everything changed. Now the Swedes say they would feel unsafe driving on the left again.

* steering wheel＝ハンドル　　vehicle＝乗り物

(1) 下線部①の They が表すものを次のア～エから選び，記号で答えよ。

ア many languages　　イ “Keep Left” signs

ウ roads near the coast　　エ European motorists

(2) 空欄(　②　)(　③　)に入る最も適切なものをあとのア～エから選び，記号で答えよ。

② ア speed up　イ slow down　ウ get off　エ stop

③ ア much　イ more　ウ little　エ fewer

(3) 下線部④の the opposite の内容を具体的に表すものを次のア～エから選び，記号で答えよ。

ア to take a risk and have an accident

イ to leave one's car at home and a car abroad

ウ to adopt a universal driving standard

エ to be more sensible

(4) 本文の内容と一致するものを次のア～エから選び，記号で答えよ。

ア イギリスとアイルランドでも車の走る側を右側に変えることを検討している。

イ スウェーデンでも昔は車は道路の左側を走っていた。

ウ ノルウェーとフィンランドの国境では今でも左側通行から右側通行に変えなければならない。

エ スウェーデンは現在再び車が走る側を道路の左側に変えることを検討している。

330 次の英文を読んで，あとの問いに答えよ。

Extremely hot weather is common in many parts of the world. Although hot weather just makes most people feel hot, it can cause serious medical problems — even death. Floods, storms and other natural events kill thousands of people every year. So ①does extreme heat. Experts say heat may be nature's deadliest killer. Last summer, for example, some towns and cities on America's East Coast set all-time temperature records. Temperatures rose as high as 42 degrees Celsius.

Doctors say ②people can do many things to protect themselves from the dangers of extreme heat. Stay out of the sun, if possible. Drink lots of cool water. Wear light colored clothing made of natural materials. Make sure the clothing is loose, permitting freedom of movement. Also, learn the danger signs of the medical problems linked to heat.

Extreme heat can lead to a serious problem called *heat exhaustion. A person suffering from heat exhaustion loses too much water through *perspiration. ③The person becomes *dehydrated. A person suffering heat exhaustion feels weak and extremely tired. He or she may have trouble walking normally. Heat exhaustion may also produce a feeling of sickness, a fast heartbeat, breathing problems and pain in the head, chest or stomach. Doctors say people with such problems should rest quietly in a cool place and drink plenty of water. They also say it may help to wash with cool water.

(出典：Voice of America Special English Heat May Be Nature's Deadliest Killer 一部改変)

＊ heat exhaustion＝熱中症，熱性疲労　perspiration＝発汗
dehydrated＝脱水症状の

(1) 下線部①の does が表すものを，下の**ア**～**エ**より選び，記号で答えよ。

ア 毎年たくさんの人が極端な暑さを感じてしまう
イ 毎年何千人もの人が病気で死んでしまう
ウ 毎年たくさんの洪水や嵐や他の自然災害が起こってしまう
エ 毎年何千人もの人が死んでしまう

(2) 下線部②の people can do many things を，本文に沿ってより詳しく説明したものとして，最も適当なものを下の**ア**～**エ**より選び，記号で答えよ。

ア people can stay in shade, wear loose clothes, and drink liquids
イ people can stay inside, wear nothing, and drink beer
ウ people can go to see a doctor or dial 911 to call an ambulance
エ people can have medical problems linked to heat

(3) 下線部③の The person becomes dehydrated の内容と一致するものを下の**ア**～**エ**より選び，記号で答えよ。

ア He / She has drunk too much water.
イ He / She has lost too much water.
ウ He / She has been sick in bed for a long time.
エ He / She has pain in the head, chest or stomach.

(4) 本文の内容と一致するものを下の**ア**～**エ**より選び，記号で答えよ。

ア 暑さは洪水や嵐のような自然災害ほどの脅威は人間にもたらさないできた。
イ 暑さは人間にとっては自然界で最も危険なものかもしれない。
ウ これから先，地球温暖化によって暑さはさらにひどくなるかもしれない。
エ 暑さ対策を充分行って，どんなに暑くてもちゃんと働ける体にしなければならない。

(5) 次の英語の問いに対する答えとして最も適切なものを下のア～エより選び，記号で答えよ。

What should people do when they feel exhausted from heat?

ア They should drink and wash with cool water, relaxing in a cool place.

イ They should keep working hard under difficult conditions.

ウ They should walk normally even though they find it hard to do so.

エ They should perspire more because sweating a lot does them good.

C

331 次の英文を読んで，あとの問いに答えよ。

Benjamin Franklin was ①born in Boston, and his family was very large. He was the 15th child in a family of 17 children!

Ben had to leave school when he was ten years old. In those days boys had to learn a trade while they were still young. Ben went to work for his father, (②) made candles and soap, but he found this work very dull. Ben liked to read and to use his mind.

One day, Ben went to his father and said, “I know you are counting on me to help you with your business but, Father, I do not want to do this work all my life.”

Ben's father thought a while. “Ben,” a he said, “how would you like to be a printer?”

“I think I would like that,” Ben answered.

“Well, your brother James is a printer. I'll arrange for you to work with him.”

Ben was very happy with ③this idea. At last he would be doing something he was sure he would like. And so he moved out of his father's house and into his brother's home. Ben was only 12 years old at this time.

James' print shop was dirty, but it had the clean smell of printer's ink. Ben enjoyed mixing the ink, setting the type and making up the sheets of rough hand-pressed paper. He had plenty of time ④to read books. He even wrote articles under a false name. His brother, not knowing that ⑤they were really Benjamin's, printed them. They were known as the “Dogood Papers.”

Ben's brother had some very strong ideas about how the colonies should be run. This made him a “radical” and he got into trouble with the government for printing his views. When James was put into prison, Benjamin ran the business and brought out a paper called the Courant. It soon became very popular.

(1) 下線部 a の文を間接話法に書き換えよ。

(2) 下線部①の born の語の原形を答えよ。

(3) 空欄(②)に入る適当な語を次のア～エから選び，記号で答えよ。

ア who　　**イ** that　　**ウ** which　　**エ** what

(4) 下線部③の this idea とはどのような idea か，日本語で答えよ。

(5) 下線部④の to read の用法と同じものを次のア～エから選び，記号で答えよ。

ア I want to drink cold water.

イ He has many things to do.

ウ She worked hard to pass the test.

エ To tell the truth, I don't like him.

(6) 下線部⑤の they は何をさしているか，本文中の語句を用いて答えよ。

(7) 次の単語の下線部と同じ発音の語を次のア～エから選び，記号で答えよ。

① still　(**ア** like　**イ** mind　**ウ** children　**エ** time)

② name　(**ア** trade　**イ** family　**ウ** want　**エ** false)

③ clean　(**ア** year　**イ** really　**ウ** leave　**エ** idea)

④ found　(**ア** trouble　**イ** about　**ウ** young　**エ** would)

(8) 次の①～⑤のうち，本文の内容に合っているものには○，違っているものには×で答えよ。

① Ben は勉強が嫌いで小学校を退学したが，本を読むことは好きだった。

② Ben は兄にすすめられて印刷工になった。

③ Ben は印刷工場のインクの匂いが我慢できなかった。

④ 兄はペンネームで書かれた記事の筆者が誰であるか知らなかった。

⑤ 兄が牢獄に入れられたため，Ben が印刷物の仕事をかわって続けた。

332 次の英文を読んで，あとの問いに答えよ。

Most of us use salt every day. We use it when we cook our food. But we think nothing of it because we can get it at a store or a supermarket at any time we like. It is there, and we use it without ①know where it comes from.

But many many years ago, in Greece, salt was not so common as it is today. It was not so easy to get it, especially for the people who lived far (②) sea. Most people used no salt in their food at that time. Only the rich people could use it because ③it was too expensive for the poor people to buy.

Salt was once so hard to get that it was used as money. Roman workers were once ④pay all or part of their wages in salt. The English word *salary* comes from the Latin word *salarium*. It means “salt money.”

In old China, salt was almost as valuable as gold. In Europe before ⑤icebox were ⑥invented, salt was used to keep meat or fish from going bad. In some parts of Africa salt is taken to market in blocks. At the market the blocks are broken（ ⑦ ）small pieces for ⑧sale. In some parts of the world there are still people who have never seen or tasted salt.

(1) 下線部①を文法的に正しく書き換えよ。

(2) 空欄②に入る適当な語を次の**ア**～**オ**から選び，記号で答えよ。

ア in　**イ** into　**ウ** from　**エ** for　**オ** beyond

(3) 下線部③を和訳せよ。

(4) 下線部④を文法的に正しく書き換えよ。

(5) 下線部⑤の複数形を答えよ。

(6) 下線部⑥の名詞型を答えよ。

(7) 空欄⑦に入る適当な語を次の**ア**～**オ**から選び，記号で答えよ。

ア on　**イ** for　**ウ** over　**エ** into　**オ** to

(8) 下線部⑧の動詞型を答えよ。

(9) 次の**ア**～**コ**のうち，本文の内容に合っているものには○，違っているものには×で答えよ。

ア われわれは何時でも好きな時に買えるので，塩の事を何も考えない。
イ 大昔のギリシャではすでに塩は多くの人に使われていた。
ウ ギリシャやローマではお金さえ払えば塩は簡単に手に入った。
エ ローマでは salarium と言う言葉が賃金の意味に使われた。
オ 古代中国では塩が金と同じくらいの価値を持っていた。
カ ヨーロッパでは冷蔵庫に塩を入れて，肉や魚の腐るのを防いでいる。
キ アフリカのある所では塩をかたまりのままマーケットで売っている。
ク アフリカでは市場でその固まりを小さく砕いて売っている。
ケ 今では世界中どこでも，塩が見られる。
コ いまでも塩を味わった事の無い人がいる。

333 次の英文を読んで，あとの問いに答えよ。

When words are spoken, they leave no permanent record. Most people do not think about words when they speak. They are, however, more careful when they write. They will probably reread what they have written, just “①to be on the safe side”. Putting words in writing makes the message more permanent. It makes us think about the consequences.

②Today the power of printed words is being undermined by computers.

*E-mail has revolutionized the style and the tone of letter writing. Because E-mail permits instant communication, it ③elicits a fast, immediate reaction, which is much closer to speech than to writing. Sometimes people "*fire off" an angry response without bothering to reread their message. We could say that ④E-mail is long-distance speech.

The speed and immediacy of E-mail have changed the rules of letter etiquette. In computer ⑤jargon, the new verb "to flame" means to send a quick, *nasty answer to an E-mail communication. An angry reply is called "flame mail". The growing frequency of flame mail indicates that computer users may need better computer manners.

Today the computer revolution is challenging the power that printed words have had during the last five and a half centuries. As we have seen, computer writing frequently copies speech rather than writing. Although the immediacy of E-mail ⑥*duplicates the spontaneity of speech, the medium of communication is written, not oral. People who use E-mail should not ignore the traditions of the written language.

＊ E-mail＝電子メール　fire off＝送る　nasty＝意地の悪い
duplicate＝複写する

(1) 下線部①③⑤⑥に最も近い意味を表すものを下のア～エよりそれぞれ選び，記号で答えよ。

① ア to memorize it　イ to criticize it
ウ to enjoy it once agein　エ to make sure of it

③ ア invites　イ discourages　ウ prevents　エ supports

⑤ ア mechanism　イ language　ウ symbol　エ skill

⑥ ア increases　イ denies　ウ copies　エ replaces

(2) 書き言葉が話し言葉と異なる点は何か，15字以内の日本語で答えよ。

(3) 下線部④のように言えるのはなぜか，20字以内の日本語で答えよ。

(4) コンピュータで通信を行う場合，どういう点に気をつけなければならないと筆者は述べているか。簡潔な日本語で答えよ。

(5) 下線部②を和訳せよ。

334 次の英文を読んで，あとの問いに答えよ。

Chickens are one of the animals that have been most completely *domesticated by man. In fact, (①) cats can still survive without man, chickens cannot. They depend on man for food and shelter. Although we think of chickens (②) a source of meat and eggs, the original reason for breeding them was for fighting. After this sport became *outlawed, more importance was placed on egg and meat production.

There are many breeds of chicken today. They are usually classified (③) American, English, Asiatic, and *Mediterranean. All major American breeds lay brown eggs and all are raised for their meat as well as their eggs. The most important English breed is the Cornish, which is raised for its meat. It is a poor egg layer, however. By far the most important egg producer in the world is the White Leghorn, which lays white eggs. It is responsible for most of the eggs you see in supermarkets.

Do you prefer brown eggs or white eggs? Some people say that brown eggs are more *nutritious. (④) prefer white eggs because they say they look prettier. Actually the *nutrition in each is about the same and it depends more on the condition of the chicken and the type of food it eats rather than on the color of the egg.

The breeding of chickens has become a complicated science and is a good example of how breeding different types of chickens together produces a newer and better type which can lay more eggs and produce more meat. As a result of scientific breeding, chickens grow more quickly and have more meat than chickens in the past.

In the past chickens were allowed to eat whatever they found in the *barnyard. Now it has become a science so that chickens receive all the nutrition necessary to produce eggs which are also nutritious and to produce chickens which are healthy and good for eating. The place where they are kept (⑤) now maintained at a temperature which is best for egg laying. Chickens are kept in wire cages. These cages are placed on top of each other in order to save space. It has also been found that keeping laying hens in cages causes them to lay more eggs.

＊ domesticated＝～を飼いならされた　outlawed＝禁止した
Mediterranean＝地中海の　nutritious＝栄養のある
nutrition＝栄養摂取　barnyard＝納屋の前庭，農家の庭

(1) 空欄(①)に入る最も適切な語を次のア～エから選び，記号で答えよ。

ア if　イ now that　ウ although　エ so far as

(2) 空欄(②)(③)に共通して入る語で最も適当な語を次のア～エから選び，記号で答えよ。

ア with　イ as　ウ like　エ to

(3) 次の英文が指す鶏種で最も適当な語を次のア～エから選び，記号で答えよ。

This breed is expected to provide us with meat, but not eggs.

ア American　イ English　ウ Asiatic　エ Mediterranean

(4) 空欄(　④　)に入る最も適当な語を次のア～エから選び，記号で答えよ。

ア Those people　イ A few of them　ウ Most　エ Others

(5) 空欄(　⑤　)に入る最も適当な語を次のア～エから選び，記号で答えよ。

ア is　イ located　ウ is set　エ is made

(6) 本文の内容と一致するものを次のア～クの中から3つ選び，記号で答えよ。

ア Generally speaking, cats are no less independent of people than chickens are.

イ Human beings first began breeding chickens because they hoped for stronger fighting cocks.

ウ It is often the case that eggs we buy at supermarkets are from White Leghorns.

エ The condition of the chicken, the type of food it eats, and the color of the egg equally affect the nutrition of the egg.

オ Chicken breeders have tried to know the way to cross, or mix, different types of chickens in order to produce a newer and better type.

カ Traditionally chickens just ate anything they found around them, but such food often lacked necessary nutrients, and they lay fewer eggs than they do now.

キ Chickens are given different food according whether they are bred for meat or for eggs.

ク It is quite natural that chickens feel stressed and lay fewer eggs when kept in cages.

335 次の英文を読んで，あとの問いに答えよ。

A new study has demonstrated the powerful connection between mind and body. American researchers say they found that something as simple as writing about a terrible experience can improve the health of some patients.

The study is believed to be the first (　A　) how writing about such an experience can $_{\text{a}}$affect disease. The findings were reported in *_The Journal of the American Medical Association_. The study was carried (　①　) at *the State University of New York at Stony Brook. It involved more than 100 people with severe forms of the breathing disease called *asthma or the bone disease called *rheumatoid arthritis.

The researchers asked all members of the group to write for 20 minutes for three days (②) a row. They asked some patients to write their feelings about the $_{b}$worst experience in their lives. For example, these patients wrote about an automobile accident, the end of a marriage, the death of a loved one or something terrible that happened when they were children. The other people were told to write about their plans (③) the day.

The health of the patients was tested for four months. The researchers say the health of many people who wrote about bad experiences improved after four months. They say 47 percent of these patients improved after writing about such experiences. Twenty-four percent of those in the other group showed a similar improvement.

Joshua Smyth of *North Dakota State University organized the study. He believes the patients (B) improved because they were able to express their emotions and $_{c}$make sense of their experiences. Mr. Smyth says the findings do not show whether the patients' health continued to improve. He also says people (C) are very sick should not consider the idea of writing instead (④) seeking medical treatment.

Earlier studies have shown that emotions can influence the development of disease.

The Journal of the American Medical Association published a *commentary on the study. David Spiegel of Stanford University in California said he was surprised by the powerful effect of writing. He said the researchers provided evidence $_{d}$that treatment with medicine is more effective when combined (⑤) the expression of stressful emotions.

＊ *The Journal of the American Medical Association*＝米国医師会発行による機関誌
the State University of New York at Stony Brook＝ニューヨーク州立大学ストニーブルック校
asthma＝喘息　rheumatoid arthritis＝リューマチ性関節炎
North Dakota State University＝ノースダコタ州立大学
commentary＝解説

(1) (①)～(⑤)に入る最も適当な語を下の**ア**～**オ**から選び，記号で答えよ。ただし，同じ語を２度以上用いてはならない。

ア with　**イ** in　**ウ** of　**エ** out　**オ** for

⑵　(　A　)～(　C　)に入る最も適当な語をそれぞれあとのア～ウから選び，記号で答えよ。

(　A　)　ア　examines　　イ　examining　　ウ　to examine

(　B　)　ア　may have　　イ　may be　　ウ　may not

(　C　)　ア　who　　イ　whose　　ウ　whom

⑶　二重下線部 a の affect とほぼ同じ意味の語を文中からさがし，1 語で答えよ。

⑷　二重下線部 b の worst の比較級を答えよ。

⑸　二重下線部 c の make sense of とほぼ同じ意味をもつものを次のア～エから選び，記号で答えよ。

ア　hear　　イ　agree with　　ウ　understand　　エ　rely on

⑹　二重下線部 d の that と同じ用法の that が使われている文を次のア～エから選び，記号で答えよ。

ア　I think that he will come to see me.

イ　All the people that were in the car were killed in the accident.

ウ　It was at the party last year that I first met Mary.

エ　We reached the conclusion that there is no easy way to learn English.

⑺　次の①～⑤のうち，本文の内容と合っているものには○，違っているものには×で答えよ。

①　Some research says that writing about bad experiences improves health.

②　The study looked at hundreds of diseases.

③　During the study, all patients improved their health after writing about anything they wanted.

④　Almost half the patients who wrote about their bad experiences, such as car crashes for example, improved their health.

⑤　Research suggests that expressing emotion may be as important as drugs in helping patients with their health.

看護医療学校受験
オープンセサミシリーズ　問題集　③
アクセス　英語

2024年２月15日　第１版第１刷

編　著　東京アカデミー

発行人　佐川　泰宏

発行所　株式会社ティーエーネットワーク
名古屋市中村区名駅 1-1-1
ＪＰタワー名古屋６Ｆ
〒450-6306　TEL　052-586-7805
FAX　052-563-2109

発売元　東京アカデミー七賢出版株式会社
東京都豊島区西池袋 1-11-1
メトロポリタンプラザビル13Ｆ
〒171-0021　TEL　03-6852-0803
FAX　03-6852-0180

印刷・製本　名鉄局印刷株式会社

ISBN978-4-86455-661-3　C7037
Printed in Japan

看護医療学校受験

オープンセサミシリーズ 問題集 アクセス ❸

英 語

平成30年告示 学習指導要領対応

解答・解説

東京アカデミー｜編

東京アカデミー七賢出版

1

(1) エ　第1文型　(2) オ　第3文型
(3) イ　第4文型　(4) ア　第2文型
(5) ウ　第5文型　(6) ク　第1文型
(7) キ　第2文型　(8) コ　第3文型
(9) カ　第4文型　(10) ケ　第5文型

2

(1) イ　(2) ア　(3) ウ　(4) オ
(5) エ　(6) ア　(7) イ　(8) オ
(9) エ　(10) ウ　(11) ウ　(12) オ

3

(1) of　(2) has　(3) it is
(4) It rains

4

(1) He gave some flowers to me.
(2) My father bought a new dictionary for me.
(3) Ms. Suzuki teaches English to us.
(4) May I ask a favor of you?
(5) My sister made a doll for me.
(6) Please lend this bicycle to me.

5

(1) He is not an ambitious boy.
(2) Can you play tennis?
(3) Doesn't George know her address?
(4) I will not do my homework tonight.
(5) You are the best skier in my class, aren't you.

6

(1) イ，オ，エ，ウ，アの順
(2) ウ，エ，オ，ア，イの順
(3) エ，オ，ウ，イ，アの順
(4) イ，ウ，ア，オ，エの順
(5) エ，オ，イ，ア，ウの順

7

(1) how old she is ⇨間接疑問文。
(2) far is it from here ⇨距離の疑問詞 how far，距離を表す主語は it
(3) Be, not to catch ⇨ Be のつく命令文，不定詞の否定は to の前に not
(4) do you, from ⇨ do you think に続く間接疑問文

8

① to　② whoever　③ the
④ sights　⑤ before　⑥ what
⑦ much　⑧ better　⑨ less
⑩ usual

9

① reminds　② of　③ brought
④ to　⑤ helped〔enabled〕
⑥ to　⑦ make　⑧ feel
⑨ prevented〔kept〕　⑩ from

10

(1) How much did this bag cost?
(2) Which do you like better, summer or winter?
(3) Whose pen did he borrow yesterday?
(4) Whose helmet is this?
(5) Who〔m〕 did you meet in the park yesterday?
(6) Where did you meet him yesterday?
(7) When did you meet him in the park?

11

(1) my calling ⇨節から句への転換。
(2) too, to
(3) If, he
(4) or ⇨命令文＋or, or は「さもないと」の意味。
(5) Nobody ⇨「だれか知っているだろうか（いや知るまい）」は，強い否定を意味する。

12

(1) Let's not go right now.
(2) What a long time it lasted!
(3) How quickly the car came running!
(4) Which do you like better, tea or coffee?
(5) Don't drink too much.

13

(3), (6), (9)
⇨(3) × diing → ○ dying
(6) ×原形 hid → ○ hide
(9) ×過去分詞 sank → ○ sunk

14

(1) rains
(2) using ⇨前置詞のあとは動名詞にする。
(3) gets ⇨主語が3人称単数，現在の習慣。
got ⇨this morning で過去だとわかる。
(4) has been ⇨現在完了継続。
(5) will do ⇨next time は「次回には」とい

う意味で現在を基準にして未来を表す。the next time は，ある特定の時を基準にしている場合に用いられる。

⑹ had given

⑺ is spoken ⇨受動態。

15

⑴ イ　⑵ ウ　⑶ エ　⑷ ウ

⑸ エ

16

⑴ organizing　⑵ have been

⑶ is closed　⑷ preparing

⑸ invited

17

⑴ ア　⑵ イ　⑶ エ　⑷ エ

⑸ ウ

18

⑴ dead ⇨死んでいる状態。形容詞を使う。

⑵ were ⇨不定詞の完了形は，文全体の動詞（are reported）よりひとつ前の時制を表す。

⑶ is ⇨期間を表す「…してから～になる」は it is〔has been〕～ since …

⑷ was ⇨不定詞を節に直したとき，時制は文全体の動詞（seemed）と一致する。

19

⑴ ア　⑵ イ　⑶ ア　⑷ イ

⑸ ウ

20

⑴ He seems to have heard the news.

⑵ I have been studying for two hours.

21

⑴ コロンブスは1492年にアメリカ大陸を発見した。

→America was discovered by Columbus in 1492.

アメリカ大陸は1492年にコロンブスによって発見された。

⑵ この花は英語では何といいますか？

→What is this flower called in English?

この花は英語では何といわれていますか？

⑶ まわりの人みなが彼をあざ笑った。

→He was laughed at by the whole crowd.

彼はまわりの人みなにあざ笑われた。

⑷ トムはスージーをそこに行かせた。

→Susie was made to go there by Tom.

スージーはトムによってそこに行かされた。

22

⑴ are, by　⑵ heard, to

⑶ shocked, at〔by〕

⑷ interested, in

⑸ known, to

23

⑴ Jane is writing a long novel.

⑵ The news will surprise her.

⑶ Who brought him up?

⑷ They speak French in Canada.

24

⑴ are not sold

⑵ was seen to

⑶ being

⑷ be asked

⑸ to

⑹ surprised at

⑺ had, been seated ⇨過去完了の受動態。

⑻ was being written ⇨過去進行形の受動態。

25

⑴ loved, by　⑵ had　⑶ Let, be, done

⑷ to, saw　⑸ looked, up, to

⑹ was, believed, have, been

26

⑴ He was seen to enter the room by me.

⑵ By whom were you shown the way? または By whom was the way shown (to) you?

⑶ It is believed that he was lazy. または He is believed to have been lazy.

⑷ I was never taken for my twin brother.

⑸ The〔Their〕 departure was put off till the next morning.

⑹ His teacher wasn't surprised at the answer.

⑺ It is said that John and Jenny have been married for five years. または John and Jenny are said to have been married for five years.

(8) I was spoken to by an American.

27

(1) This book was written by him.
(2) The train was delayed because of a heavy snow.
(3) She was spoken to by a stranger in the town.
(4) English is spoken all over the world.

28

(1) Are, able, to
(2) ought〔have〕, to
(3) have〔ought〕, to
(4) may, must
(5) may, well
(6) can't, too

29

(1) 乳房レントゲン検査が広まる以前は，そのような女性は乳ガンと診断される前に，ほかの原因で死んだかもしれない。⇨推量の助動詞 may「～かもしれない」の過去 may have＋p. p.「～したかもしれない」 might have＋p. p. も同じ意味。
(2) 彼らは彼女のことを「ランプの婦人」と呼んだものだった。というのも彼女は夜，彼らが大丈夫かどうかを見るためランプを手に病院の中を歩きまわったからであった。⇨ used to(過去の習慣を表す)

30

(1) ウ ⇨ would rather have bought「むしろ～を買ったほうがよかったのに」という仮定を表す。
(2) エ ⇨「明日のだいたいこの時間には，彼女はロンドンに到着してしまっているだろう」という未来完了。
(3) ウ ⇨ had better の否定は had better not(＋動詞の原形)
(4) エ ⇨ Must ～？の否定の答えには don't have to または need not（～する必要がない)を用いる。
(5) イ ⇨ when 以下は know の目的語となる名詞節。
(6) ウ ⇨ start の前の should を省略した形。

31

(1) ウ　(2) ア　(3) ア　(4) ウ
(5) イ　(6) イ

32

(1) ① イ　② ウ
(2) イ

33

(1) ① イ　② ウ　③ エ
(2) a イ　b ウ

和訳

客室乗務員：お客様，何をなさっていらっしゃるのですか。もう離陸は止められないのですよ。
乗客：でもそうしてもらわなくちゃ困るんだ。私は2時間後にはロサンゼルスにいなくてはならんのだ。絶対に行かなくちゃならんのだ。あの飛行機に乗らなくては。
客室乗務員：では航空券を拝見させてください。
乗客：航空券は持っとらん。でも到着したら買うと約束する。
客室乗務員：無理です。2時間後に別の便がございますから，それになさってください。
乗客：娘が重病なんだ。3時間後，ロサンゼルスで手術を受けるんだ。私がそこにいなくては！　娘といっしょにいてやらなくては！
客室乗務員：でも無理です。航空券をお持ちでないのですから。
乗客：着いたら買うと約束する。頼むから航空券のために娘の所に行ってやれないなんてことにしないでくれ。

34

多くの偉大な人々が，絵がどのようにして描かれるべきかを世に示そうと試みてきたが，彼らに言えることのすべては，レオナルド・ダ・ヴィンチによって言われていた。彼が芸術について書いたことは芸術家の知識の基礎である。

35

(1) to learn　名詞的用法
(2) to help　形容詞的用法
(3) to see　副詞的用法

(4) to keep　名詞的用法
(5) To master　名詞的用法

36

(1) to play　(2) go　(3) to go
(4) mend　(5) get

37

(1) enough
(2) to be seen ⇨ be＋to 不定詞の受動態。
(3) enough not, sing ⇨不定詞の否定は to の直前に not を入れる。
(4) to have been
(5) made to work
(6) laugh ⇨ cannot help ～ing＝cannot but＋原形不定詞「～せずにはいられない」。

38

(1) **ア** 予定　(2) **エ** 意図　(3) **ウ** 可能
(4) **オ** 運命　(5) **イ** 義務

39

(1) 覚えておくべきことは，その人に同じ部屋で語りかけているかのように言うことを手紙に書く，ということだけだ。
(2) たいていのアメリカ人は，自分の生まれた場所に留まっているのが必要だということに，もっともな理由があるとは思っていない。⇨ to remain 仮主語 it の真主語を表す不定詞

40

(1) Is this (the first time for you to meet) Mr. Ito?
(2) We (had Tom sing a song).
(3) It (is not so difficult how to solve the question).
(4) I (can't but feel sorry for her).
(5) It (seemed impossible for us to climb that side of the mountain).
(6) He (spoke loudly enough to be heard by everyone).
(7) One day, the (old woman went to the river to do) the laundry.
(8) She (was surprised to see a big peach flowing) down the river.
(9) She (tried to grab the peach), but she couldn't.

41

(1) It is strange for him to say so.
(2) She seems to have been absent from school yesterday.
(3) The stone was too heavy for Jim to move.
(4) Shigeo is rich enough to〔so rich as to〕buy anything.

42

(1) My dream is to take my time and go around the museums in Europe.
(2) I told him not to open the window.

43

(1) packing　(2) to come
(3) seeing　(4) saying
(5) lending

44

(1) my ⇨動名詞の主語が文全体の主語と食い違っている場合，動名詞の主語は，所有格か目的格にして動名詞の直前に置く（you …文全体の S，I …動名詞の S）。
(2) of ⇨動名詞が後にあるので前置詞（句）が置かれる。instead of「～のかわりに」「～しないで」。
(3) of, been ⇨(2)参照。
(4) because of ⇨「～のために」「～の理由で」。
(5) no knowing
(6) her being

45

(1) **イ-エ-オ-ア-ウ**
⇨He never goes fishing without taking his son.
never〔cannot〕… without ～ing で「…のときは必ず～する」
(2) **イ-エ-ア-オ-カ-ウ**
⇨The book is worth reading twice.
(3) **エ-オ-イ-キ-ウ-ア-カ**
⇨A slight fever kept me from going to work.
keep＋O＋from＋～ing で「O が～することができない。」
(4) **ウ-カ-コ-ク-イ-ケ-ア-エ-キ-オ**
⇨It goes without saying that regular exercise plays an important role in the stress management.
It goes without saying that …「…は言

うまでもない」

(5) エ-イ-ア-オ-ウ

46

(1) He is proud of being rich.

(2) There is no returning on the road of life.

(3) They never meet without quarreling.

(4) I regret not having seen the movie.

47

(1) エ　(2) オ　(3) ア　(4) イ

(5) ウ

48

(3)

⇨(1) have been studying 現在完了進行形の一部。

(2) 現在分詞 standing by the door が girl を修飾。

(3) enjoy の目的語としての動名詞。不定詞は不可。

(4) 分詞構文＝He picked up a stone, and he threw it at dog.

49

(1) ① 彼は今日その仕事をしたのを覚えている。
② 彼は今日その仕事を忘れずにしなくてはならない。

(2) ① ミホは試験にきっと受かる。
② ミホは試験に受かることを確信している。

(3) ① 彼はタバコを吸うのをやめた。
② 彼はタバコを吸うために立ち止まった。

50

(1) イ　(2) ウ　(3) ア　(4) エ

(5) ウ　(6) ウ　(7) ウ　(8) ア

(9) ウ　(10) イ

51

(1) stolen　(2) drowning　(3) granted

(4) understood　(5) burning

(6) lying

52

(1) Dressed in poor clothes, the girl was ashamed of herself.

(2) Arriving at the station, Mr. Tanaka found his train gone.

(3) Many days having passed, people forgot all about it.

(4) Judging from the look of the sky, it may rain this afternoon.

53

(1) 1 interesting ⇨ interesting は「物・事・人」が「興味を引き起こす」, interested は「人」が「興味を持っている」

(2) 1 Seen

(3) 3 made by

54

(1) She was (at the appointed place on time).

(2) Jim (kept me waiting for an hour).

(3) I (had a terrible time finding a parking lot).

(4) He (never goes out fishing without taking) his son.

55

(1) written in a hurry

(2) having set

(3) Not knowing what to do

(4) had my bicycle stolen last

56

(1) (Did you have your watch fixed at the clock shop)?

(2) I hear there is (an express leaving this station at nine) in the morning.

(3) Jim was very (angry because he was kept waiting for two hours) or so.

(4) I (always keep my dog tied to) a tree in the garden.

(5) (There being no vacant seat), I kept standing. [as が不要]

(6) There are some people (waiting to come) in. [who が不要]

(7) (Tom was sitting on a bench with his eyes closed). [in が不要]

57

(1) It being too cold, nobody went out.

(2) He always studies, watching TV.

58

(1) being ⇨ was being fought 過去進行形の受動態。

(2) dying ⇨ 現在分詞。men を修飾「死にかけている人」。

(3) shone ⇨ shine の過去形。

(4) wounded ⇨ wound は「～を傷つける」，wounded soldier は「傷つけられた兵士」

(5) lying ⇨ lie の現在分詞。soldiers を修飾。

(6) whom

(7) better ⇨ be better off「状態がよくなる」。

(8) suffering ⇨ was suffering 過去進行形。

(9) over ⇨ be over「終わる」。

(10) running ⇨現在分詞叙述用法。

和訳　残酷な闘いが行われていた。地面は死人や死にかけた人間で覆われていた。空気は暑く，息苦しかった。太陽は血とほこりの中に横たわっている傷ついた兵士たちの上に容赦なく降り注いだ。

これらの兵士のひとりに，ある貴族がいた。その優しさと親切のためにみなが愛した人だった。それなのに今，彼は戦場で最もかわいそうな人と少しも変わらなかった。彼は傷ついていた。そしてまもなく死ぬだろう。痛みとのどの渇きでひどく苦しんでいた。

闘いが終ったとき，彼の友人たちが彼を助けに急いだ。ある兵士が手にコップを持って走ってやってきた。しかし，その貴族は別の兵士にその水をやったのだ。

59

(1)
- ① 彼には医者をしている二人の息子がいる。
- ② 彼には二人の息子がいて，二人とも医者である。

(2)
- ① その人形の片目は閉じている。
- ② その人形は目が1つで，その目は閉じている。

(3)
- ① 彼は人を驚かせる奇術師になった。
- ② 彼は奇術師になったが，そのことは我々を驚かせた。

60

(1) イ　(2) ウ　(3) イ

(4) ア ⇨ I talked about the castle で先行詞は「物」，目的格。目的格は省略できる。

(5) エ

(6) ウ ⇨ all (that) he could (do) for his son の関係代名詞の目的格と，前と同じ動詞 do の省略。

(7) ア　(8) ア　(9) イ　(10) ア

61

(1) whose

(2) that ⇨ all が先行詞についている場合，that を用いる。

(3) Whoever　(4) but　(5) when

(6) where　(7) What

(8) who または that　(9) which

(10) what

62

(1) for which ⇨ you told a lie for the reason の the reason が関係代名詞に。

(2) had bought　(3) matter how

(4) can't〔never〕，without

(5) what

63

(1) I (gave her what little money I had).

(2) Now (is the time when we need such) a great stateman as he.

(3) There is (nobody that I know is as efficient) as you.

(4) You should not (put off till tomorrow what you can do) today.

(5) (There are some people who have little to eat).

(6) The quickest way (to master a foreign language is to spend several years in the country where it is) spoken.

64

(1) 2　what

(2) 3　where

(3) 2　which

(4) 2　who〔that〕

(5) 5　ever seen

65

(1) Please give me back the book (which) I lent you two months ago.

(2) All we can do is to wait for her.

66

(1) 水分は体の熱を皮膚の表面へ運び，そしてそこで熱は汗によってなくなる。

(2) 患者は思いをめぐらし，頭に浮かぶどんなことも言うように求められる。

(3) アメリカの作家で講師でもあり，体は不自由であっても，何百万人もの人をその業績で激励したヘレン・ケラーは，1880年，アラバマに生まれた。

(4) 子供が一生を通じていつまでも残る食事作法を学ぶ（または学ばない）ところは，家族の食卓においてである。

(5) 私たちがわからず，支配できない思考や感情の大部分を，彼は無意識と呼んだ。

67

(1) イ ⇨ times は「～倍」。 (2) オ

(3) キ (4) エ (5) ウ

68

(1) happier (2) fastest

(3) latest ⇨ at latest「遅くとも。」

(4) prettier (5) cities

69

(1) イ (2) ウ ⇨程度の by「～だけ」。

(3) エ (4) エ (5) エ (6) イ

(7) ア (8) イ (9) ウ (10) イ

70

(1) senior

(2) the cleverest boy

(3) as, as または so, as

(4) any

(5) the finest

(6) less

(7) better than

71

(1) 2 much, even, far など

(2) 2 safer (3) 4 ever

(4) 3 as

72

(1) No (other mountain in Japan is higher than Mt. Fuji).

(2) She (earns three times as much as I) do at her part-time job.

(3) (I would rather walk than go by taxi).

(4) If you go on a diet, (you eat less food than usual) in order to lose weight.
⇨ than usual「いつもよりも」。

(5) He is (no more a good player) than I am.

(6) I found (the book much more interesting than I had) expected.
⇨ find＋O＋C

(7) He's as (honest a man as ever lived).
⇨ as ～ as ever lived「この上なく～」。

(8) The lake (is deepest at this point).
the が不要 ⇨同一物のある部分を他と比較して，「最も～」という時には the をつけない。

73

(1) 彼女は去年よりずっと上手に絵が描ける。

(2) 私の収入は君の収入の２倍である。

(3) できるだけ速く泳いでみなさい。

(4) 遅かれ早かれ，その花は開いてくるでしょう。

(5) アメリカ人は，例えば，ある程度の年齢に達しても，日本人ほど中年だと感じないようだ。

(6) やがてコンピュータは，少なくともいくつかの点で単なる人間よりも利口になるだろう。そしてこのコンピュータ革命の先頭に立っているのは日本とアメリカであり，それぞれが更に高性能なコンピュータを開発するために競い合っている。

74

(1) That girl swims better than anyone else in her class.

(2) We must find effective ways to reduce the garbage as early as possible.

75

(1) ウ (2) オ (3) ア (4) カ

(5) イ (6) ク (7) キ (8) コ

(9) エ (10) ケ

76

(1) or (2) so (3) and (4) nor

(5) for

77

(1) or, Unless

(2) so, that, cannot, it

(3) sooner

(4) Whenever

(5) that, could〔might〕

(6) that he

(7) though〔although〕, raining heavily

78

(1) ウ (2) キ (3) カ (4) エ

(5) コ

79

(1) **イ**　(2) **イ**　(3) **ウ**

(4) **エ** ⇨ The moment＝As soon as「～するとすぐに」。

(5) **ウ** ⇨ if 節は am not sure の目的節で「彼が遅れて来るかどうかは確かではない」の意。

(6) **イ**「今や～なので」。

80

(1) She was (in such a hurry that) she couldn't stop to talk with me.

(2) (It will not be long before my father) gets well.

(3) Not (till then did I realize the danger of) the situation.
⇨否定の副詞が文頭にあるので助動詞＋主語＋動詞の倒置が起きている。

(4) Mary didn't learn Spanish even (though she lived in Mexico) for a year.

(5) (Leave early so that you won't miss the bus).

81

(1) **エ**　(2) **ウ**　(3) **オ**　(4) **ア**
(5) **イ**　(6) **ク**　(7) **コ**　(8) **カ**
(9) **キ**　(10) **ケ**

82

(1) **ア** ⇨様態を表す。「～のように，～のとおりに」。

(2) **エ** ⇨同格の that「～という」。

83

(1) これらやほかの汚染物質の結果として湖や川の中には，非常に汚れてそこに住む魚が死んでしまうものもある。

(2) 漢字の書き方を学習することは常に日本の教育の中心であった。そしてたとえどんな機械が発明されようとも，続けられるべきである。

84

(1) He as well as you was surprised at the news.

(2) It is believed that she knew the fact. または It is believed that she has known the fact.

(3) On going to bed, he heard the strange sound.

85

(1) If I had money, I could buy my own house.

(2) I wish I had proposed marriage to her.

(3) If I had known your address, I would have written to you.

86

(1) 彼女の手厚い看護がなかったら，彼は死んでいただろう。

(2) あなたの忠告がなかったなら，たいへんな誤りを犯していただろう。

(3) 私は忙しかった。そうでなければ君に電話していたのに。

87

(1) had had　(2) were
(3) had realized　(4) stopped
(5) known

88

(1) were not for
(2) had not been
(3) had told
(4) If, had
(5) If
(6) would stop

89

(1) **エ**　(2) **エ**　(3) **ア**　(4) **イ**
(5) **イ**　(6) **ウ**　(7) **ウ**

90

(1) You (should have come to tell it) to me earlier.

(2) …to work (less and to spend more time with) their children.

(3) (I wonder what Akemi would have done) if she had known the fact.

(4) (What would become of David if his wife were to) die?

91

(1) To hear him　(2) Were
(3) as it were または so to speak
(4) knew

92

(1) 君はもっと丁寧に話せばうまくいくだろう。

(2) もし時間があれば遊びに来てください。

(3) すべての電流が断ち切られるならば，何が起こるかということを想像することによって，電気の重要さを理解し始めることができる。電灯は消えるだろう。電気を使う道具，機械は止まるだろう。電車や市街電車は動かなくなるだろう。

(4) 黄熱病という流行病がパナマ運河の建設をすんでのところで阻止してしまうところだった。もし３人の決然とした医師たちがいなかったならば，貨物船は大西洋から太平洋へ行くのにいまだにわざわざ南アメリカの先端を回って航海しなければならないであろう。

93

(1) They looked as if they had seen a ghost.

(2) If I had a sister, I would be very happy.

(3) I wish he were still alive.

94

(1) ア (2) エ (3) エ (4) ア

95

(1) he would, me

(2) if I knew

(3) to, her

(4) had been

(5) I had eaten

(6) not

(7) yesterday, asked, if

96

(1) 彼は翌年16歳になると言った。

(2) マイクは昨日彼女に会ったと言った。

(3) 先生は光陰矢の如しと言った。(不変の真理のため時制の一致が行われない)

97

(1) Ken said (that) he had met that girl the day before.

(2) He asked her if he might use her camera.

(3) She asked me where I was going.

(4) The doctor advised me not to smoke too much.

98

(1) Today she said, "It will rain tomorrow."

(2) Jack said to me, "I have been to Europe five times."

(3) She said to me, "Do you want this ?"

(4) I said to them, "Please come at five o'clock."

99

(1) She asked him if he would have some coffee.

(2) I asked her if she had ever been abroad.

(3) I said to my brother, "What is the matter with you ?"

(4) He told me never to forget that knowledge is power.

100

(1) He said (that he wished she were there).

(2) He prayed (God to bless me).

(3) I told him (to work hard and he would succeed).

(4) The lady (asked me to move my car).

(5) He (suggested not saying anything) about it till they heard the facts.

101

(1) He said to them, "Go away and come back to me in an hour." 彼は彼らに言った。「行きなさい。そして１時間したら，私のところに戻って来なさい。」

(2) I said to him, "Didn't you have any good food ?" 私は彼にそれがどうだったのか聞いた。彼の返事はこうだった。「ひどいもんです。私はどこでもおいしいお茶を飲むことができませんでした。ああ，戻れてありがたい。」私は彼がそこにいる間おいしい食べ物を何も食べなかったのではないかと聞いた。

102

(1) He said to me, "Do you know her name ?"

(2) Father says to us, "Don't waste time."

103

(1) He asked me if I knew her name.

(2) Father tells us not to waste time.

104

(1) any ⇨ too ～ to は否定の意味を持つので，「もうこれ以上～ない」の any を使う。

(2) None ⇨ but＝except「～以外の」
「バカでなければだれもそんなばかげたことを信じないであろうに」。

(3) Nor ⇨「…も～また～ない」

(4) did ⇨動詞の時制を見ること。

(5) were ⇨強調する前の文は，You were wrong.

(6) by

105

(1) it was

(2) there are, errors

(3) 後の happy

(4) the reason または why

106

(1) last

(2) afraid not

(3) to

(4) both

107

(1) never, without ⇨「～するときは必ず…する」。

(2) Who

(3) What makes

(4) Mind, nothing to do

(5) prevented〔kept〕

(6) brought

(7) good speaker

108

(1) I had no doubt about it at all〔whatever〕.

(2) It was John that〔who〕made the big kennel.

(3) Hiroko did inform you of her arrival.

109

(1) Scarcely had he seen the policeman when〔before〕he ran away.

(2) Helen did not play the violin, neither〔nor〕did Bob.

(3) It was not until yesterday that I knew her name.

110

(1) (Little did I imagine that) she would come.

(2) She (tried to look much younger than she really was).

(3) It (won't be long before Ted comes back).

(4) (Child as he is, he can answer the question).

(5) (His illness prevented him from attending the meeting).

(6) It is (the dog that bit my) child.

111

(1) do → am　　(2) feeling → feel

(3) no longer → any longer または
doesn't work → works

(4) he hung → had he hung

112

(1) 私が無事に戻ってきたのを見たときの，母の喜びは大変なものだった。

(2) しかしながら，すべての日本人が金持ちだというわけではない。たいていの中流階級の人々は，豊かな生活をしているアメリカ人やヨーロッパ人より，質で劣っている生活を送っているのだ。⇨部分否定 not all

(3) 重要な言葉を用いるときは必ず，その言葉のある文を理解するよう努めるのだ。
⇨ cannot ～ without …，二重否定「～するときは必ず…する」。

(4) 彼女の驚いたことに，社長は彼女の申し出を受け入れた。

113

(1) I can hardly〔scarcely〕believe such a story.

(2) Never have I been abroad.

(3) It was getting dark and, what was worse〔to make matters worse〕, it began to rain.

114

(1) ウ　(2) イ　(3) ア　(4) オ
(5) エ　(6) コ　(7) カ　(8) ケ
(9) ク　(10) キ

115

(1) to

(2) to

(3) on ⇨手段を表す。

(4) by ⇨程度を表す。

(5) of ⇨ instead of で「～のかわりに，～しないで」の意味。
(6) on
(7) on
(8) with ⇨ be wrong with で「～が故障している」。
(9) on
(10) in, of
(11) to
(12) from
(13) with
(14) with
(15) from
(16) with
(17) of
(18) in

116

(1) エ (2) イ (3) ケ (4) キ
(5) オ (6) ア (7) ケ (8) ク
(9) コ (10) カ

117

(1) サ (2) オ (3) イ (4) サ
(5) カ

118

(1) ウ ⇨ある範囲を越えている状態。
(2) キ
(3) ア ⇨ go on ～ing で「～し続ける」。
(4) ク ⇨～しながら
(5) コ ⇨同格「～という」。
(6) イ ⇨ (動作･行為の過程を示して)「…中で」。
(7) エ ⇨ in favor で「～に賛成で」。
(8) カ ⇨ persuade … into ～ ing「…を説得して～させる」。
(9) ケ (10) オ

119

(1) at (2) on (3) to (4) to
(5) for〔to, of〕

120

① ケ ② シ ③ カ ④ ク
⑤ ケ ⑥ キ ⑦ ア ⑧ カ
⑨ キ ⑩ イ ⑪ ケ ⑫ ケ
⑬ オ ⑭ エ ⑮ コ ⑯ ク
⑰ オ ⑱ キ ⑲ サ ⑳ エ

121

① コ ② ウ ③ ク ④ ア

122

(1) ア (2) ウ (3) ア (4) イ
(5) ウ

解説

(1) 「トムが話に割り込んできたとき，私たちは楽しい会話をしていたところだった。」
cut in「割り込む，邪魔をする」に最も近いのは，interrupted「遮る，中断する」。
(2) 「会社には，遅刻に対して厳しい規則がある。」
hard and fast「非常に厳重な，がんじがらめの」に最も近いのは，strict「厳しい」。
(3) 「あなたが早く決心したらいいのになあ。」
make up one's mind「決心する」
(4) 「ヘンリーは祖父にとても似ている。」
take after …「…に似ている」
(5) 「私が困っているときはいつでもそばにいて支えてください。」
stand by「支援する」

123

(1) ウ (2) ウ (3) ウ (4) イ
(5) ウ (6) ウ

解説

(1) 「雨のせいで試合は延期された。」
put off＝postpone「延期する」
(2) 「彼らが伝統に反することは考えられない。」
out of the question「考えられない，問題外の，不可能な」
(3) 「アメリカ合衆国の国旗の星は州を表している。」
stand for＝represent「表す」
(4) 「正直さは結局のところ最も良い策である。」
in the long run「結局のところ，長い目で見れば」
(5) 「彼女は自分の行為を説明するよう求められた。」
account for＝explain「説明する」
(6) 「彼はすぐにそれをすることを約束した。」
right away＝immediately「すぐに，た

だちに」

124

(1) イ (2) エ (3) ア (4) ア
(5) ウ

解説

(1) 「1週間で減量するのを助けるという製品にだまされてはいけない。」
take in「人をだます」(しばしば受身で)
ア 信じる イ (人を)だます
ウ 予期する エ (人を)喜ばせる

(2) 「ケイトは若い頃ヨーロッパをかなり旅行したものだ。」
get around＝get about「旅行する，動き回る」
ア 紹介する イ 暮らす
ウ 塗る，描く エ 旅行する

(3) 「一度習慣にしてしまったら，喫煙をやめるのはとても難しい。」
ア (習慣などを) やめる
イ 続ける
ウ 従う，ならう
エ 扱う

(4) 「考え直した結果，君と一緒に行かないことに決めた。」
ア 考え直したあとで
イ 義務を負わずに
ウ 受け取り次第
エ 十分に前もって

(5) 「このテーブルは本当に重い。手を貸してくれない？」
ア つかまえて イ 車に乗せて
ウ 手助けして エ 必要として

125

(1) anxious (2) strong
(3) mature (4) mysterious
(5) important (6) hungry
(7) successful

126

(1) ア (2) ウ (3) エ (4) ウ
(5) ア (6) ア (7) ウ (8) イ
(9) イ

127

(1) 現在の市長。市長は出席していた。
(2) ある人。彼が来るのは確かである。
(3) 亡くなった父。私の父は遅れた。
(4) 日本にはほとんど友人がいない。日本に数人友人がいる。

128

(1) a few (2) well (3) five
(4) small (5) living

129

① エ ② ケ ③ カ ④ ア
⑤ ク ⑥ イ ⑦ サ ⑧ コ
⑨ オ ⑩ ス

130

(1) イ (2) カ (3) ケ (4) エ
(5) ウ

131

① イ ② ケ ③ カ ④ コ
⑤ オ ⑥ ウ ⑦ ク ⑧ ア
⑨ キ ⑩ エ

132

① エ ② ウ ③ カ ④ オ
⑤ ア

133

(1) either, better ⇨ know better than to 不定詞は，「～するほどバカではない」の意味。
(2) up
(3) seldom
(4) all ⇨ all the better for で，「～だからなおいっそう」という意味。

134

(1) fluently, speaker
(2) enough to

135

(1) カ (2) ア (3) イ (4) エ，オ
(5) ウ (6) キ

136

(1) ① 彼女は今日はとても具合がいいようだ。
② 彼女は今日はとても上手に歌う。
(2) ① 私は昨晩それをとてもうまく作った。
② きれいにしていなさい。
(3) ① あなたの父さんはもう出発したの？
② あなたの父さんはすでに出発してしまったの？(yet を用いた場合と違って，動作の早く終わったことに対する驚きなどの感情を含む。)

(4) ① 彼女は英語を一生懸命勉強する。
② 英語を勉強するのはむずかしい。

137

① ウ　② イ　③ ア　④ エ
⑤ イ

138

(1) I have never seen a panda.

(2) Fortunately, he could pass the examination.

(3) I'm not so interested in soccer.

139

何度も危険にあった後，彼の船は座礁し，彼は自分の船から去らなければならなかった。しかし，幸運にも彼は小さな島の海岸に着くことができた。

140

(1) All の前　(2) well の後
(3) spoke の後　(4) him の後
(5) We の後　(6) kind の後

141

(1) ウ　(2) ウ　(3) エ　(4) ウ
(5) エ　(6) ア

142

(1) one　(2) All, their　(3) yours
(4) some　(5) either　(6) none

143

(1) it　(2) Help yourself, They
(3) It, another　(4) Anything

144

(1) it　(2) it　(3) one　(4) It

145

(1) that → those

(2) is → does

(3) is → are, that → those

(4) 誤りなし

146

(1) 英国の食べ物については，いくらでも論じることができます。それはひどいものだと思う人もいれば，素晴らしいと思う人もいます。

(2) 親から子へと伝えられるものは，正確には何なのか。

147

(1) none ⇨「あなたには関係のないことだ。」

(2) impossible to ⇨「次に何が起こるかは，わからない。」

148

(1) yours　(2) yourselves　(3) it
(4) they　(5) it　(6) it

149

(1) To my disappointment, I could not make myself understood in English.

(2) It was not long before the patient came to himself.

150

(1) サ　(2) オ　(3) イ　(4) キ
(5) セ　(6) ケ　(7) カ　(8) エ
(9) シ　(10) ス　(11) ク　(12) ウ
(13) コ　(14) ア

151

(1) mother　(2) tree　(3) foot
(4) musician　(5) departure

(6) hypotheses ⇨「仮説」の意味。-sis[-sis], -ses[-siːz]

152

(1) August　(2) nation　(3) adult
(4) soldier　(5) century

153

(1) ア　(2) エ　(3) イ　(4) ア
(5) エ

154

(1) エ　(2) ウ　(3) イ　(4) ア
(5) オ

解説

(1) 病院で医師から治療を受けている人⇨患者

(2) 商品やサービスを購入したり利用したりする人⇨消費者

(3) イベントや試合を見ている人⇨観客

(4) 車，飛行機，船で旅行しているが，それを動かしたりその中で働いたりはしていない人⇨乗客，旅客

(5) イベントや特別な行事に招待されている人⇨（招待された）客，来賓客

155

(1) カ　(2) コ　(3) ク　(4) ケ
(5) ウ　(6) オ　(7) エ　(8) ア
(9) イ　(10) キ

解説

(1) 水に完全に囲まれた土地の1区画⇨島

(2) 人が見に行けるよう多くの種類の動物が飼育されている場所⇨動物園
(3) 困難を引き起こす状況⇨問題
(4) 高くて細い建物⇨タワー，塔
(5) 国や州などの主要な政府がある重要な都市⇨首都
(6) 特定の科目やスポーツ，技術を教える人⇨指導者，講師
(7) 望んだり，とても起きてほしいと思ったりするもの⇨夢
(8) 人が生きてきた，または，何かが存在していた年の数⇨年齢
(9) 人がどのように考え，感じ，動くのかを制御する，頭の内側にある器官⇨脳
(10) 働いて稼ぐもの，物を買うのに使うもので通常はその価値が印刷された硬貨か紙幣の形のもの⇨お金

156

(1) coffee　(2) piano
(3) clinic　(4) computer
(5) virus　(6) protein
(7) handkerchief　(8) soccer
(9) knife　(10) volunteer

157

(1) ウ　(2) ア　(3) ウ　(4) エ
(5) ア　(6) ア

158

(1) ア　(2) エ　(3) ア　(4) ウ

159

(1) child's → children's
(2) furnitures → furniture, are → is
(3) homeworks → homework
(4) two shoes → two pairs of shoes
(5) the train → trains

160

(1) biography　(2) neighbor
(3) sweat　(4) bicycle
(5) insect

161

(1) ア　(2) ウ　(3) イ　(4) ウ

解説

(1)「初老の人々は自分の権利を主張し始めている。」
the elderly「初老層」
＝the aged「高齢者」
(2)「彼は途中で退席することでその映画に対する嫌悪を表した。」
disgust for 〜「〜に対する嫌悪」
＝dislike for 〜「〜への嫌悪」
(3)「彼の仕事のスケジュールによって，彼らの旅行期間が決定した。」
the duration of 〜「〜の期間，継続」
＝the length of 〜「〜の(時間の)長さ，期間」
(4)「このルールはあらゆる時と場所で有効だ。」
hold good「有効である，あてはまる」
＝be valid「有効である，通用する」

162

(1) ウ　(2) ア　(3) イ　(4) エ
(5) ア　(6) イ　(7) ア　(8) エ
(9) ア　(10) ア　(11) イ　(12) ア
(13) エ　(14) ア　(15) ウ　(16) エ
(17) ア　(18) ア　(19) エ　(20) ア

163

(1) a, the　(2) the　(3) a
(4) ×, ×　(5) an, ×

164

(1) the が不要
(2) younger → the younger
(3) a such → such a
(4) the most → most,
United → the United

165

a → the
「世界中でもっともよく食べられる野菜は何ですか。」

166

私はなぜ，母が妹たちのためにハロウィンパーティをすることに決めたのかわかっている。母は妹たちが家にいれば，彼女らを監視できると気付いたからだ。

167

(1) a big
(2) a difficult
(3) the young
(4) the fourth, the year

168

(1) 学校に校長は1人しかいないのが普通。of our school という形容詞句で限定され

るので the をつける。

(2) 学校に教師は何人もいるのが普通。He はその中の不特定の 1 人なので a をつける。

(3) この the は of our school が teachers を限定しているためのもの。「教師全員」を意味する。

(4) 無冠詞複数形は全員ではなく，不特定の「一部の教師」を表す。

169

(1) エ　(2) イ　(3) エ　(4) イ
(5) ア　(6) ア　(7) イ　(8) イ
(9) ウ　(10) ウ

170

(1) ウ　(2) ウ　(3) イ　(4) エ
(5) ア　(6) エ　(7) イ　(8) エ
(9) イ　(10) エ

171

(1) ア　(2) ア　(3) イ　(4) イ
(5) ア　(6) ウ　(7) ア　(8) ア
(9) ウ　(10) イ　(11) ア　(12) ア
(13) イ　(14) エ　(15) イ　(16) ア
(17) エ　(18) ア　(19) イ　(20) イ
(21) ア　(22) ア　(23) イ　(24) ウ
(25) イ　(26) ア　(27) ウ　(28) ア

172

(1) イ　(2) イ　(3) エ　(4) ウ

173

(1) イ　(2) ア　(3) イ　(4) ウ
(5) ア

174

イ，エ，ク，サ，チ

175

ア，エ，ケ，ス，セ

176

(1) ア　(2) ウ　(3) イ　(4) イ
(5) エ

解説

(1) ア ho-tél　イ chár-ac-ter
ウ ím-pulse　エ ín-stru-ment
(2) ア díf-fer-ence　イ íg-no-rance
ウ oc-cá-sion　エ en-ter-táin
(3) ア óp-po-site　イ oc-cúr
ウ vol-un-téer　エ vól-ume
(4) ア pér-son-al　イ di-réc-tion
ウ góv-ern-ment　エ un-der-stánd
(5) ア cón-fer-ence　イ cón-trar-y
ウ in-vi-tá-tion　エ pre-císe

177

(1) イ　(2) オ

解説

(1) ア succéss　イ ínfant　ウ repórt
エ uníque　オ prefér
(2) ア phótograph　イ mánager
ウ ópposite　エ dángerous
オ commércial

178

(1) イ　(2) ア

解説

(1) [séz]
ア [wí:k]　イ [héd]　ウ [hí:t]
エ [stéik]　オ [déindʒə(r)]
(2) [mʌ́sl]
ア [tʌ́f]　イ [kɔ́:f]　ウ [máuθ]
エ [mjú:zik]　オ [jú:θ]

179

(1) エ　(2) ウ　(3) ア　(4) エ
(5) ウ

解説

(1) [rí:snt]
ア [éinʃənt]　イ [dékərèit]
ウ [finǽnʃəl]　エ [səsáiəti]
(2) [kʌ́ntri]
ア [ɔ:lðóu]　イ [dáut]
ウ [sʌ́ðə(r)n]　エ [θɔ́:t]
(3) [imǽdʒin]
ア [kǽpətl]　イ [fɔ́:ls]
ウ [méidʒə(r)]　エ [séikrid]
(4) [ikspǽnd]
ア [igzǽkt]　イ [igzǽmpl]
ウ [igzíst]　エ [èksəbíʃən]
(5) [fíə(r)]
ア [bέə(r)]　イ [wέə(r)]
ウ [klíə(r)]　エ [ə́:(r)θ]

180

(1) ○　(2) ×　(3) △　(4) △
(5) △　(6) ×

解説

(1) [hélθi]　[θáuz(ə)nd]　[θíŋ]
3 つとも同じ。

(2) [kǽnsə(*r*)] [méidʒə(*r*)] [hɔ́:l]
3つとも異なる。
(3) [diskʌ́s] [mʌ́sl] [jú:nit]
2つ同じ。
(4) [inʌ́f] [θrú:] [fáit]
2つ同じ。
(5) [θə́:(*r*)sti] [də́:(*r*)ti] [dʒu:lái]
2つ同じ。
(6) [gráund] [kúd] [kóuld]
3つとも異なる。

181

(1) ア (2) イ (3) ア (4) イ
(5) ウ

解説

(1) néwspaper (2) arránge
(3) ínteresting (4) agréement
(5) recreátion

182

(1) ウ (2) イ (3) ア (4) エ
(5) ウ

解説

(1) ア be-gín イ gui-tár
ウ vol-un-téer エ e-nóugh
(2) ア nóte-book イ po-líce-man
ウ yés-ter-day エ Ín-ter-net
(3) ア sur-príse イ áir-port
ウ hós-pi-tal エ hám-burg-er
(4) ア Ko-ré-a イ be-twéen
ウ i-dé-a エ búsi-ness
(5) ア fór-eign イ Éu-rope
ウ a-grée エ sci-en-tist [sáiəntəst]

183

(1) ア (2) ア (3) ウ (4) イ
(5) イ

解説

(1) ア [síns] イ [áilənd]
ウ [(h)wáit] エ [kláim]
(2) ア [igzǽmpl] イ [ikskjú:z]
ウ [ikspénsiv] エ [iksplé in]
(3) ア [séi] イ [néitʃə*r*]
ウ [séz] エ [féis]
(4) ア [díə*r*] イ [lə́:*r*n]
ウ [híə*r*] エ [klíə*r*]
(5) ア [míst] イ [stá:*r*tid]
ウ [láikt] エ [stɔ́pt/stápt]

184

(1) × (2) × (3) × (4) ○

185

イ，オ，ク，シ，ソ

186

(1) イ (2) ア (3) エ (4) ア
(5) ウ

187

オ

188

(1) ウ (2) ア (3) イ (4) ウ
(5) エ

解説

(1) ア [héd] イ [hévən]
ウ [ə́:(*r*)θ] エ [hélθ]
(2) ア [pílou] イ [bráit]
ウ [máin] エ [aidíə]
(3) ア [hauziz] イ [lǽfs]
ウ [séz] エ [tɔiz]
(4) ア [kóut] イ [tóust]
ウ [brɔ́:d] エ [góul]
(5) ア [θróu] イ [máuθ]
ウ [θɔ́:t] エ [ðóu]

189

(1) ウ (2) イ (3) ウ (4) エ
(5) イ

解説

(1) ア for-gét イ mo-rále
ウ úp-ward エ ex-íst
(2) ア fúr-ni-ture イ he-ró-ic
ウ dóc-u-ment エ cát-a-logue
(3) ア ín-ter-est イ síg-na-ture
ウ vol-un-téer エ sát-is-fy
(4) ア cor-réct イ con-fíne
ウ suc-céss エ ús-age
(5) ア vól-ume イ trans-fér
ウ wór-ship エ tér-ror

190

(1) ウ (2) エ (3) エ (4) イ
(5) ア (6) イ

解説

(1) ア advíce イ caréer
ウ míschief エ occúr
(2) ア páttern イ próduct

ウ préface　エ prefér
(3) ア méchanism　イ cálendar
ウ éducate　エ entertáin
(4) ア áverage　イ devélop
ウ índustry　エ úniverse
(5) ア nécessary　イ mathemátics
ウ politícian　エ energétic
(6) ア accésory　イ ágriculture
ウ demócracy　エ photógraphy

191

(1) ウ　(2) エ　(3) エ　(4) ア

解説

(1) ア [ripέər]　イ [pripέər]
ウ [wíəri]　エ [swέər]
(2) ア [péiʃənt]　イ [féivərət]
ウ [béikən]　エ [lǽtər]
(3) ア [əsémbli]　イ [distrés]
ウ [mʌ́sl]　エ [sízərz]
(4) ア [ikspérəmənt]　イ [kəmplí:t]
ウ [ikstrí:mli]　エ [imí:diət]

192

イ，オ

解説

ア [bɔ́:l]/[téik]　イ [sí:]/[pí:s]
ウ [lɔ́:ŋ]/[kʌ́p]　エ [tú:θ]/[béið]
オ [zú:]/[nɔ́iz]

193

(1) ア　(2) イ　(3) イ　(4) エ
(5) エ

解説

(1) ア dám-age　イ mis-táke
ウ oc-cúr　エ per-fórm
(2) ア én-er-gy　イ ex-ám-ine
ウ hés-i-tate　エ sát-is-fy
(3) ア mag-nét-ic　イ pól-i-tics
ウ dra-mát-ic　エ cli-mát-ic
(4) ア i-dén-ti-ty　イ a-bíl-i-ty
ウ tech-nól-o-gy　エ ín-ter-est-ing
(5) ア chár-ac-ter　イ mán-ag-er
ウ cár-pen-ter　エ pio-néer

194

(1) イ　(2) ウ　(3) イ　(4) イ
(5) ウ

解説

(1) pre-díct
ア con-strúct　イ díf-fer
ウ con-frónt　エ ap-pláuse
(2) éx-e-cute
ア fás-ci-nate　イ déd-i-cate
ウ em-bár-rass　エ sép-a-rate
(3) ín-tel-lect
ア fác-ul-ty　イ at-tríb-ute
ウ íg-no-rant　エ ád-e-quate
(4) bi-óg-ra-phy
ア an-tíc-i-pate　イ man-u-fác-ture
ウ i-dén-ti-fy　エ hy-póth-e-sis
(5) phy-sí-cian
ア dis-tríb-ute　イ en-déav-or
ウ cón-cen-trate　エ in-súr-ance

195

(1) ウ　(2) イ　(3) ア　(4) ア
(5) ウ　(6) イ　(7) エ

196

(1) take〔have〕　(2) take
(3) suffering　(4) feel　(5) use

197

(1) エ　(2) ア　(3) イ　(4) エ
(5) ウ

198

(1) ウ　(2) オ　(3) カ　(4) ク
(5) キ

199

(1) ウ　(2) オ　(3) ア　(4) イ
(5) エ

200

(1) ウ，エ　(ウ，ア，エ，イの順)
(2) イ，ウ　(イ，エ，ウ，アの順)
(3) エ，ウ　(エ，ア，ウ，イの順)

201

(1) キ　(2) オ　(3) ウ　(4) イ

202

(1) エ　(2) イ　(3) ア　(4) エ
(5) エ

203

(1) ウ　(2) ク　(3) エ　(4) オ
(5) ア　(6) ウ　(7) ア　(8) オ
(9) エ　(10) カ

204

(1) ア　(2) ウ　(3) イ　(4) エ
(5) ウ　(6) エ

解説

⑴「ちょうど今，あなたの家で何が起きていますか。」

at the moment「(現在時制で) ちょうど今」「(過去時制で) ちょうどそのとき」の意。まさに進行中のことを表していると考えられるので，**ア**が入る。

⑵「若かったとき，学校にジーンズを履いていきましたか。」

used to ～「(以前は) ～したものだ」という過去の習慣を示す表現。

⑶「その鳥は鷲であるはずがない。それはとても小さすぎる。」

cannot be ～「～であるはずがない」

⑷「彼女はこれらの絵画のうち両方とも好きです。」

both of 限定複数名詞で「～の両方とも」の意。

⑸「『あなたは自分で手術ができるほど熟練してはいない』と外科医は言った。」

not … enough to～「～するのに足りるほど…でない」

⑹「情報を教えてくれませんか。」

information は不可算名詞なので an をつけず，複数形もとらない。

205

⑴ **ウ**　⑵ **エ**　⑶ **ウ**　⑷ **ウ**

⑸ **イ**　⑹ **エ**　⑺ **エ**

解説

⑴「何のために，そのような場所に行ったのですか。」

What ～ for?「何のために～ですか？，なぜ～ですか？」

⑵「あなたは両親に頼るべきではない。」

depend on ～「～に頼る」

⑶「ケイトはトムから何の便りもない。そのことが，彼女を不安にさせています。」

which は前の文章全体を指す関係詞の非制限用法である。

⑷「スティーブは家の支払いを終えたいと思っています。」

finish ～ing「～し終える」

⑸「あなたが支払うのが現金かクレジットカードかは重要ではない。」

whether A or B「AかBか」

make no difference「違いはない，重要でない」

⑹「バスの便がなかったので，私たちはタクシーに乗らなければならなかった。」

There being …「…がある (あった) ので」(独立分詞構文)

⑺「もし昨夜私がぐっすり眠っていたならば，今ごろそんなに眠たく感じないだろうに。」

今と昨夜と出来事の時間がずれているので，if 節の中は仮定法過去完了にする。

206

⑴ **エ**　⑵ **イ**　⑶ **ウ**　⑷ **ウ**

⑸ **ア**　⑹ **エ**　⑺ **ア**　⑻ **エ**

⑼ **エ**　⑽ **ア**

解説

⑴「彼が村に戻ったら，私たちは彼に手紙を書くだろう。」

when 節は副詞節なので，「村に戻る」という未来を表す言葉も現在形で表す。

⑵「彼の言う通りにしなさい。」

as ～「～のように，～の通りに」

⑶「彼は定期的に行っていたものでしたが，今は行きません。」

used to ～「(以前は) よく～した (ものだ)」

⑷「物音一つ聞こえませんでした。」

not a ～「ただ一つ (一人) の～もない」

⑸「彼らは何が起こったかを警官に伝えました。」

tell A B「AにBを伝える」

⑹「夏には多くの人々がそこへ行きます。」

a lot of 複数名詞＝lots of 複数名詞「たくさんの～」

⑺「今のところ私の姉はそこに行っていない (行ったことがない)。」

現在完了形 (継続，経験) で表す。

⑻「私は長い間，彼から連絡をもらっていません。」

hear from～「～から手紙 (連絡) をもらう，便りを聞く」

現在完了形 (継続) で表す。

⑼「私は父にあなたを手伝うように頼むでしょう。」

ask O to do「Oに～するように頼む」

⑽ 「その命を救われた人は私の父です。」
　所有格の関係代名詞 whose が入る。

207

⑴ **ウ**　⑵ **ウ**　⑶ **ア**　⑷ **イ**
⑸ **ウ**

解説

⑴ 「私は毎朝散歩に出かけるのを楽しんでいます。」
　enjoy ～ing「～を楽しむ,～して楽しむ」
　go for a walk「散歩に行く」

⑵ 「私の父が亡くなって10年になる。」
＝My father died ten years ago.
＝It is〔It's been〕ten years since my father died.

⑶ 「彼は若い医師にきちんと世話をされた。」
＝A young doctor took good care of him.
　take good care of ～「～をきちんと世話する」

⑷ 「日が暮れてから一人で外出してはいけない。」
　had better do「～したほうがよい」の否定形は had better not do「～しないほうがよい」
　You が主語の場合，肯定文は「～しなくてはいけない」，否定文は「～してはいけない」の意。

⑸ 「たくさんお金があったら，外国に行けるだろうに。」
　現在の事実とは反対の仮定を表しているから，仮定法過去を用いる。

208

⑴ **ウ**　⑵ **ウ**　⑶ **エ**　⑷ **イ**

解説

⑴ 「あなたがた全員が時間通りにくる必要はない。」
　「あなたがた全員が時間通りに来ないといけないわけではない。」
　There is no need for 人 to ～「人が～する必要はない」
　not all ～「すべてが～とは限らない」(部分否定)

⑵ 「我々の上司はミスを指摘するのが上手い。」
　「我々の上司はかなりよく我々のミスを見つけることができる。」
　be good at ～ing「～するのが上手い」
　quite well「かなりよく，上手に」

⑶ 「ビルはクラスで一番背が高い。」
　「ビルはクラスの他の誰よりも背が高い。」
　比較級 than any other …「他のどの～よりも…」

⑷ 「私たちは赤ちゃんをとても注意深く見守るべきだ。」
　「私たちの赤ちゃんはとても注意深く見守られるべきだ。」
　受動態の形で表現した文。

209

⑴ make you　⑵ so, that
⑶ whose eyes　⑷ was heard to
⑸ of him to lend

解説

⑴ 「毎日走れば，あなたはより強くなるでしょう。」
　「毎日走ることがあなたを強くするでしょう。」
　無生物主語の構文。A will make 人 …「Aは人を…にするだろう（Aをすれば，人は…になるだろう）」

⑵ 「彼女はとても具合が悪いので，働くことができない。」
　「彼女はとても具合が悪いので働くことができない。」
　so … that ～「とても…なので～」

⑶ 「ディーン・スミスは青い瞳の男性ですか。」
　「ディーン・スミスはその瞳が青い男性ですか。」
　関係代名詞 whose「その人の…が～であるところの」

⑷ 「私たちは彼が助けを呼ぶのを聞いた。」
　「彼は助けを呼ぶのを聞かれた。」
　hear A do「Aが～するのが聞こえる」の受動態では，do が to do となる。

⑸ 「彼は親切にも私にたくさん CD を貸してくれた。」
　「こんなにたくさん CD を貸してくれるなんて彼はとても親切だ。」
　It's kind of A to ～「～するとはAは親切だ」

210

(1) What (2) keep (3) little
(4) headache (5) in (6) thirties
(7) Millions (8) where (9) free
(10) what ⇨ A is to B what C is to D.
「AとBの関係はCとDの関係に等しい」
(11) on earth (12) not always
(13) from behind (14) when to
(15) had been (16) for, in, life
(17) works for, company
(18) call, soon, get

211

(1) イ (2) ア (3) エ (4) イ

212

(1) ウ (2) ウ (3) エ (4) エ
(5) ア (6) イ (7) ア (8) ウ
(9) エ (10) イ (11) ウ (12) イ

213

(1) ウ (2) エ (3) イ (4) ア
(5) ウ (6) エ (7) イ (8) エ
(9) ア (10) ウ (11) ウ (12) エ
(13) イ (14) エ (15) イ (16) ウ
(17) ア (18) ウ (19) イ

214

(1) ケ (2) ア (3) イ (4) ク
(5) キ (6) エ (7) ウ (8) コ
(9) カ (10) オ

215

(1) イ (2) エ (3) イ (4) ア
(5) エ

解説

(1)「しばらく座ったままでいてください。」
remain ～「～のままでいる」
seatは「…を着席させる」の意であるため，過去分詞形。

(2)「冬はもうすぐです。」
around the corner「間近に，近づいて」

(3)「明日，教科書を買うのを覚えていなければならない。」
remember to ～「忘れないで～する」

(4)「彼は庭に犬をつないだままにしていた。」
犬はつながれるのだから，過去分詞形。

(5)「もし私があなたならば，彼女を助けただろうに。」
仮定法過去なので，would＋動詞の原形。

216

(1) エ (2) ウ (3) エ (4) ウ
(5) エ

解説

(1) A：「何人子どもがいますか。」
B：「娘が一人と息子が二人います。」
子どもの人数を答えているため，how many 複数名詞～で尋ねる。

(2) A：「デイビス先生は多くの生徒たちに好かれていると思いますよね。」
B：「全く同感ですし，私も彼のことが好きです。」

(3) A：「テレビを消してくれませんか。私はこの本を読みたいのです。」
B：「見ているんですけど。」
will you ～?「～してくれませんか」

(4)「私たちの旅行の計画について話し合いましょう。」
discuss は他動詞なので，そのまま直後に目的語が置かれる。

(5)「だから私は大学へ行きたくないのです。」
that is why～「そういう理由で～，だから～」

217

(1) more (2) hunger (3) short
(4) peace (5) mice (6) public
(7) succeed

解説

(1) 形容詞：比較級 (2) 名詞：形容詞
(3) 反意語 (4) 反意語
(5) 単数：複数 (6) 反意語
(7) 反意語

218

(1) ア (2) イ (3) エ (4) ウ
(5) イ (6) エ

解説

(1)「私の娘は歴史も数学も好きです。」
both A and B「AとBの両方」

(2)「事故の数は近年，着実に増加しつつあります。」

(3)「あなたはどのくらいの頻度でその美容院へ行きますか。」
ア どのくらい（距離）
イ どのくらい（時間）
ウ how many 複数名詞（いくつ）

エ　どのくらい（頻度）

(4)「その国は自然資源に恵まれている。」

rich in ～「～に恵まれて」

(5)「パーティーがキャンセルされても，私のせいではない。」

ア　blame には所有格をつけない。I am to blame.＝It's my fault.「私に責任がある」

(6)「マイクはいつも定刻に到着する。彼はとても時間に正確である。」

ア　飽き飽きする，うんざりする

イ　勤勉な　　ウ　神経質な，気の弱い

エ　きちょうめんな，厳密な

219

(1) イ　(2) ウ　(3) エ　(4) ウ

(5) ア　(6) エ

解説

(1)「私は夜更かしすることに慣れていない。」

be used to ～ing「～することに慣れている」の意。be used to の後には名詞・動名詞がくる。

(2)「学ぶのに遅すぎるということはない。」

ことわざである。⇨「六十の手習い」

(3)「彼はここ3日間ずっと病気で寝込んでいる。」

(4)「あなたの温かい手紙にとても勇気付けられます。」

feel〔be〕encouraged by …「…に勇気付けられる」

(5)「ロングスカートをはいている女性はどなたですか。」

wearing は the lady を修飾する現在分詞。

(6)「満月は今夜見られる。」

月は人によって「見られる」のだから，受動態の be seen が入る。

220

(1) ア　(2) エ　(3) ウ　(4) イ

(5) ア

解説

(1)「いつ私たちが USJ に行けるのか教えてください。」

let me do「私に～させて」

(2)「私たちが彼女の計画に賛成できない理由が2，3ある。」

a few reasons を先行詞とする関係副詞 why を用いる。

(3)「先日見た映画は興奮したよ。」

excite ～「～を興奮させる」（動詞）

excited「（人が）興奮した」（形容詞）

exciting「（人を）興奮させるような」（形容詞）

(4)「彼女が病院に着くまでに暗くなっているだろう。」

by the time S＋V ～「Sが～するまでに」という時を表す副詞節では，主節に未来を表す will が含まれていても，現在時制を用いる。

(5)「医師はその患者に1週間ベッドに横になっていることを強く求めた。」

insist that S＋(should)＋動詞の原形「Sが～することを強く要求する」

should は主に省略される。

221

(1) ウ　(2) ア　(3) ウ　(4) ア

(5) イ　(6) ウ　(7) ア　(8) イ

解説

(1)「大雨のため試合は延期された。」

put off ～「～を延期する」

(2)「その話を彼女に理解させるのは不可能だ。」

make 人 do「人に～させる」

her の後ろには原形の understand が入る。

(3)「昨夜，私たちは高校時代のことを楽しく語り合った。」

enjoy ～ing「～して楽しむ」

talk over ～「～について語り合う」

(4)「家に着いたとき，雨が降り始めた。」

接続詞 when「～のとき」

while「～の間に」

(5)「朝の3時か4時まで起きて読書していることが時々ある。」

sit up ～ing until …「…まで起きて～している」

(6)「彼はこれまでで最高の芸術家だ。」

as ～ as ever lived「これまでで～」

(7)「山田さんはかなり高齢だけれども，テニスがとても上手だ。」

though＋節「～だけれども」

in spite of＋名詞「～にもかかわらず」

unless＋節「もし～でなければ」

(8) 「そのバッグの値段がとても高いので買えなかった。」

the price is high「値段が高い」

222

(1) have been (2) All, have

(3) my〔me〕watching (4) But for

解説

(1) 「彼はお金持ちだったらしい。」

It seems that ～「～らしい，～のようだ」

that 節が過去のことを表している場合，不定詞の完了形を用いて書き換える。

(2) 「あなたは名前と住所を書きさえすればよい。」

You have only to ～＝All you have to do is (to) ～「～しさえすればよい」

(3) 「テレビを見てもよろしいでしょうか。」

Would you mind if I ～?＝Would you mind my〔me〕～ing?「私が～したら気になりますか。」の丁寧な表現。名詞節を動名詞を使って書き換える。通常，if I の後は仮定法過去として過去形が用いられるのが正式だが，現在形が用いられる場合もあるので注意する。Do you mind if I ～の文では現在形。

(4) 「音楽がなかったら，私たちの生活は砂漠と同じくらい乾いたものになるだろう。」

If it were not for ～＝But for ～「～がなかったら」

223

(1) イ (2) エ (3) ウ (4) ウ

(5) イ

解説

(1) 「その交通事故は速すぎるスピードで運転している若者によって起きた。」

a young man ～ing「～している若者」

名詞を修飾する分詞が後に置かれた形。

(2) 「ロープがなかったら，登山者は落ちて死んでいただろう。」

仮定法過去完了 If it had not been for ～「～がなかったら」の If が省略されて it と had が倒置された形。

(3) 「メンバー全員が7時までに戻らなければならない。」

by the time＋節「～が…するまでに」

by ～「～までには」(期限)

until ～「～まで」(期間)

(4) 「彼は胃を診察してもらうために医師のところへ行った。」

have＋O＋過去分詞「Oを～してもらう」

(5) 「今の彼女は10年前のかつての彼女とは全く違う。」

what she used to be「昔の（かつての）彼女」

224

(1) イ (2) ウ (3) ア (4) イ

(5) ウ

解説

(1) 「近い将来，あなたに会えるのを楽しみにしています。」

look forward to ～「～を楽しみにして待つ」

to のあとは名詞・動名詞がくる。

(2) 「思いついた理由を教えてくれませんか。」

the reason why S＋V「Sが～する（した）理由」，come up with ～「～を思いつく」

(3) 「デニスはクラスの他の誰よりも一生懸命勉強する。」

比較級 than any other 単数名詞「他のどの～よりも…」で，最上級の意を表す。

(4) 「この橋は何年も（ずっと）工事中である。」

under construction「工事中」

(5) 「私は中年の男性がその家に入るのを確かに見た。」

see A do「Aが～するのを見る」

go の場合は行く先を表す副詞（to～）などが後ろに必要である。

225

(1) ウ (2) エ (3) ア (4) イ

(5) ア

解説

(1) 「外国に行ったとき，人混みの中で財布を盗まれた。」

have＋O＋過去分詞「Oを～される」

(2) 「君は熱心に勉強をしなかった。だから試験に失敗した。」

That's why ～「それが～の理由である，

だから～なのだ」

(3) 「私たちは土曜日，彼の車で海岸に行きたいの。というのも私たちの車はまだ修理できてないだろうから。」

repair「～を修理する」なので our car が主語のこの文では「修理される」となるように受動態を用いる。

will have＋過去分詞（未来完了）で未来のある時点での完了や継続などを表す。「土曜日の時点でまだ修理が終わっていないだろう」という意味にするには won't have been repaired の形となる。

(4) 「そのことは忘れるようにしよう。だってそれは心配する価値がないのだから。」

be worth ～ing「～する価値がある」

(5) 「彼女はとても気が動転しているので，私たちは彼女をそっとしておく方がよい。」

had better ～「～する方がよい」，leave … alone「（人を）そのままにしておく，邪魔をしない」

226

(1) Shall I　(2) will give
(3) It being　(4) ordered, not
(5) having said　(6) that, recover
(7) without visiting
(8) have only
(9) to come　(10) who has
(11) here, we come
(12) not either, or
(13) boring, made me
(14) could have spoken
(15) According to
(16) stupid of you
(17) I must do
(18) made up of

227

(1) エ　(2) ウ　(3) ア　(4) イ
(5) エ

228

(1) サ　(2) ケ　(3) チ　(4) オ
(5) ウ　(6) コ　(7) カ　(8) タ
(9) セ　(10) イ

229

(1) イ　(2) ウ　(3) エ　(4) イ
(5) エ　(6) ア　(7) イ　(8) ウ
(9) エ　(10) ウ

230

(1) オ，②　(2) イ，①　(3) ア，④
(4) エ，⑤　(5) ウ，③

解説

(1) A：わかりません。
B：答えはすぐ目の前にありますよ。

right under one's nose「すぐ鼻の先で，すぐ目の前で」

(2) 「リンダは審美眼があります。」

have an eye for ～「～を（～に関して）見る目がある」

(3) 「彼女は額にしわを寄せながら，『それはしたくない』と言いました。」

wrinkle one's brow「額にしわを寄せる」
knit〔bend〕one's brows「眉をひそめる」

(4) 「私は科学が好きではないので，彼の講義を理解できない。」

above one's head「理解を越えていてわからない」

(5) A：うまくいくよう祈っててね！
B：幸運を祈っているよ。

cross one's fingers for A「A の幸運を祈る」

231

(1) オ　(2) ア　(3) オ　(4) オ
(5) イ

解説

(1) 「そのグループはひそかに集まった。どんな外的要因にも左右されたくなかったからである。」

質問：この文で，exは何を意味していますか。

external「外的な」↔ internal「内的な」

(2) 「これらは私たちがローマを訪れた時に撮った写真のいくつかです。」

先行詞がないので関係詞は入らない。接続詞 when が入ると判断する。

(3) 「彼はもう何年もコーチをしているので，試合のルールの全てに精通している。」

be familiar with ～「～に精通している」

(4) 「恐ろしい叫び声が聞こえて目が覚めてしまった。」

wake up「目が覚める」（自動詞）

「目を覚まさせる」(他動詞)
wake-woke-woken
be woken up by 〜「〜で起こされる」

(5) 「私の責任ではないです。私がそこで働き始める前にその決定は下されていたのです。」
take a decision「決定を下す」
before 以下が過去形なので，それより前のことを表すには過去完了形を用いる。

232

(1) I have (never seen such an exciting movie) as this.
(2) I will give you (the answer about this matter as soon as I can).
(3) She (did not know anything about this).
(4) It is difficult to (communicate our feelings to others without) using the language.
(5) She (was injured while playing volleyball).

233

(1) **ア, ウ** (カ, ア, イ, キ, ウ, オ, エの順)
(2) **ア, ウ** (エ, ア, イ, オ, ウの順)
(3) **ア, エ** (イ, ア, ウ, オ, エの順)
(4) **オ, カ** (イ, オ, ウ, ア, カ, エ, キの順)
(5) **キ, ア** (オ, キ, イ, カ, ア, ウ, ク, エの順)
(6) **ア, カ** (ウ, ア, オ, イ, カ, エの順)
(7) **カ, オ** (エ, カ, ウ, ア, オ, イの順)
(8) **イ, エ** (カ, イ, オ, ア, エ, ウの順)
(9) **イ, エ** (オ, イ, ア, カ, エ, ウの順)
(10) **ア, ウ** (エ, ア, カ, オ, ウ, イの順)
(11) **エ, オ** (ア, エ, カ, ウ, オ, イの順)
(12) **ウ, オ** (エ, ウ, ア, カ, オ, イの順)
(13) **ウ, エ** (キ, ウ, カ, ア, エ, オ, イの順)

234

(1) **ウ, ア** (オ, ウ, イ, ア, カ, エの順)
(2) **ウ, カ** (オ, ウ, ア, カ, エ, イの順)
(3) **ア, オ** (ウ, ア, エ, オ, イの順)
(4) **ウ, エ** (カ, ウ, ア, エ, オ, イの順)
(5) **オ, ウ** (ク, オ, カ, ウ, イ, エ, キ, アの順)
(6) **ア, イ** (オ, ア, エ, イ, カ, ウの順)
(7) **ア, ウ** (イ, ア, カ, ウ, オ, エの順)
(8) **イ, ア** (エ, イ, カ, ア, ウ, オの順)
(9) **カ, オ** (エ, カ, イ, オ, ウ, アの順)
(10) **ア, カ** (エ, ア, ウ, カ, イ, オの順)

235

(1) **ウ**　(2) **ウ**　(3) **カ**

解説

(1) I'm advised to finish jogging before it gets dark.
「暗くなる前にジョギングを終えるよう助言された。」
advise to do「〜するよう助言する」
finish 〜ing「〜し終える」

(2) I think it's too difficult for me to read this book.
「私にはその本は難しすぎて読めないと思う。」
too … for 人 to 〜「(人)には…すぎて〜できない」

(3) She was so intelligent that she was able to solve this math question.
「彼女はとても頭がいいのでこの数学の問題を解くことができた。」
so 〜 that …「とても〜なので…」

236

(1) (What do you want me to do)?
(2) (Help yourself to anything you like).
(3) You (should have told me that earlier).
(4) How (much longer are you going to stay) in Japan?
(5) Be sure to (write home as soon as you're settled).
(6) When we write, (is the use of a period after 'Mr' optional or not)?
(7) (Ms. White's teaching has made me interested in studying English).
(8) I thought (it useless to argue with her about) politics.
(9) (I doubt whether the topics you have chosen are worth discussing).
(10) I'm just (wondering if there is anybody living in) this old mansion.
(11) He (pulled me by the sleeve when he caught sight of her).
(12) (More and more people are attending night classes in America).
(13) (John was lying on the bed with his

eyes closed).

(14) (I wonder if there is any sugar left in the bottle).

(15) (The doctor gave me some medicine to be taken three times a day).

(16) (It was two days ago that he left the hospital).

(17) (She is thought to have been a fine nurse).

(18) (I saw her leaving the sick room with tears in her eyes).

(19) (Sunday is the day when we receive no visitors).

(20) (The examination is too hard for old people to put up with).

237

(1) ア (ウ, イ, オ, ア, エ, カの順)
(2) エ (イ, ア, キ, エ, カ, ウの順)
(3) オ (ク, ウ, イ, オ, キ, カ, アの順)
(4) ク (エ, ア, イ, ク, ウ, オ, キの順)
(5) イ (ア, オ, エ, イ, カ, ウの順)

238

(1) ①エ ②キ ③カ ④オ ⑤イ ⑥ア
(2) ①キ ②イ ③エ ④カ ⑤オ ⑥ウ
(3) ①エ ②キ ③オ ④ウ ⑤カ ⑥イ
(4) ①イ ②オ ③キ ④カ ⑤エ ⑥ア

239

(1) エ He (went to sleep with the radio on).

(2) ウ Be (careful not to make such a mistake again).

(3) エ You (can read this book without a dictionary).

(4) ウ I (was spoken to by a stranger in front of the bank).

(5) イ Don't (use words whose meanings are not clear to you).

240

(1) ウ, イ (2) イ, ア (3) カ, ウ
(4) エ, オ (5) ア, エ

解説

(1) There were (no children playing because it was dark).
playing は children にかかる現在分詞。

(2) We visited (the town famous for its beautiful castle).

(3) Mimi (did not know what to give him).
what to do ～「何を～すべきか」

(4) It will (not be long before Mark comes back).
It is not long before ～「ほどなく～」

(5) He saw (a small picture which did not have a price on it).
「値段のついていない」という部分は「絵の上に値段がついていない」と言い換えれば, it は picture を指すことがわかる。

241

(1) エ, オ (2) オ, ア (3) ア, ウ
(4) キ, エ (5) ア, イ

解説

(1) He's (proud of his son having married her).
be proud of ～「～を誇りに思う」

(2) You (are old enough to know the fact).
形容詞＋enough to ～「～するのに十分…」

(3) I (feel as if I were flying in the air).
as if ～「まるで～であるかのように」

(4) It (goes without saying that we all support your claim).
it goes without saying that ～「言うまでもなく～」

(5) It (is of importance to us whether she likes our cooking or not).
または It (is of importance to us whether or not she likes our cooking).
whether ～ or not「～かどうか」

242

ウ

解説

After a major disaster we should pay close attention to mental health as well as physical health.
pay attention to ～「注意を払う」
A as well as B「BだけでなくAも, BはもちろんAも」

243

(1) (My father has been sick in) bed

since last night.

(2) (You do not have to come here).

(3) (Is this book yours)?

(4) Nothing (is more important than helping each other).

(5) (The stone was too heavy for her to lift).

解説

(1) 寝込んでいる⇨「継続」なので現在完了形。

(2) do not have to ～「～する必要がない」

(4) Nothing ～ 比較級 than …「…ほど～なものはない」で最上級の意を表す。

(5) too ～ (for 人) to …「あまりに～なので，(人には)…できない」

244

(1) イ，オ　(2) イ，ウ　(3) エ，ア
(4) エ，カ　(5) エ，カ　(6) オ，エ

解説

(1) (Someone suggested going to the movies), but I never wanted to go.

suggest ～ing「～しようと提案する」

(2) Whenever she doesn't get a strike, (she blames it on the ball).

blame A on B「AをBの責任にする」

(3) She can be rude; (at the same time everyone likes) her.

at the same time「同時に，それでも」

(4) I (drew the rope as tight as I could).

as 形容詞 as I can「できるだけ～」

(5) (No matter how old I get), I'm always young at heart.

no matter how 形容詞「どんなに～でも」

(6) You learn much about what to do and (what not to do from your) mistakes.

what to do「何をすべきか」

245

(1) エ，ア　(2) ウ，エ　(3) ウ，オ
(4) オ，ア　(5) ウ，オ　(6) エ，ウ

解説

(1) This is (the only way to deal with) this situation.

deal with ～「～を扱う，処理する」

(2) It's very (kind of you to invite) us this evening.

be kind of A to ～「～するなんて，Aは親切である」

(3) If you (cannot keep a promise you'll lose) trust of your friends.

keep a promise「約束を守る」

(4) The (capacity to know how others feel) is important on the job and in the family.

others「他人」

(5) (We see fewer and fewer women carrying babies) on their backs these days.

fewer and fewer …「…がどんどん減って」

(6) Please (turn off the radio so that I) can get to sleep quickly.

so that「～するために，～となるように」

246

(1) ア　(2) イ　(3) ウ

解説

(1) Don't speak with your mouth full.

with＋名詞＋形容詞で付帯状況を表す。

(2) You have grown much taller since I saw you last.

比較級を強める場合，much などを前につける。

(3) This book is easy enough for young children to read.

… enough to ～「～するのに十分なくらい…」の構文で意味上の主語 (for＋人) は enough と to の間に置く。

247

(1) ① オ　② カ
(2) ① カ　② オ
(3) ① カ　② オ
(4) ① イ　② オ
(5) ① オ　② エ

解説

(1) This is the only way that was left for us.

the only way「唯一の方法」のように，先行詞を強く限定する修飾語 (all, every,

the only など）がつくとき，関係代名詞にはthatが用いられる。

be left for ～「～に残されている」

⑵ Who do you think wrote the novel？

Who wrote the novel？「誰がその小説を書いたか？」は疑問詞が主語なので，do you think を加えるには，疑問詞＋do you think＋動詞 ～?の語順になる。

⑶ He is the last man to do such a thing.

the last man to ～「最も～しそうにない人」

such「そのような～」の意で，後に続く名詞を強調する形容詞の働きをする。

⑷ Turning to the right, you will find a large temple.

turn to the right「右へ曲がる」

⑸ Had I had enough money, I could have bought the book.

仮定法過去完了の If が省略され，倒置が起こり，助動詞が主語の前にきた形。条件節には過去完了形（had＋過去分詞）が，帰結節には助動詞の過去形＋現在完了形（could have＋過去分詞）がくる。

248

⑴ ウ　⑵ イ　⑶ エ　⑷ エ

⑸ ア

解説

⑴ Please explain clearly (so that everybody can understand you).

⑵ Can you (tell me where you got the) sweater？

Can you tell me where ～？「～はどこか教えてくれませんか」

where の後は S＋V の語順。

⑶ I'm sure it will help me a lot if you (reply as soon as you can).

as soon as one can「できる限り早く」

⑷ Will (you tell me where I am)？

「ここはどこだか」

＝「私はどこにいるのか」

⑸ You should do (what you would like to do).

what S＋V「Sが～すること」（関係代名詞節で目的語として用いられている。）

249

⑴ ① ウ　② エ

⑵ ① オ　② ア

⑶ ① ウ　② ア

⑷ ① ア　② イ

解説

⑴ I dropped in at the barber's to (have my hair cut on) my way home.

have＋O＋過去分詞「Oを～してもらう」

on one's way home「帰り道の途中で」

⑵ Accurate (experiments will enable you to) find what is wrong.

無生物主語の構文。A will enable 人 to do「A は人を～できるようにするだろう（Aをすれば人は～できるだろう）」

⑶ (As is often the case with) people who are proud, he is unaware of his rudeness.

as is often the case with …「…の場合よくあることだが」

⑷ Perhaps you (would be kind enough to) open it.

Perhaps you would be kind〔good〕enough to ～「できましたら～していただけないでしょうか」は依頼のかなり丁寧な表現。

250

⑴ エ　⑵ ウ

解説

⑴ It's very kind of you.(I cannot thank you too much).

cannot ～ too …「いくら～してもしすぎることはない」

⑵ What (if it were not for rain forests) on the earth？

what if ～「～したらどうなるか」

if it were not for ～「～がなかったとしたら」

251

⑴ ① ウ　② イ

⑵ ① ア　② イ

⑶ ① ア　② オ

⑷ ① イ　② エ

⑸ ① ア　② エ

解説

(1) Scarcely had I got on the train when my cell phone started to ring.
「電車に乗るとすぐに私の携帯電話が鳴り始めた。」
scarcely … when ～「…するかしないうちに～」
I had scarcely got on ～ の scarcely が強調されて「副詞＋V＋S」という語順になり，I と had が倒置された形。

(2) In the past, cancer was thought of as an incurable disease and its victims were normally not to be told the name of their disease.
「以前は，がんは不治の病と考えられていたので，がんにかかった人は普通，その病名を告げられないことになっていた。」
think of A as B「AをBとみなす」のAを主語にすると受け身になるので，A is thought of as B となる。

(3) What do you think made her change her mind?
「何故彼女が心変わりしたと思いますか。」
What made her change her mind?に do you think が挿入された形の間接疑問。

(4) A well-balanced diet is essential for good health. It contains all the substances without which our bodies would not function properly.
「バランスのよい食事は健康に不可欠である。それにはそれなくしては人間の体がきちんと機能しない成分がすべて含まれている。」
the substances を先行詞とする関係詞中で，前置詞が関係代名詞の前に置かれた形。

(5) After the interview, he was given the job right away.
「面接後，彼はすぐに仕事を与えられた。」
right away「すぐに，直ちに」

252

(1) Bring me a cup of coffee, will you?
(2) How beautifully Jane sings!
(3) Not knowing what to do, I asked for his advice.
(4) I wish you had not told him about the plan.
(5) Weren't those books returned to the library by them?
(6) When she looked into the room, she saw her sister crying.
(7) The sky was filled with clouds. ⇨ be filled with ～「～でいっぱいである」
(8) When and where were you born?
(9) She seems to have been ill for a long time.
(10) He is tall enough to reach the ceiling.
(11) He was lying on his bed with his eyes wide open.
(12) I suggested to her that she (should) come in and take a seat.
(13) Traveling is the most pleasant thing of all.
(14) He said, "I bought this book here yesterday".
(15) They built the house in 1964.
(16) Hardly had he opened the door when〔before〕the telephone rang. ⇨ hardly を文頭に出すと，そのあとは〈had＋主語＋過去分詞〉の語順となる。
(17) His name is known in foreign countries as well as in Japan. ⇨ not only A but (also) B＝B as well as A
(18) It was last Sunday that I saw her in front of the church.
(19) Please tell me where you found the cat.

253

(1) イ → is あるいは has been
(2) イ → had
(3) ア → What
(4) イ → driving
(5) ウ → was
(6) エ → that
(7) ウ → others
(8) イ → soccer
(9) イ → so
(10) ウ → knew ⇨ as if＋仮定法過去(まるで～であるかのように)
(11) イ → to run ⇨ 知覚動詞(see)の文が受

動態のとき to-不定詞

⑿ ア → have known ⇨ 現在完了(継続)

254

(1) confusing → confused

(2) which → when

(3) 2つ目の that → what

(4) too → either

(5) can → could

(6) visit → visiting

(7) activity → activities

(8) being → to be

(9) break → broken

255

(1) I heard someone close the door.

(2) It is dangerous for children to play near the railroad.

(3) Say that you love me.

(4) I want to be a nurse.

(5) She has been in Kanazawa since she finished her school.

(6) Almost all the mothers have trouble in raising their children. ⇨ almost は副詞なので直接名詞を修飾できない。

(7) Every student of the nursing school is so cute and smart. ⇨ every のあとには単数形の名詞

(8) The patient in room 205 had her money stolen.

(9) Teacher: Which is larger, America or Japan? Student: America is, sir.

256

(1) エ (2) ア (3) イ (4) ア

(5) イ

257

(1) ウ (2) イ (3) ア (4) イ

(5) イ (6) イ

258

(1) ウ，ア，エ，イの順

(2) ウ，ア，エ，イの順

(3) エ，ウ，ア，イの順

(4) ウ，ア，エ，イの順

(5) イ，エ，ア，ウの順

259

(1) ウ (2) エ (3) ア (4) イ

(5) イ

260

(1) would

(2) thanks

(3) depends

(4) done

(5) looking

和訳

(1) A：私たちと一緒に来ませんか。

B：できたらいいのですが。

(2) A：もう少しいかが。

B：いえ，結構です。

(3) A：パーティーに行きますか。

B：ええっと，状況次第です。

(4) A：彼女のスピーチを聞き逃しちゃったよ。どうだった。

B：とてもよくできてたよ。

(5) A：いらっしゃいませ（何かお探しですか）。

B：見てるだけですから，ありがとう。

261

① ウ ② オ ③ ア ④ イ

⑤ エ

和訳

A：こんにちは。いらっしゃいませ。

B：エレノア・チャールズといいます。（7時に5人で予約しているのですが。）

A：少しお待ちください…（はい，チャールズ様。こちらへどうぞ。）

B：ありがとう。

A：（こちらのテーブルはいかがでしょうか。）

B：いいですね。えっと5人で頼んだのですが，今夜は私たち4人だけなんです。

A：（わかりました。では，皆さまお揃いですね。

B：そうです。

A：（お食事の前に何かお飲み物はいかがですか。）

B：お酒は飲まないんです。ソフトドリンクをいただきます。

A：はい。何がよろしいですか。

B：ジンジャエール1つとコーラ2つ，アイスティー1杯ください。

A：わかりました。すぐにお持ちします。

262

① ア ② カ ③ ウ ④ イ

和訳

M：大丈夫？何があったの？
S：りんごの木から落ちて腕の骨を折ったんだ。
M：（痛むの？）
S：もう痛くないよ。でもお医者さんが3週間はギプスが必要だって言ってたよ。
M：3週間も！どうやってそうなったの？
S：りんごの木に登って滑ったんだ。
M：（救急車を呼んだの？）
S：いや。トムのお父さんが車に乗せていってくれた。庭で車を洗ってて，僕が叫ぶのを聞いたんだ。
M：（木登りはだめだと言ったのに。）
S：わかってるよ，でもそんなに高いのには登ってないんだ。ほんの小さな木だったんだよ。
M：（腕だけで済んでよかったわ。）
S：うん，でも10月まではギプスをしてなければいけない。サッカーのシーズン始まりには参加できないよ。
M：サッカーのシーズンは次があるでしょ。

263

(1) イ　(2) ア　(3) イ　(4) エ
(5) ア

解説

(1) A：お名前をいただけますか。
B：(はい。リナ・ホーンと申します。)
A：“ホーン”の綴りは最後にeがつきますか？
B：そうです。
ア　わかりません。
イ　はい。リナ・ホーンと申します。
ウ　誰に話しているのですか。
エ　シカゴ出身です。

(2) A：また会えて嬉しいよ。元気だった？
B：(元気にしてるわ。あなたは？)
A：元気だよ。ありがとう。
ア　元気にしてるわ。あなたは？
イ　早すぎて言えない。
ウ　長いこと病気なの。
エ　私も。ちがう？

(3) A：すみませんが，市役所行きのバスはこれであっていますか。
B：（残念ながら違うようです。6番のバスに乗ってください。）
A：ありがとう。助かりました。
ア　市役所行きのバスはどこで乗れますか。
イ　残念ながら違うようです。6番のバスに乗ってください。
ウ　いいですよ。いつでも来てください。
エ　このバスであっているかどうか，わかりません。

(4) A：ご注文はお決まりでしょうか。
B：(本日のおすすめ料理は何か教えてくれますか。)
A：はい。フィッシュアンドチップスのグリーンサラダ付きがございます。
B：いいですね。それをいただきます。
ア　まだ決めている最中です。あとで来てくれますか。
イ　菜食者向けのメニューを持ってきていただけますか。
ウ　まずワインを楽しみたいのです。銘柄をいくつか挙げてもらえますか。
エ　本日のおすすめ料理は何か教えてくれますか。

(5) A：まず初めに，来週の予定を話し合いましょう。
B：そうですね。火曜日の朝と木曜日の午後は来られます。
A：（完璧ですね。私も同じ日にこちらにおります。）
B：それはよかった。それなら土曜日の朝にこちらに来る必要はなくなると思います。
A：はい，来なくてもよいですよ。
ア　完璧ですね。私も同じ日にこちらにおります。
イ　土曜日の朝もあなたは来るべきだと思います。
ウ　土曜日の朝も来てくれるよう頼まなければいけません。
エ　申し訳ありませんが，あなたがどちらの日に来るべきか私どもは決めることができません。

264

(1) エ　(2) イ　(3) エ　(4) エ
(5) ウ

265

① エ　② キ　③ イ　④ ア
⑤ カ

266

① ウ　② カ　③ オ　④ イ
⑤ エ　⑥ ア　⑦ キ

267

① ク　② キ　③ ケ　④ オ
⑤ ア

268

① オ　② エ　③ イ　④ ア
⑤ ウ

269

① コ　② ア　③ カ　④ ク
⑤ ウ

270

(1) ウ　(2) エ　(3) ア　(4) ウ

解説

(1) ア「いいわね」
　イ「大変ね」
　ウ「顔色がよくないわ」
　エ「悲しそうね」
(2) ア「もうお医者さんに診てもらったの？」
　イ「今までに同じような兆候があったの？」
　ウ「困ったことがあったの？」
　エ「薬は飲んだ？」
(3) ア「焼き加減はどうだったの？」
　イ「どれくらい（何度）食べるの？」
　ウ「いつ食べたの？」
　エ「どんな材料を使ったの？」
(4) ア「薬局で薬を買ってくるわ」
　イ「気晴らしに少し外に出よう」
　ウ「病院へ連れて行くわ」
　エ「横になっておかなきゃ」

和訳

アリス：ハイ，クロエ。ただいま。今日はどうだった？
クロエ：それが…あまりよくないの。
アリス：何かあったの。顔色がよくないわ。
クロエ：ひどい腹痛と熱が出て，午後ずっと具合が悪かったの。
アリス：薬は飲んだ？
クロエ：うん，でも全然効き目がないの。ますます気分が悪くて。
アリス：何か食べた？
クロエ：あまり。お昼にハンバーガー食べただけ。
アリス：焼き加減はどうだったの？
クロエ：レアよ。
アリス：レアなの！？
クロエ：私はいつもレアでハンバーガーを食べるの。
アリス：クロエ，食中毒かもしれないわ。
クロエ：えっ！私はどうしたらいいの？
アリス：病院へ連れて行くわ。行けそう？
クロエ：う～ん，かなり弱ってる。午後もずっともどしていたの。
アリス：でも，行ってみましょう。まずお医者さんに診てもらう必要があるわよ。

271

① オ　② ア　③ エ　④ ウ
⑤ カ　⑥ イ

和訳

ジェイニー：どなたですか。
和田さん：(私は歯科衛生士です。)
ジェイニー：私に何をなさるのでしょうか。
和田さん：私はあなたに歯の磨き方をお話ししたいのですが。
ジェイニー：(痛くなりますか。)
和田さん：もちろんそんなことはないです。(鏡を見てください。)
ジェイニー：はい。
和田さん：まず，このように歯の外側を磨いてください。ご自分でやってみてください。
ジェイニー：はい。(これでいいですか。)
和田さん：いいですね。では，歯の外側の周りを最初から最後までやってみてください。このように，一つ一つの歯を10回磨きながら。
ジェイニー：(これはくすぐったいですね。)
和田さん：同じように歯の内側もやってください。
ジェイニー：楽しいですね。
和田さん：(さて，嚙み合わせの面を磨いてください。)
ジェイニー：これは楽しい。
和田さん：それでは，同じように上の歯も

すべてやってください。舌を磨くのを忘れないで。

ジェイニー：はい。

272

(1) ① **ア**　② **エ**

(2) ③ **エ**　④ **イ**

(3) ⑤ **ウ**　⑥ **イ**

(4) ⑦ **ウ**　⑧ **イ**

(5) ⑨ **ウ**　⑩ **ア**

解説

(1) A：もしもし，ソフィアはいらっしゃいますか。

B：申し訳ございませんが，今は外出中です。

(2) A：土曜日にトニーがパーティーを開くことをスージーに伝えてくれませんか。

B：もちろんですとも。

A：それから，彼女に私と一緒に行きたいかどうか聞いておいてください。

B：ピーター，了解です。彼女に伝えておきます。

ask A if ～「Aに～かどうか尋ねる」

(3) A：ルームメイトの広告の件でお電話しています。まだルームメイトをお探しでしょうか。

B：はい，探してます。

A：まぁ，よかった！私はちょうどそのことに興味をもっているのです。

call about ～ 「～の件で電話をする」

(4) A：見てごらん。彼らはお似合いの夫婦じゃない？

B：ええ，本当にそうね。私は彼らをよく知ってるの。二人ともとても気さくで，社交的なのよ。

(5) A：このあたりでパスポートの写真を撮ってもらえるところを知りませんか。

B：ええっと，ちょっと考えさせてくださいね。あぁ，ショッピングセンターにいいところがあります。

命令形で用いた let は「～させてください」の意。

273

(1) **ウ**　(2) **エ**

解説

(1) カエ：こんにちは，シュン。

シュン：こんにちは，カエ。君の机の上はいったいどうしたんだい。

カエ：留学に向けて最終計画の段階で，これらは書類と項目リストよ。

シュン：ワクワクするね！君がもうすぐ出発することを忘れていたよ。本当にこの留学を楽しみにしているに違いないね。すでに荷物をつめているものね。

設問：この会話はどこでなされていると思いますか。

ア　旅行代理店　　**イ**　シュンの部屋

ウ　カエの部屋

エ　ホストファミリーの家

シュンがカエの机の上のものについて尋ねていることから，カエの部屋であると読み取れる。

what's all this ～?「いったいこれ（この～）はどうしたことか。」

(2) カエ：ええ，それでちょっと散らかってるの。まだ何を持っていくべきかわからなくて。これは多すぎると思う？

シュン：そのようだね。気候はどんな感じなの。

カエ：ちょうどここと同じような四季よ，だいたいここより暖かいことを除いては。

シュン：わかった。ええっと，大抵の人は必要以上のものを持ってくると思う。向こうでいつでも安く服を購入できるし，必要ならば家から送ってもらうこともできるよ。

設問：会話のこの部分に基づいて，シュンが提案していることは何ですか。

ア　カエは目的地の天気には注意深くなるべきだ。

イ　シュンは旅行に行く時，十分に服を持っていかない。

ウ　カエは安い洋服を持って旅行に行くのが好きだ。

エ　カエはそんなに多く持っていくべきではない。

会話の内容から，たくさんの服を持っていかなくてもよい理由をシュンがカエに伝えているので，シュンの提案していることはエだとわかる。

274

(1) **ウ**　(2) **イ**　(3) **ア**　(4) **エ**
(5) **オ**

解説

(1)　A：すみませんが，バス停はどちらにありますか。
　B：すみません。わかりません。私はこの辺りはよく知らないんです。
　A：いずれにしても，ありがとうございます。
　stranger「不慣れな人，不案内な人」

(2)　A：どうされましたか。
　B：高熱があって，鼻水がでます。
　A：インフルエンザのようですね。
　空欄の次に the flu という言葉があるので，病院での会話であることが想定できる。

(3)　A：何かお探しでしょうか。
　B：今のところ大丈夫。ありがとう。見てるだけです。
　A：何かお手伝いできることがあれば，お声掛けくださいね。
　I'm just looking.「見てるだけです。」店員から May I help you? と話しかけられた際，特に何も探していないときや，ぶらぶらと商品をながめたいときなどの返答の一例である。

(4)　A：いつ映画を見に行きたい？
　B：月曜日の夜はどう？混んでないだろうから。
　A：ごめん。平日の夜はアルバイトがあるの。
　Aが「平日の夜はアルバイトがある」という理由で断っていることから，Bは平日の曜日を提案したと考えられる。

(5)　A：すみません，今日は有機栽培のりんごはありませんか。
　B：こちらではそれを販売しておりません。
　A：いえ，売ってますよ。昨日いくつかありましたよね。私は見ました。
　B：まぁ，すみません。新人なんです。

275

① **イ**　② **キ**　③ **エ**　④ **オ**
⑤ **ア**

解説

トム：ねえ京子，①正直なところ，ここにいるすべての人は似ているのだろうと思っていました。

キョウコ：（笑いながら）私が初めてアメリカに行ったときに，みんな似ているのだろうと思っていたから，面白いです。

トム：②それを聞いてびっくりです！アメリカが移民の国であることはみんな知っているけれど，それにしても日本には外国人があまりいないと思いました。

キョウコ：たいていの人々が認識している以上にここでは多様性がありますよ。日本には③多くの韓国人や中国人がいます。また，近年では日本は今まで以上にたくさんの国の人々に就労ビザを発行しました。

トム：とある人を見たときにどの国の出身かすぐに見分けられますか。

キョウコ：ええっと，実際に，私はずっと④日本人は他の民族とは違うと思っていましたが，誰が日本人で誰がそうでないかを見分けることができないことがよくあると気付くようになりました。

トム：アメリカでは，⑤見かけでその人がアメリカ人かどうかを見分けることはできません。ある程度までは日本でも同じようなことだと思います。

① to be honest with you「正直なところ」

③ 前の文で「日本も多様性がある」と述べていることから，それに合うように，日本にどのような人がいるのかを考えると導くことができる。

276

① **カ**　② **オ**　③ **ケ**　④ **イ**

和訳

A：こんにちは，テディ。

B：あ，やあ。ここで何しているの，チャティ。
A：ここに両親を見送りに来たの。
B：どちらへ行かれるの？
A：ハワイよ。
B：偶然だね。僕もそこへ飛行機で行くんだ。
A：ハワイへ？（信じられないわ。）去年の夏，そこでひどい夏休みだったのよね。
B：そうだよ。でもまた行くんだ。
A：あなたの泊まったホテルは改修工事中だったのを覚えてるわよ。（電気がつかなかったのよね。）だから部屋でろうそくを灯さなくちゃいけなかった。調理場が改修中だったからレストランも閉まってた。そのホテルの名前はホワイト・ダブだったわよね。
B：そう，その通り。（すごい記憶力だね！）うん，昨年の夏休みはすっかり台無しだった。
A：じゃあもちろん別のホテルを選んだんでしょ。
B：えっと実は，君がまさに言ったそのホテル，ホワイト・ダブに滞在するよ。
A：まさか。冗談でしょ。
B：いや，本当さ。（今頃はもう改修が完了したはず。）そうなら，今年の夏は心地よい環境で休みを楽しめるよ。
A：何言ってるんだか。ともかく幸運を祈るわ。帰ったら電話してね。
B：わかった。ハワイ土産に何か素敵なものを買ってくるよ。

277

⑴ **ア**　⑵ **ウ**　⑶ **ウ**

解説

⑴ 客：こんにちは。このキーボードを返品したいのですが。
店：（かしこまりました。何か問題がありましたでしょうか？）
客：これは PC 用で，私は Mac を使っているのです。妻が間違えて違うものを買ってきたのです。
ア　かしこまりました。何か問題がありましたでしょうか？
イ　クレジットカードで支払いましたか？
ウ　これまでに Mac を使ったことはありますか？
エ　申し訳ありません。当店はあと5分で閉店いたします。
オ　それをお包みいたしましょうか？
＊参考…PC の生まれたアメリカでは，「PC」は Windows 搭載機のことを示し，Macintosh 搭載機と言い分けている。

⑵ 女性：マーク？マーク・ジョンソンですか？
男性：（マヤ！ずいぶん久しぶりだね。）
女性：元気だった？
ア　今，仕事してるの？
イ　僕だよ。君なの？
ウ　マヤ！ずいぶん久しぶりだね。
エ　スーザン，元気だったかい？
オ　いつ卒業したの？

⑶ 男性：川下のほとりでピクニックするのはどう？
女性：（駐車場から遠すぎるわ。）
男性：僕がそこまで運転して，荷物を全部降ろして，それから車を駐車しに戻るよ。
ア　先週そこへ行ったのよ。もう一度は，あんまり行きたくない。
イ　ここから駐車場はかなり遠いの？
ウ　駐車場から遠すぎるわ。
エ　代わりにバーベキューしに行きましょう。
オ　サンドウィッチとケーキなら作るのに時間がかからないわ。

278

① **ウ**　② **ア**　③ **エ**　④ **イ**　⑤ **ウ**

和訳　ナンシーとキヨシは夏休みの計画について話している。

ナンシー：ちょっと考えてみて。夏休みが2週間後に始まるわよ。1学期はあっという間に終わっちゃったね。（もう計画立てたの？キヨシ。）
キヨシ：いや，はっきりしたのはないんだけど，気分を換えて飛び出してどこか外国に行きたい。
ナンシー：いい考えね。（どこへ行く予定なの？）

キヨシ：はっきりと決めてないけど，今回はヨーロッパのどこかを考えてる。
ナンシー：今回？（じゃあこれまでに外国へは行ったことがあるの？）
キヨシ：うん，高校生のときに一度だけアメリカに行ったことがあるよ。すごく良かったんだけど，でも…
ナンシー：今回はむしろ別のどこかへ行きたいのね。
キヨシ：（ああ，でもそれだけじゃないんだ。）知っての通り，僕はクラシック音楽が大好きで，ヨーロッパでコンサートに行くというこの夢をずっと見続けてきたんだ。
ナンシー：（でも，オーケストラが夏休みを取らない？）8月に良いコンサートを探すのに困ったりしないかしら。
キヨシ：いや，そんなことないんだ。僕の音楽の先生は「ドイツとオーストリアでは年中毎日必ずどこかでコンサートがある」って言っているよ。

would rather do「むしろ～したい」

279

① カ　② ウ　③ オ　④ ア
⑤ イ　⑥ エ

280

① ウ　② キ　③ カ　④ ア
⑤ エ

281

(1) ウ，イ　(2) エ，ウ

解説

(1) The (batteries in my alarm clock must have been) dead.

ケン：トム，遅いよ。何があったの。
トム：ごめんね。寝過ごしてしまったよ。目覚まし時計をセットしていたのに，鳴らなかった。目覚まし時計の電池が切れてしまったに違いないよ。

must have p.p.「～だったに違いない」

(2) Does it (hurt more when you lie down or when you get) up?

カレン：腰が激しく痛みます。
ナンシー：ええっと。横になっているときと起きているときとではどちらが痛みますか。
カレン：わかりません。ほとんど差がないように思います。

lie down「横になる」

282

① Tell me about yourself.
② My parents moved there because they wanted to farm.
③ send me to college, where I majored in business
④ Have you ever had job interviews with other firms〔companies〕before?
⑤ I'd really like to be somebody

解説

A：さて，ジャクソンさん，今日は雨の中ご足労頂きありがとうございます。
B：とんでもないです。面接をしてくださり，ありがとうございます。
A：ご自身のことを話してください。
B：私はカンザス州で生まれました。両親は農業をしたいと思ってそこへ引っ越したのです。しかし農場がひどい火事になって，それで…破産したのです。
A：それからどうしたのですか？
B：そうですね，私の両親には園芸の才がありました。彼らは非常に懸命に働き，園芸用品店の経営を継ぎました。私を大学に行かせるだけのお金をとっておいてくれて，私はそこで経営を専攻しました。
A：他の会社で面接を受けたことはありますか。
B：実は，ありません。
A：あなたのキャリア上の目標は？
B：私は野心家だと思っていますので，金融界でひとかどの人物になりたいと本気で思っています。

③ major in ～「～を専攻する」
④ have a job interview with ～「～で面接を受ける」
⑤ somebody「ひとかどの人物，大物」

283

(1) 私はそのおもしろい話に笑わずにはいられなかった。

(2) その箱はからっぽだとわかった。
(3) 一般的に言って，人が何でもおいしく食べるなら，それはその人が完全に健康であることを示している。

284

昨日，私はスーパーマーケットで旧友のひとりに会いました。彼は現在，年老いた母親の世話で毎日とても忙しいと言っていました。

285

(1) How long have you been coughing?
(2) When did you hurt your foot〔leg〕?
(3) I will take your blood pressure.

286

(1) What is this flower called in English?
(2) Most Japanese houses〔あるいは Most of the Japanese houses〕are made of wood.
(3) The older he became, the harder he studied.
(4) How long have you been in America?
(5) Either you or I am wrong.
(6) I have not seen him for three years. I wonder where he lives now.

287

(1) ウ　(2) イ　(3) エ　(4) ウ
(5) ア

解説

(1)「ビルが火事だ！すぐに逃げなければならない。」
ア　数分後に　イ　しばらくの間
ウ　今すぐ　エ　時間通りに
(2)「あなたは小さな白い花で満開の桜の木を見たことがありますか。」
blossoms「花，開花」
(3)「多くの人々は冬に備えて果物や野菜を保存します。」
エ　keep in good condition「良い状態を保つ」
(4)「メアリーの先祖はまず，1500年代にヨーロッパからカナダに到着しました。」
ア　近所の友人　イ　兄弟姉妹
ウ　ずっと昔からの親類
エ　おじ，おば
(5)「私の家族は東京から離れた郊外に住んでいます。私たちは都心に着くまでに長い間，運転しなければなりません。」
ア　離れた　イ　外国の
ウ　近くに　エ　類似した

288

(1) 時は金なり。
(2) まさかの時の友こそ真の友。
(3) 健康は富にまさる。
(4) 良薬口に苦し。

289

(1) The doctor did his best to cure her disease.
(2) Modern society has greatly changed by the invention of the computer.

290

A：Do you think I'll be able to get〔find〕a good job after I graduate?
B：It depends (on) how hard you study.

291

(1) ウ　(2) エ　(3) ア　(4) イ
(5) オ

解説

(1)「学ぶのに遅すぎるということはない。」
⇨「六十の手習い」
(2)「賢い人には1つの言葉で十分である。」
⇨「一を聞いて十を知る」
(3)「ホメロスでさえ時には居眠りする。」
⇨「猿も木から落ちる」
「弘法も筆の誤り」も同じ意味である。
(4)「同じ羽を持つ鳥は群れを作る。」
⇨「類は友を呼ぶ」
(5)「二人の頭脳は一人に勝る。」
⇨「三人寄れば文殊の知恵」

292

A：The twenty first century has finally come.
B：Yes. I hope a lot of good things will happen.
A：Yes, but it seems that there will be big changes such as globalization and IT revolution.
B：We also have problems in education and environment.
A：In any case, all we can do is do our best.

293

(1) ウ　(2) ク　(3) イ　(4) オ
(5) カ　(6) ケ　(7) エ　(8) コ
(9) ア　(10) キ

294

(1) 援助　(2) 病気
(3) 有機の，器官の　(4) 洪水，出血多量
(5) 保菌者　(6) 処方箋
(7) 延命治療　(8) 優越感

295

(1) イ ⇨ shoulder
(2) ウ ⇨ terminal は「末期の」の意。

296

(1) cough　(2) headache
(3) nausea　(4) diarrhea
(5) stomachache　(6) constipation
(7) toothache　(8) fever

297

(1) ア　(2) イ　(3) ウ　(4) エ
(5) ウ　(6) イ　(7) ア　(8) ウ
(9) エ　(10) ア

298

(1) stress　(2) brain
(3) heart　(4) sweat
(5) dentist　(6) ear
(7) operation　(8) diet

299

(1) エ　(2) ア

300

(1) イ　(2) ア　(3) エ　(4) ア

和訳　教養を深める読書のためには，著者が述べる事について批判的な目を注ぐべきである。しかしながら残念なことに，文字どおりにしか読めない読者が多すぎる。批判的な目を注いで読むことを知らない人たちの多くは，他人の考えに支配されてしまう。彼らは印刷されている事はなんでも真実であると受け入れがちである。困ったことに，そのような人々は真実と意見を区別しない，推論したりしない，あるいは著者の先入観に気づかないという理由で読みまちがえてしまう。

批判的に読むためには，自分自身の先入観や偏見にも気づく必要がある。私たちは物事にあまりにも偏見を持ってしまうことがあるので自分自身で推論したり考えたりすることができない。もし私たちが近所の人，政治家，他の国々に関する否定的な言葉をだれかが言いふらしているのを聞いたとしたら，それが真実なのか単なる考えなのかを確かめずに信じてしまいがちである。

私たちはみな，先入観をもっている。著者でさえもっている。それゆえ批判的な読者として，自分自身の先入観で自分の理解力を妨げないように注意すべきである。同じように，私たちは真実を調べるまで影響されないように著者の先入観を認識する必要がある。

301

(1) ウ　(2) イ　(3) ア　(4) ア
(5) エ

和訳　活気のある生活は人が長生きをする手助けとなると研究者たちは長い間信じていた。しかし，新たな証拠が少なくとも男性にとって長寿という利益を作り出すのはまさに結婚であることを示唆している。研究者たちは，45～64歳の未婚男性は同じ年齢の既婚男性に比べて２倍もの人が10年以内に亡くなりそうだということをも見い出した。男性にとって結婚がもたらす健康上の影響はどう説明されるのか。未婚男性のうち栄養不足で非常によくたばこを吸ったり，酒を飲むことは，短命とかかわりがあると言う研究者もいる。

302

(1) ① printed　② helps
(2) a オ　b カ　c エ　d イ
e ウ　f ア
(3) ・めんが短い。
・ぬるいお湯でも調理できるようにしている。
(4) 〈解答例〉 It is important to study the tastes and lifestyles of the people to sell food in other countries. [18 words]

和訳　海外を旅行する多くの日本人はおみやげに即席めんを買って帰る。けれども，もしあなたが彼らが買うめんのパッケージをよく調べてみると，ごく小さな活字でプリントされている「メイド・イン・ジャパン」をしばしば見つけることになるだろう。

毎年, 約130億食の即席めんが世界の90カ国で売られている。日本以外で消費されている84億食のうち，約70%が日本から輸入されたものか，売られたものかである。日本の即席めんは世界中で食べられている。

日本の会社がめん業界をほとんど征服してきた理由は，各国の人々の味覚を注意深く研究し，それらの味に合わせためんを売るからである。

もちろん，しょうゆ味のヌードルは他のアジア諸国で人気がある。けれども，ある生産者は，アメリカ向けにビーフ，チキン，ポークという３つの味を発展させた。その会社は，アメリカ人が舌の味覚よりも風味についてより関心があることを学んだ。そのため，アメリカ人が好きな風味の３種類を売り出した。

即席めんは地方の生活様式にぴったり合わせられている。アメリカの西海岸では，天気が良く，屋外で食べられるため，めんは主にカップに入ったものが売られている。東海岸では，めんは家庭で調理されるので，袋に入ったものがほとんど売られている。

アメリカやヨーロッパで売られているめんは短い。これは，フォークでより簡単に食べやすくしているだけではなく，音をたてて食べるのを防ぐことにも役立っている。そして，そこでは多くの人々が熱湯を嫌うので，めんはぬるま湯でさえも調理できるように設計されている。

303

(1) for
(2) ② spoken　④ Making
(3) ウ　(4) ウ
(5) ・外国人と話を始める前に話すことを用意するようにすること。
・できるだけ何度でも英語を使ってみること。
(6) 〈解答例〉
・Making friends with foreign people is a lot of fun〔または very enjoyable〕.
・I find〔take〕 great pleasure in making friends with foreigners.

和訳　現代の世界では，人々がお互いに理解し合うことはますます重要になっている。そして，人々にとって英語はとても役に立つ言語である。というのは英語は世界中で大勢の人々によって話されているからだ。英語はまた多くの国々で外国語として学校で教えられてもいる。

英語で外国の人々とコミュニケーションしたいなら，ここにとても大事な２つのことがある。まず，外国人と話を始める前に話すことを用意しておこう。自分の好きな話題で会話を始めよう。準備していれば，英語でコミュニケーションすることがずっと簡単になるだろう。次に，できるだけ何度でも英語を使ってみよう。最初はたくさん間違えるかもしれないが，心配しなくてもよい。間違えることはあなたにとってとても重要な一歩である。

これらの２つのことを忘れないで。コミュニケーションができれば，外国人はあなたを理解してくれる。あなたも彼らを理解するだろう。

304

(1) ①～④ 和訳 参照。
(2) a　食べ過ぎと運動不足
b　より伝統的な文化
c　Americans are または they are
d　young

和訳　アメリカ人は健康意識や若者重視の傾向がある。フィットネス計画や健康器具は数知れぬほどあり，それらのうちのいくつかは日本のテレビで宣伝されてさえいる。①アメリカ人は若々しくいることに重きをおき，食事やフィットネスや健康を永久的に若くいられる方法と見なす。しかしながら概して，アメリカ人は食べ過ぎと運動不足の傾向にあり，目的を達成させるためにもがき続けている。

②年齢は確かに経験，成熟，知恵という点で美徳であるが，アメリカでは大して価値づけはされない。若さの自由，柔軟性，活力はより魅力的でとても求められる。アメリカ人はだんだん年をとっている間でさえ，彼らの若々しさを維持したいと考える。これは年齢を重ねることがとても尊敬されるという，より伝統的な文化とは対照的である。

アメリカ人は年齢について大変敏感でしばしば年齢を尋ねられるときに拒否することがある。人々は，しばしば「年齢がどうして重要なの」「あなたには関係ない」と言ってこのような質問に答える。「(年齢とは対照的に) 私はかくかくしかじかの若さです」と言って答える人すらいる。このようなすべての反応はアメリカでは若くいたい，若さを表現したいという欲望や欲求を示す。

アメリカの観点は若々しい。人々は若く見られたいだけでなく，若さを感じふるまいたいとも考える。アメリカ人は一般的に年にふさわしいふるまいをすることにあまり賛成していない。中年を定義する不思議な年齢はない。③例えば，アメリカ人は日本人ほどある程度の年齢になっても中年だとは感じにくい。アメリカ人は彼らが感じるのと同じ年齢であると信じるのが好きだ。もしあなたが若いと感じるならばあなたは若い。多くのアメリカ人はこのことを信じ，人生において若々しい展望を維持し，取り入れる。④このことより，個人主義と高い離婚率とともに，若さと魅力的な精神と身体を維持することがより一層必要とされる。

305

(1) His legs and wings had become too sticky with the honey for him to use.

(2) 和訳参照。

(3) イ　(4) ウ　(5) ウ

(6) the flame

(7) ア

(8) ① creep　② crept　③ become
④ became　⑤ kept　⑥ kept
⑦ begin　⑧ begun　⑨ catch
⑩ caught

和訳　ある日，とあるハエがハチミツのつぼに止まり，ハチミツを大変気にいって縁にそって食べ始めた。

しかし，すぐに彼はつぼの縁から中の方へと少しずつはっていき，ついには体がべったりくっついて動かなくなってしまった。彼の足も羽もハチミツでねばねばになり，使いものにならなくなってしまった。

ちょうどその時一匹の蛾がそばに飛んできて，もがいている彼を見ながら，「おや，なんてお馬鹿なハエなんでしょう。(2)きみはそんなふうに捕まってしまうほど欲張りだったのかい。きみの食欲は度が過ぎていたんだよ。」と言った。

その哀れなハエは何も言えなかった。やがて夕方になり，その蛾はランプのまわりをぐるぐる飛んでいたが，しだいに炎に近づいていき，ついには炎へ飛び込み，焼けて死んでしまった。

「何てことだ。」「きみもお馬鹿さんなのかい。きみはぼくがハチミツに目がないことを笑ったけれど，炎とたわむれると危ないという分別がなかったんだね。」とそのハエは言った。

他人の誤ちは自分のものよりも目につきやすいものである。

306

(1) a less　b less　c more
d less　e less

(2) 心臓発作

(3) 気を楽にする

(4) イ

(5) そのアドバイス（飲食の量を減らし，十分な睡眠をとり，あまりくよくよせず，あまり働かない）に従うことは，私にはできません。

和訳　ジョーンズ氏はとても出世したビジネスマンである。彼は非常に懸命に働くが，睡眠時間は短く心配症である。先週彼は健康診断を受けにかかりつけの医者のところへ行った。医者は注意深く彼を診察した。「ねえ先生，結果はどうですか？」診察後，彼は尋ねた。

「結果はあんまりよくないですよ」と医者は答えた。「私からのアドバイスとしては，少なめに食べて，少なめに飲んで，もっと睡眠をとって，あまりくよくよせず，あまり働かない―ですね」

「ご忠告，ありがとうございます」ジョンは言った。「でも，それに従うなんて私には無理ですよ。私は忙しい人間です」

「もし私のアドバイスに従わなければ心臓発作になりますよ。たやすく起こるんです。のんびりやって力まないようにしなくてはいけません」

「どうやって？こんなに忙しいのに」

「ご自身を成功した人間だと言えますか？」医者は尋ねた。

「はい，言えると思います」ジョーンズ氏は答えた。

「では，質問させて下さい。成功の代償って何でしょう？」

「うーん，よくわかりません」

「では私が言いましょう。それは死です」

307

(1) ① tell ② take ⑥ spend
⑦ be ⑨ say

(2) ③ daughter ④ last ⑤ day
⑧ turn〔put, switch〕on
⑩ light

(3) かなり

(4) **ア，エ**

和訳 ある近所の人が2歳半になる彼の息子と行った旅行について話してくれた。それは初めてその父子が彼らだけで出かけた時であった。

最初の晩，彼らはホテルで過ごした。父親は自分のベッドを少年のベッドの近くに寄せ，二人共（毛布に）くるまると，彼は明かりを消した。数分後，「真っ暗だよね？」と小さな声がした。「うん，かなり暗いな。でも万事オーケーさ」と父親は言った。更に数分の沈黙がありそれから小さな手がのびてきて父親の手をつかんだ。小さな少年は言った。「ただ手を握っていてあげるよ，パパが恐くならないようにね」

308

(1) the written word

(2) the telephone (the radio, the televidion)

(3) in fact

(4) **ア** × **イ** ○ **ウ** × **エ** ×

和訳 人間は意思伝達ができる。他の動物たちもだ。しかし，人間は時間と空間の壁を越えて意思伝達ができるが，他の動物はそれができない。というのは，人間だけがあらゆる発明の中でも最高の秘策，書き言葉をもっているからである。この書き言葉と比べると，電話やラジオ，テレビは子どものおもちゃ同然のものである。実際には，つい最近，人間は話し言葉を用いて自然な声が届くよりも広範囲にわたる空間を征服したのだが，長い歴史の流れを通してずっと，書き言葉は人間と国家をより密接にするという点で，計り知れないほど利便をもたらしてきた。実際，我々が口伝えの伝承のみに頼らなければならないとしたら，そもそも歴史自体についてほとんど知識をもつことができないだろう。

309

(1) ① **エ** ④ **ウ** ⑤ **イ**

(2) **ア** (3) **エ**

(4) ⑥ to travel short distances
⑦ the more severely handicapped

(5) **和訳** 参照。

和訳 たくさんの身体障害者は，毎日の生活の中で直面している多数の困難を克服するために助けを必要としている。これらのうちの一つに，高所に到達する際の困難がある。ほとんど問題なくなんとかやっていける人もいれば，助けが必要な人もいる。最近，身体障害者が彼らの障害を克服するのに役立つためにたくさんの機械的かつ電子工学的な補助器具が使用されている。マイクロコンピュータとよばれる大変小さなコンピュータが工場にある機械を制御するために長年使われている。この科学技術を使用した機械は，いま身体障害者がもっと普通の生活を送るのに役立つように作られている。

身体障害者はしばしば家の内側と外側の両方で動き回るのに困難をかかえている。ほとんどの車は部分的に障害があるドライバーによる使用に適応し得るが，オートマチックトランスミッションは，彼らが運転するにはより簡単である。車イスによりたくさんの身体障害者は短距離旅行を比較的容易にできるようになったが，より重い障害を持つ人には電力の備わった特別な車イスが必要だろう。彼らは普通の車イスを動かす力を欠いているので，1本の指や，つま先の動きや，息でさえも操作できる1本のレバーによって動かすことができる特別な車イスを使う。電動の車イスは，時々折りたたんで車で運ばれるが，手動車イスより大きい。そのため，(5)車イスに座ったままで，直接乗車できる昇降機を特別に備え付けられた車もある。

310

(1) made

(2) fond

(3) May I または Can I

(4) a from b of c to

(5) ① an operation ② crutches

和訳 ある紳士が小さな村にある病院に入って来た。彼はスキーで足を骨折したスーという姪を訪ねて来た。彼がスーに彼女の大好きなキャンディの箱をあげたとき，スーはどんなに喜んだことか。彼女のおじは，それを開けるように言った。しかし彼女は後々のためにそれをとっておいてもよいか尋ねた。おじが去るとすぐに彼女は松葉づえをついて廊下を通って行った。彼女はがんで苦しんでいる60歳の婦人の部屋へ行った。彼女は，スーが初めて病院にやって来たとき，特に優しくしてくれた。今度はスーが彼女の優しさに恩返しをしたかった。笑顔で彼女は自分の部屋に戻った。

しばらくして，婦人は手の中にキャンディを持って部屋を出た。彼女はゆっくりある部屋に向かって歩いた。14歳の若い男の子であるボブは，手術から回復してきていた。ベッドの脇にあるキャンディを見つけたら，彼はどんなにうれしがるだろう。彼女はスーのように笑顔で自分の部屋に戻った。

311

(1) **イ** (2) **エ** (3) **エ** (4) **ア**

和訳 ニューヨークを移動する手段はいろいろある。実を言うと，私は歩くのが一番好きである。なぜかわかるだろうか。確かに他の方法より安い。それに加えて，ニューヨークを歩くことはたいていいつも（他の方法よりも）わくわくする。ご存知のように，ストリートミュージシャンやパフォーマー，様々な面白い服装をした人たちなど，ニューヨーク市内の通りには見るべきものがたくさんある。

ニューヨークを訪れる観光客にとって，バスは地下鉄ほど評判のよいものではないけれども，地域の人の中には，（地下鉄よりも）清潔だからバスを好む人もいる。おそらく，地域の人がバスを好む最大の理由は，より安全だからである。それで，バスは高齢者や夜遅く移動する人たちの間で，より評判がよいのである。バスのよくない点は，地上を運行するので，ラッシュ時の間はとても遅いということである。

ニューヨークの地下鉄のシステムには良い点も悪い点もある。1日24時間運行するというのは多分，世界で唯一のシステムだろう。それは便利であるが，同時に多くの問題を引き起こす。決まった清掃の時間がないため，地下鉄の車内や駅はひどい悪臭がするのだ。

312

(1) **エ**

(2) もしあなたがストレスを感じていたり，悲しかったり，退屈であるなら

(3) **ウ**

和訳 私たちがどんなにたくさんもっていても，もっと欲しいかのように思われることが時々ある。しかし，それを得ることが私たちにとって必ずしもよいとは限らない。クローゼットや食器棚，ガレージの中をちょっと見てごらん。あるいは，鏡の中の自分を見てごらん。実際にそこから始めよう。渇望，つまり食べ物への強い欲望は，健康に特によくないものとなり得る。これはその渇望をコントロールする方法である。

次に渇望を覚えたとき，ストレスを感じていたり，悲しかったり，退屈であったりするかどうか自分に問いかけよう。もしそうなら，感情的な虚しさを埋めるために食べているかもしれない。1週間，もしくはそれ以上，「欲望の日記」をつけて，何か食べたいという強い欲望に襲われたときにはいつでも，必ず自分の気分をメモしなさい。ストレスが原因なら，重圧を軽くするために，もっと運動しよう。孤独感がポテトチップスやアイスクリームに走らせるなら，友人に電話するとよい。現実の飢えを満たすのはたやすいということを覚えておいて欲しい。どんな食べ物でもよいのだ。それに反して，感情の飢えはしばしば，アイスクリームやファストフードのような特定の

ものへの欲望として現れる。

313

(1) ①，② 和訳 参照。

(2) 家族，高校や大学の学級，会社，地域社会

和訳 ①日本人は自分たちを一個人というよりむしろ，家族や会社，国家等の集団の一員として考える傾向がある。家族は基本的な集団であり，それが高校・大学の同級生の集団そして会社の集団，さらには市町村等の地域の集団というように発展していく。そして現在では国家集団としての自覚が再びよみがえりつつある。

家族は両親とその子供，それに祖父母が同居するか，近くに住んでいれば加えて構成される。②実際，ここ15年の間に日本の家族構成は3世代構成から西洋風の2世代構成へと，とって変わってきている。すなわち，昔していたほど，祖父母は結婚した子どもとその孫たちとともに住んでいないのである。

314

(1) **イ**　(2) **ウ**　(3) **ア**　(4) **エ**
(5) **ウ**　(6) **ア**

和訳 血液は，水が一連の規則正しい水道管を規則正しく流れるようには，人間の体を流れない。心臓から体中にポンプで押し出される血液が通る管は，動脈である。しかし，心臓からいくらか離れている動脈は，毛細血管と呼ばれるごく小さな管になるまで繰り返し分かれ続ける。そして血液は，動脈を通るよりも一層ゆっくりとこれらの管を流れる。

毛細血管は，人間の毛髪の50倍細い。だから，血球は縦一列にそれらを通る。血液が1本の毛細血管を流れるのに約1秒かかる。

血液は絶え間なく心臓を流れる。一定量の血液が心臓を通るのに約1.5秒かかる。血液が心臓から肺へ流れ，そして心臓に戻る。これには，約5～7秒かかる。

血液は心臓から脳へも流れ，そして心臓に戻る。これには約8秒かかる。血液がしなくてはならない最も長い旅は，心臓から胴や足を通ってつま先まで行き，それから心臓まで戻ってくるものである。これには，約18秒かかる。

血液が体全体を循環するのに必要な時間，すなわち，心臓から肺へ，そしてまた心臓へ，そして体中へ，そしてまた心臓へめぐりめぐるには，約23秒かかる。

しかし，体調が血液の流れる速さに影響する。例えば，熱や運動によって，心拍数は増加し，血液は2倍の速さで流れる。たった1つの血液細胞が，1日で体中を約3000回も駆けめぐる。

315

(1) a **オ**　b **カ**　c **ク**　d **エ**
e **イ**

(2) ① **オ**　② **イ**　③ **エ**　④ **ウ**

和訳 地球の表面のほとんどは水で覆われている。水は深かったり浅かったり，色が濃かったり淡かったり，冷たかったり温かかったり，澄んでいたり濁っていたり，穏やかだったり荒れていたりするだろう。水は海水だったり淡水だったりするだろう。

陸は地球の表面の3分の1以下を覆っている。それは広々とした草原，深い森，砂漠あるいは雪に覆われた山であったりするだろう。様々な種類の生命がほとんどいたる所で見つけられる。しかしながら，生命が存在するためには，特定の環境が現存しなければならない。

316

(1) A after　B before

(2) C **アまたはウ**　D **ア**　E **イ**

(3) a **ア**　b **ウ**　c **エ**　d **イ**

(4) 和訳 参照。

和訳 人々が住むためにアメリカへ思いきってやってきたのは，コロンブスがアメリカ大陸を発見してからまさに何年も経ってからであった。(4)探険のために来た人も少しはいたが，来ることを決心した多くの人々はヨーロッパでは幸せではなかった。彼らの中には国の統治の仕方が好きではない人もいた。法律が定めている王の宗教に従いたくない人もいた。

多くの人が富と自分自身の土地を夢見た。彼らが新世界について聞いたすべてのことは，より良い世界について約束されたよう

だった。

ついに岸に到着して，さみしい荒野しか見なかった最初の人々はさぞかし奇妙に思い，ぎょっとさせられたに違いない。そこには家もなく，学校もなく彼らのあとに残してきた文明に似たようなものや，彼らがいつも知っているものは何もなかったのである。

317

(1) **イ**
(2) ② younger ③ older
(3) ④ **イ** ⑤ **エ** ⑥ **ウ** ⑦ **ア**
(4) しみ，そばかす
(5) one third

和訳　ベビーブーム世代も年を重ねている，つまり彼らは1946年から1964年までの間に生まれた人口の３分の１にあたるのだが，多くは（自分が年をとってきたことを）認めようとしない。

30才から50才の1200人以上を対象にした調査によると，大部分（76%）の人たちが実際の年令よりも自分は若く見えると確信している。大部分（73%）の人たちは一世代前の50才の人たちは今日の50代よりもさらに年をとって見えると考えている。

ベビーブーム世代も年をとるにつれ，66%は体重増加を，30%が抜け毛が多くなったのを，28%が顔のしみの増加を，24%が髪が白くなってきたことを心配している。

人の年齢を判断する時，多くのベビーブーム世代（58%）は顔のしわかまたは茶色いしみがあるかどうかによって(判断に)影響を受ける。それ以外の少数派は，白髪(46%)，肥満（37%）そして抜け毛（34%）で影響を受ける。

ベビーブーム世代の３分の１以上(37%)は女性よりも男性の方が上品に年をとると考えているし，22%は女性の方が上品に年をとるとしている。大部分（77%）の人たちは男性よりも女性の方が年を重ねるにつれ顔の容貌について心配していると考えている。

318

① I wish he were really still alive.
② The name Kurosawa is well known in the western countries.
③ There is little chance for the public to see his works directly.

和訳　イギリスの映画監督アレックス・コックスは黒沢明と彼の作品を紹介するドキュメンタリーテレビ番組を製作している。彼が初めてそのドキュメンタリー番組の構想を企画したのは10年以上も前の事である。しかしその構想が財政上実行可能となったのはまさに黒沢明の死後であった。

「本当に彼がまだ生きていればなあと思います。」とコックスは言う。

コックスはスティーブン・スピルバーグやフランシス・コッポラ，マーティン・スコルセッシ，ベルナルド・ベルトリッチなど黒沢明に影響を受けた様々な世界的な監督と対談する計画を立てている。

「黒沢という名前は，欧米でよく知られているが，一般の人々は彼の作品を実際に見る機会がほとんどないのです。」とコックスは言う。彼はそのドキュメンタリー番組によって黒沢明の国際的名声が高まるとよいと思っているとつけ加えた。

319

(1) **オ** (2) **イ** (3) **オ** (4) **ウ**
(5) **イ** (6) **ウ**

解説

(1) **ア** 組織　**イ** 出口　**ウ** 権威
エ 発明　**オ** 紹介，入門
第１段落の内容から，化学実験セットは子どもにとっては化学の世界への入門であることが分かる。
(2) 下線部①は化学工学者がどのような位置づけであるかを説明した文章中にあるため，「中間的な人」と理解するのが望ましい。
(3) １つ前の文がヒントになる。them の「彼ら」とはアルコール飲料を作っていた古代文明の人々のことを指す。call A B で「AをBと呼ぶ」の意であるため，Bにあたる that は人間を表す言葉を指すと推測できる。よって正解は**オ**となる。
(4) **ア** 生産する　**イ** 知る
ウ 要求する　**エ** 作る
オ 使う
下線部③は「創り出す」の意。「まだそ

の語が創り出されていなかったので，彼らをそう呼ぶ者は誰もいなかった」という文にこれらを代わりに当てはめていくと，**ウ**の「要求する」が全く別の意味となる。

(5) **ア** あまり遅くでなく
イ 間もなく，すぐに
ウ 今までずっと
エ 最近
オ 最近

Not long afterwards「間もなく，ほどなくして」の意であるため，ほぼ同じ意味になる表現は**イ**となる。

(6) 次の「製造するために最も良い方法を選べるように，工場の設計，気候，エネルギー源，その他における違いをコンピュータに与えることができる」という文がヒントになる。その目的に応じて「コンピュータの使い方」が異なり，うまく使うことで化学工学者の仕事が改善されていったのである。

和訳 私たちの多くは子どもの頃，プレゼントとして化学実験セットを受け取ったことを覚えている。それらは小さかったけれども，それでも危険をはらんだ玩具であり注意深く使われなければならなかった。それはとても小さな規模であったけれども，それにもかかわらず，これが化学の世界あるいは化学者と呼ばれる科学者への入門であった。ところで，化学者と化学工学者との間の違いとは何だろうか。言い換えれば，化学工学とは何であって，それは化学とはどのように異なるのだろうか。

化学工学者は科学者とエンジニアとの中間的な人である。彼は，完全な化学の知識を持っていなければならないが，他の何かも持っていなければならない。彼は自身の実験室の外での自分の知識の応用の仕方を知らなければならない。重要で幅広く使われている大量の化学薬品を製造することができなければならない。このように，化学工学者の主な目的は長期にわたり大量の化学薬品を製造することができるように，大工場を設計し管理することである。資金もまた一つの要因であるから，それらの化学薬品をできるだけ安く製造することが重要であった。古いエネルギー源を使うためのより安くよりよい方法を見つけることも，化学工学者の仕事の一部であった。

化学工学は新しく思えるが，実際はとても古い。発酵の過程をつかみ，それを用いて多量のアルコール飲料を作っていた古代文明の人々は，実際に化学工学者であった。まだその語（化学工学者）が創り出されていなかったので，彼らをそう呼ぶ者は誰もいなかった。実際に，その語自体は今世紀の始め頃になってようやく使われ始めた。それでも，彼らはそうであったということだ。

よりよい製造過程への要求が始まったのは，19世紀の，産業革命の間であった。それゆえ，製造について理解している化学者により大きな需要があった。自動車が発明されたあと間もなく，それらにガソリンが使われてから，石油産業は以前よりもずっと重要な分野になった。化学工学者が重要になったのはまさに石油産業が成長したからであった。というのは，より良く，より安く，石油からガソリンを作る方法のために様々な企業の間でたくさんの競争が行われたからである。

現代，コンピュータの使用が化学工学者の仕事を格段に改善した。製造するために最も良い方法を選べるように，工場の設計，気候，エネルギー源，その他における違いをコンピュータに与えることができる。

化学工学者の仕事について，他にどんな例が考えられるだろうか。あなたはあなた自身の言葉で化学者と化学工学者の違いを説明できるだろうか。

320

(1) a **ア** b **オ** c **ク** d **カ** e **イ**

(2) ① wrote ③ built

(3) curious

(4) **イ**

(5) 知的関心〔知的興味〕

(6) （飛行機の）翼への風の効果を調査すること。

(7) ① ○ ② × ③ ×

解説

(1) a　be made of ～「～で作られる」

b　形容詞＋enough to ～「～するのに十分…」

c　environment を説明する関係副詞なので，where が適切。

d　not only ～ but also …「～だけでなく…も」

e　succeed in ～ing「～するのに成功する」

(2) ともに過去形にする。

① write－wrote－written

③ build－built－built

(4) **ア**　北極圏内の　　**イ**　大西洋の

ウ　太平洋の

(5) 第2段落第3文に述べられている。

(6) 第3段落最終文に述べられている。

(7) ①　第1段落の内容に一致する。

②　自動車販売ではなく，自転車販売である。

③　ゲティズバーグではなく，キティホークである。

和訳　オーヴィルとウィルバーのライト兄弟が子どもだった頃，彼らの父親から安い玩具をもらった。コルクと竹でできた飛ぶ玩具であった。本体は紙でできており，動力は輪ゴムによるものだった。その玩具は自力で居間を横切って，飛んでいくことができた。

二人は魅了された。兄のウィルバーは，見つけられる限りの翼や空飛ぶマシーンについてのあらゆる本や新聞記事を読み始めた。オーヴィルは後に「知的関心を追い求めるための，また好奇心を呼び起こすものは何でも調査するための，子どもにとっていつもたくさんの励みとなるものがある環境の中で成長できるなんて，よくよく幸運であった。」と書いた。彼は読んだものから，空中で人間を運ぶ飛行機を作ることができると確信するようになった。

生活していくために，1892年に二人の兄弟はオハイオ州のドレイトンで自転車の商売を始めた。自転車を販売したり修理したりすることは，生活費を生み出したが，彼らは他のことに打ち込んだ。自転車店の裏の作業場で，彼らは自転車だけでなく，グライダーや凧を作った。これらのグライダーや凧は，風の翼への効果を調査するのにきわめて重要なものであった。

1900年に兄弟はキティホークの近くにテントを立てた。彼らは大きなグライダーを組み立て，大西洋からの強風の中でそれをテストし始めた。ときどき，兄弟のうち1人は人が乗る凧のようにグライダーに乗ったものだった。その「パイロット」は翼が風でどのように動くかを学ぶために，コントロールを操った。彼らは数百メートルにわたって空中を飛び続けることに成功した。

321

(1) **イ**	(2) **イ**	(3) **エ**	(4) **ウ**
(5) **ア**	(6) **イ**	(7) **イ**	(8) **ウ**

解説

(1) both A and B「AもBも両方とも」

(2) 文脈から判断するとよい。「イギリスで起こることはどこか他のところで起こることと同じではないということをイギリス人が主張しているのが，その言葉の中に見えるので，…」

空欄を含む文と前の文とのつながりに注意する。

(3) appear from nowhere「どこからともなく現れる」

(4) not only A but (also) B「AだけでなくBも」

(5) whatever「どんな～でも」，「どんな～を…しようとも」，「どんな～が…しようとも」

(6) 和訳 参照。

(7) may well～「～するのももっともだ」

(8) **ア**　イギリスの気候は特有であると冒頭で述べられている。また，第2段落第1文に一日の間に4つの季節を経験できる国はイギリス以外にはないと述べられている。

イ　天気を予測するのは難しいとあるため，不一致。

ウ　第4段落に一致する内容が述べられている。

エ　第4段落の最終文にイギリスの天気はイギリス人に順応性を持たせる手助

けとなってきたと述べられているため，不一致。

和訳 「他の国には気候がある，イギリスには空模様がある。」この言葉はイギリス人が自国における特有な気象条件を説明するのにしばしば使うのだが，的を射ているし，真実でもある。イギリスで起こることはどこか他のところで起こることと同じではないということをイギリス人が主張しているのがその言葉の中に見えるので，それはうまく表現されているのだ。数日よりも長い間イギリスに滞在している外国人であれば誰でも，その真実を確かめられるだろう。

言われてきたことだが，たった一日の中で4つの季節を経験できる国はイギリス以外にはどこにもない。一日は穏やかな春の朝のように始まる。1時間ほど経つと，黒い雲がどこからともなく現れ，雨が激しく降り出すかもしれない。昼ごろには，およそ8℃かそれ以上気温が下がり，本当に冬のように感じる。その後，午後遅くには空が晴れ，太陽が輝き始める。そして，日が沈む前の1，2時間の間は夏のようになるだろう。

①イギリスでは，最も極端な天候を除けば，ほとんどあらゆる種類の天候を経験することができる。(外国人の中には，1年のうち10か月間，イギリスは濃い霧ですっぽり覆われてしまっているという印象を受ける人がいるらしいが，これは真実ではない。)問題は，異なるタイプの天気がいつ生じるのか，私たちには全くわからないことである。一日のうちに異なる天気をいくつか経験するだけでなく，夏に冬のような天気を，あるいはその逆もまた同様に経験することがあるかもしれない。

天気についてのこのような不確かさはイギリス人の性格に確実に影響を与えている。それによって例えば，彼らは用心深くなる傾向がある。太陽が輝く晴れた日の朝にイギリス人がレインコートを着て，傘を持って出かけているのを見たら，外国人は笑うかもしれない。しかし，その日の後半には，自分が笑ったことを後悔するのも無理はない。イギリスの天気はイギリス人に順応性を持たせる手助けにもなってきたのである。

イギリスがかつて世界中の多くを植民地化した理由の一つは，外国でイギリス人がどんな天気の状態に遭遇しようとも，彼らはすでに自国でそのようなことを経験していたからだと言われてきた。

それからもちろん，天気の多様性は常に話題を提供する。どんなに口数の少ないイギリス人でもいつも天気を論じる準備はできている。そして，彼は時には天気についてひどく不平を言うけれども，可能であったとしても，天気を他国の予測ができる気候と交換しようとは思わないだろう。

322

(1) ② カ　③ ウ　④ ア　⑤ キ　⑥ コ　⑦ オ

(2) a エ　b ウ　c イ　d イ

(3) a spent　b taking

(4) ① 「早歩き」でがん予防

⑧ 少しの変化を作るだけで，あなたはがんの危険を減らすことができる。

(5) サイクリング，水泳，ダンス，ガーデニング，掃除機をかけること

解説

(1) ② 専門家　③ 適度な

④ 肉体の　⑤ 強調する

⑥ 増加　⑦ 数

(2) a 関係代名詞の非制限用法なので，which が適切である。

b set aside「(時間などを)とっておく」

c the fact は事実という意味では that 節とともに用いる。

d 文脈から判断することが望ましい。「乳癌や大腸癌を含めてある特定のがんは，早歩きなどのような適度な運動を規則正しく行う人々にはあまり見られないという確証がある」であるから，この文意にあてはまるようにするには，less が適当である。

(3) a time にかかる分詞である。時間は費やされるから，過去分詞形にする。

b instead of ～「～の代わりに」の意。～にあてはまる部分なので動名詞の taking にする。

(4) 和訳 参照。

(5)　第２段落の最後の文に挙げられている。

和訳

①「早歩き」でがん予防

人々がよりもっと早歩きをしていれば，イギリスでの毎年およそ１万件の乳癌と大腸癌は予防できただろうと専門家が主張している。世界がん研究基金（WCRF）の科学者たちは，心臓の鼓動を速くさせるどんな適度な活動でも同じことをもたらすだろうと述べている。例えば，一日に45分間の適度な運動は約5,500件の乳癌を予防することができるとデータは示唆している。肉体運動は肥満を防ぐ手助けになり，その肥満ががんの危険要因である。

WCRF の研究チームは運動に費やした合計の時間こそが重要だと彼らの報告の中で強調している。あなたは運動するために，毎日30分とっておく必要はない。（運動時間の）合計が同じになりさえすれば，短い一期間の運動でも同じくらい有益だと慈善団体は述べている。早歩きと並んで，数に入れることのできる他の活動にはゆったりとしたペースのサイクリングや水泳，ダンス，ガーデニング，他の家事をしながら掃除機をかけることなども含まれると WCRF は述べる。

科学長であるレイチェル・トンプソン博士は毎日の日課に少しの変化を作ることによって，人々はかなりの健康増進を果たすことができると述べた。「今となっては肉体的な運動をすることはがん予防に重要であるという確固たる証拠があります。運動の量を比較的控えめに増すだけでも，毎年イギリスにおける何千ものがんの症例を防ぐことができます。これらの数字は利益を得るために，毎日ジムに通う必要は無いことも示しています。⑧少しの変化を作るだけで，あなたはがんの危険を減らすことができるのです。そして，このことは多くのがんの症例が早歩きと同じくらい簡単な何らかの事を通して防ぐことができるという事実によって，強調されています。散歩を趣味にすることや，バスや車に乗る代わりに店まで歩くことですら，人々は彼ら自身の健康にまったくの違いを生じさせることができるのです。」

イギリスのがん研究所の科学情報マネージャーであるヘンリー・スコウクロフトはこう述べる。「あなたはがんの危険を減らすために運動選手になる必要はありません。乳癌や大腸癌を含めてある特定のがんは，早歩きなどのような適度な運動を規則正しく行う人々にあまり見られないという確証があるのですから。」

323

(1)　a　空気（大気）　b　海
　　c　土地　　　　　d　鳥
　　e　植物

(2)　ウ　(3)　ア　(4)　ウ　(5)　イ

(6)　ア

解説

(1)　下線部①のあとに続く二文に書かれている。

(2)　one's own …「～自身の…」

(3)　下線部③の That は直前の文の内容を指す。

(4)　look around「見回す」
　　other＋名詞「別の，他の，違った～」

(5)　another は「もうひとつ」の意である。前の文で one earth と書かれているので，それに対して「もうひとつの地球」を示す。

(6)　ア　第１段落の最終文において坪田愛華は1991年に亡くなったと述べられているため，誤りである。
　　イ　第２段落の内容に一致する。
　　ウ　第３段落の第５文に書かれている。
　　エ　最終段落の第３，４文に書かれている。

和訳　１杯の味噌汁をきれいな水に変えるために7,000杯の水を必要とすることを知っているだろうか。樹齢15年の大木から約700枚しか紙袋が得られないことを知っているだろうか。坪田愛華はこのようなことについて考え，地球の未来を心配した。彼女は1991年に，たった12歳のときに亡くなったが，彼女は非常に重要な事実を発見した。

私たちの地球には長い歴史があるが，多くの人々は①今危機にあると言っている。私たちは空や海，陸を汚染してきた。あまりにも多くの種類の動物，鳥，植物の命を奪ってきた。これらは他の人々の問題ではなく，私たちの問題である。愛華は「私たちができることはないかしら」と考えた。

地球を救うためにできることはたくさんあるということを彼女は見出した。例えば，私たちは割り箸を使うのをやめることができる。もし私たちが自分の箸を持参すれば，外食のときにそれを使うことができる。それは，多くの木を伐採する必要がないことを意味している。私たちは買い物に行くとき，店で紙袋やビニール袋を受け取る代わりにマイバッグを使うことができる。あるいは，リサイクルのために使用済みの空き缶を集めることもできる。④<u>もしあなたが周りを見回せば，地球のために良いことは他にもたくさん見つかるだろう</u>。

私たちに地球はたったひとつしかない。地球をもうひとつ作ることはできない。きれいな地球のために，すべての国々が力を合わせよう。手遅れになる前に地球を救うために私たちができる全てのことをしなければならない。私たちは美しい地球への愛華の夢を忘れてはならない。

324

⑴ ① **ウ**　② **エ**　③ **イ**　④ **イ**
　⑤ **ア**　⑥ **エ**　⑦ **エ**　⑧ **イ**

⑵ ① 断食をやめる
　② 神のご加護があらんことを

解説

⑴ ① 第１段落の第２文の前半を参照。
　② 第１段落の第２文の後半を参照。
　③ “etiquette”という単語はもともとフランス語であるが，スペイン語になっても元の意味を保ったとある。
　④ 第１段落の第４文を参照。
　⑤ 第１段落の第４，５文を参照。
　⑥ 第１段落の第７文を参照。
　⑦ 第１段落の最後の２文を参照。
　⑧ 冒頭に述べられている。

⑵ **和訳** 参照。

和訳 すべての研究の中で最も興味深い分野の一つが，単語や語源についての研究である。それぞれの言語はいくつかの古い言語から成り立っている。そしてある言語の単語は，２つか３つの異なる言語をさかのぼって語源にたどり着くこともある。また，一つの言語のある単語は他の言語の一部になり，新しい意味をもつようになるかもしれない。“etiquette”という単語の語源はフランス語で，もともと標札や標識という意味であったが，スペイン語になっても，その元の意味を保持していた。だから，スペイン語では今日でも“etiquette”という単語は店がスーツやドレス，瓶につけている小さな札を示すのに使われている。しかしながら，フランス語の“etiquette”という単語は，徐々に違った意味を持つようになった。後に，宮廷で重要な式典の間，出席者がどのような服装を身に着け，どのように振舞うべきか，“etiquette”という小さな紙片に指示を書く慣行となったのだ。このようにして，“etiquette”という単語は，人々が守るべき一連の正しい礼儀作法を示し始めた。この意味で，この単語は英語にも渡った。

“breakfast”という単語を考えてみよう。「断食する」ということは，一定の期間食べないでいることである。したがって，食事をとらない夜を何時間か過ごしたあとの朝に，「①<u>断食をやめる</u>」のである。

“Good-bye”という日常の英語表現を考えてみよう。ずいぶん昔は，人々はお互いに別れ際に「②<u>神のご加護があらんことを</u>」と言っていた。この表現が何百万回も繰り返され，次第にそれは“Good-bye”と短縮されるようになったのだ。

325

⑴ a **イ**　b **エ**　c **オ**　d **ウ**
　e **ア**

⑵ **和訳** 参照。

⑶ According to the world view Larry learned

⑷ 〔解答例〕母親に甘やかされて育ち，自分には自分の思い通りにする資格があるという感覚を過度に持ってしまったから。

解説

⑴ a　the second ～「～した途端に」
　c　due to ～「～による，～のために」
　d　put up with ～「～を我慢する」

e　stand up for ～「(権利など) ～を主張〔要求〕する」

(2)　have O around「Oを家に招く」
want O to ～「Oに～してもらいたい」

(3)　according to ～「～によれば」
the world view「世界観」

(4)　第3段落前半部分，第4段落前半部分に書かれている。

和訳　まさに欲しいものをまさに欲しいときに得られないだろうと気づいた途端，手厳しい批評家になる人がいる。そういう人たちには，ぶつける（ぶちまける）感情が際限なくあるようだ。自分には何でも思い通りにする資格があると考える不寛容な，甘やかされた人にありがちだ。

サラは，自分と子どもたちがたえず夫ラリーにおびえていることに気づいた。①彼は子どもたちに，彼らの友人を家に招いてほしくないと思っていた。彼の睡眠の邪魔だったからである。もちろん彼の友人は，彼の望むときにはいつでも，訪ねて来ることができた。彼は子どもたちが好む音楽を流すことを許さなかったが，自分の（好む）音楽は自分の好きなだけ大きな音量で流すことができた。彼は静かで従順な家族であることを要求し，それがかなわないとサラと子どもたちを情け容赦なく責め立てた。

サラはラリーの非難の裏にある意図を調べ，ラリーのふるまいは彼が甘やかされていたことと彼には過度の権利意識があることによるものだと判断した。彼の（感情の）爆発は頻繁に起こったが，ただ単に彼らの怒りや不満をぶつけていただけではなかった。彼は本当に自分の思い通りになることを求めていたのだ。

ラリーが成長していくとき，彼の人生における大きな問題も小さな問題もすべて母親が解決してきた。彼はとてもすばらしく特別だから，普通の人と同じような不満や不快を我慢する必要はないと母親から教えられてきた。ラリーが身につけた世界観によれば，彼はどんなことでも自分の思うようにしてよく，自分を妨げようとする人は罰せられ，命令に従うようにならないと気がすまない。

ラリーの行動パターンを変えるためにサラは長い間戦っていたが，能動的対処方法が彼女を手助けした。そして，子どもたちは自分たちの家庭を楽しむための権利を主張している。

326

(1)　1809年，アメリカ合衆国マサチューセッツ州ボストン

(2)　父親は赤ん坊の頃，母親は2歳の頃。

(3)　Edgar Allan Poe

(4)　**イ**，**オ**

(5)　1845年，彼がようやく有名になった時。

(6)　たいていのアメリカ文学作品は現実主義であるのに，ポーの作品の関心や書き方は少しも現実主義ではなかったから。

(7)　江戸川乱歩

解説

(4)　**ア**　第2段落第1文にイギリスの学校に通っていたとある。
　ウ　第2段落第6文に2年間兵役についていたとある。
　エ　第2段落第12文に作品が出版されても給料はあまりよくなかったとある。

(5)　下線部の直前の文に着目する。until は否定文で使うと，「…（する）までは～しない，…してようやく～する」の意。よって直前の文は「彼は1845年までは有名にならなかった」と訳せるため，1845年は彼がようやく有名になった時だとわかる。

和訳　エドガー・ポーはマサチューセッツ州ボストンで1809年に生まれた。彼の両親は役者であった。当時，俳優業は最良の社会によって受け入れられていなかった。父親が家族の元を去ったとき，エドガーは赤ん坊だった。母親を亡くしたとき，彼は2歳だった。彼は裕福な実業家，ジョン・アランの家に引き取られた。そして彼は新しい名前を受けた。エドガー・アラン・ポーだ。

エドガーはイギリスとヴァージニア州リッチモンドで学校に通った。彼は若い頃，シャーロッツヴィルにあるヴァージニア大学に通っていた。彼は善良な学生だった。ジェファーソン・リテラリー・ソサイアティ（文学サークル）の一員だった。そして

その後，エドガーはボストンへ行き，月刊誌のライター兼編集者として働き始めた。２年間，軍隊で兵役にもついた。エドガー・アラン・ポーは懸命に働いた。彼は編集者として成功した。３冊の詩集を出版した。小説も書き始めた。彼の５作品は1832年，ペンシルヴァニア州フィラデルフィアで一つの出版物として印刷された。しかし，給料はあまりよくなかった。生活は厳しかった。彼は貧しさで，心と体に病を抱え困っていた。ポーはうつ病にかかった。恐怖から逃れるために酒を飲んだ。アルコールは彼に非常に悪い影響を与えた。

あらゆる危機を経て，エドガー・アラン・ポーは多くの小説や詩，作品批評を書いた。小説のいくつかは賞を獲得した。だが，彼は1845年までは有名にならなかった。それは『大鴉（おおからす）』という詩が出版された時であった。たいていのアメリカ文学作品は現実主義である。しかしポーの関心と書き方は全く現実主義ではなかった。ポーの作品はフランスで最も賞賛された。彼は多くのフランスの作家に大きな影響を与えた。ポーの最も有名な詩は『大鴉』である。その詩を愛する人たちがいる。それは音楽のようだという。一方，その詩を嫌う人たちもいる。強制的で不自然に感じる，よくない音楽のようだという。

327

(1) 和訳 参照。

(2) ア ○　イ ×　ウ ×　エ ○

(3) ア ímages（画像）
　イ convénient（便利な）
　ウ ísolated（孤立した）
　エ nówadays（今日では）

(4) Cell phones will never replace face-to-face communication.

解説

(1) ① in which 以下は the few countries in the world を先行詞とする関係詞節。
　② カンマからカンマまでは挿入句。

(2) ア 「携帯電話通信はアメリカで始まった。」
　冒頭の第２文の内容に合っている。
イ 「日本は携帯電話の利用者数が世界で最も多い。」
　本文によればアメリカ，中国に次ぐ数と述べられている。
ウ 「人は通話のためだけに携帯電話を利用する。」
　第２段落に通話以外の用途が挙げられている。
エ 「日本の携帯電話はあまり重くない。」
　第３段落第２文に very lightweight「とても軽い」という表現があり，内容に合っている。

和訳 現代では，携帯電話は広く一般に普及している。携帯電話の根本的な着想は1947年に，アメリカのパトカーの車内で移動電話通信を利用したことから始まる。しかし，最初の携帯電話通信は1973年まではなされていなかった。1987年までには，100万人以上のアメリカ人が携帯電話を使うようになっていた。今日では，6,900万人以上のアメリカ人，6,500万人以上の中国人，6,300万人以上の日本人，5,500万人以上のドイツ人，4,300万人以上のイギリス人が携帯電話を使っている。

携帯電話は特に日本で普及しているようだ。①日本は一般の電話よりも携帯電話の方が多いという世界中でも数少ない国の１つである。日本のどこに行っても，携帯電話を使っているのを見かける。日本人は電子メールやテキスト・メッセージを送受信したり，ウェブを拾い読みしたり，ゲームや買い物をしたりするために携帯電話を使う。

日本には世界でも最高レベルの携帯電話システムやサービスがいくつかある。電話機がとても軽量で，液晶表示画面にフルカラー画像を表示できる。利用者がスナップ写真や短い動画までも撮影して友人に送信できるようにカメラも内蔵されている。日本の携帯電話は使いやすくて便利だ。

多くの他の国と違って，サービスもとてもよいし，②トンネルや地下のショッピングモールも含めて，携帯電話が使えない場所はないようだ。

そう，携帯電話は素晴らしい。しかしながら，問題が１つある。現代の日本人の多くがかなりの孤独を感じている。この理由の1つは，情報交換に携帯電話を利用するということである。

意思伝達は1つの技術であり，どんな技術でも同じく実践が必要だ。携帯電話は決して面と向かってのコミュニケーションの代わりにはならないだろう。人間は対面して相手と話さないなら，必ず孤独な気持ちになるであろうから。

328

(1) **ア**　(2) **エ**　(3) **エ**　(4) **イ**
(5) **イ**

解説

> お見逃しなく！
> 世界で最も有名なシャツがただ今当店にてセール中！
> 豊富なカラー，サイズ，デザインを取り揃えています！
> 洗濯機 OK，アイロンがけ不要
>
> ご両親やご友人，あなたの愛する人へのプレゼントに最適

(1) この広告はどこから出ているものですか。
(2) この店のセール商品について正しくないものはどれですか。

> メモ　　：ジョナサン・エドワーズ　様
> 日付　　：8月31日
> 時間　　：午後12時30分
> 昼休みの間に Info Tech のメアリー・ケイ様よりお電話あり
> 電話番号：713-5506（内線）22
> 伝言　　：
> 来週までに車の見積りを頂きたいです。
> お電話お待ちしております。
> 受　　　：ジョー・スミス

(3) このメモを書き留めた人は誰ですか。
(4) この伝言を受けたのはいつですか。
英語では昼の12時は 12:00 p.m. または noon と表現する。
(5) 電話を待っているのは誰ですか。

329

(1) **イ**　(2) ② **イ**　③ **エ**
(3) **ウ**　(4) **イ**

解説

(1) 思い出させるために役に立つものであると述べているので，前文の “Keep Left” signs「左側通行の標識」だと判断できる。
(2) ② このようにするか事故に遭うかもしれない危険を冒すかのどちらかだと述べているので，スピードを落として後ろにつくという内容が最も適切である。
③ それまでの内容から，自分の車を置いてきて右ハンドルの車を借りれば，外国人が関与する事故は少なくなると判断できる。
(3) これは，前文のイギリス人，アイルランド人が言っていること（左側通行の国では右ハンドルの車を運転する）に対する the opposite「反対のこと，対立すること」である。ヨーロッパ人は，「この2つの国ではルールに合わせる」のではなく，「この2つの国がルールを合わせる」べきだと考えている。つまり，**ウ**の「共通の通行基準を採用すること」を指している。
(4) **ア** そのようなことは述べられていない。
イ 最終段落に述べられている。
ウ ヨーロッパの基準を採用し，すべて変更されたと述べられている。
エ 今では再び左側通行にすると危険を感じるだろうと述べられている。

和訳 日本では車線は左側通行だが，アメリカ，カナダとヨーロッパ本土の国はすべて右側通行である。イギリスとアイルランドのみ日本と同じである。これが大きな混乱の原因となる。

日本にいるアメリカ人ドライバーは二重の衝撃を受けている。というのは狭い道を運転することにも順応しなければならないからだ。ヨーロッパ人ドライバーはイギリスにしばしばハンドルが左側に付いた自分の車を持ってくる。沿岸付近の道路には，多くの言語で書かれた「左側通行」の標識がある。

それらは（左側を通行することを）思い出させるために役に立つが，反対側にハンドルがある車を運転するのが明らかに難しいことについてはどうすることもできない。

もしそのドライバーが他の乗り物を追い

越したいと思ったとき，彼はそんなに先まで見ることはできないだろう。スピードを落として後ろにつかなければならないか，危険を冒して事故に遭うかもしれないかのどちらかだ。自国に自分の車を置いて，イギリスやアイルランドで右ハンドルの車を借りれば，外国人ドライバーが関与する事故がより少なくなるだろう。これはイギリス人とアイルランド人が言うことであるが，ヨーロッパ人は反対のことを言う。

彼らはこの2つの国が右側通行に移行したら，より賢明なことであると考えている。それならヨーロッパとアメリカにおいて唯一単純な基準になるだろうにと。

1960年代初頭まで，スウェーデンも左側通行だった。車はノルウェーやフィンランドの国境で通行を（左から右へ）変えたのであった。スウェーデン政府は，スウェーデンがヨーロッパの基準を採用することを決めて，すべて変更した。今では，スウェーデン人は再び左側通行で運転したとすれば危険を感じるだろうと言う。

330

(1) **エ**　(2) **ア**　(3) **イ**　(4) **イ**
(5) **ア**

解説

(1) So＋do〔does〕＋S「Sもまたそうする」
この does は直前の文の kill thousands of people を指す。

(2) 下線部②の次に示されている内容である。
ア 陰にいて，ゆったりした服を着て，水分をとることができる。⇨正しい。
イ 室内にいて，何も身につけず，ビールを飲むことができる。⇨誤り。
ウ 医師に診せるか，911に電話して救急車を呼ぶことができる。⇨誤り。
エ 暑さに関連する医学上の問題を抱える可能性がある。⇨誤り。

(3) 下線部③の前の文を説明するものとして「そういう人は脱水症状になる」と言っている。
ア 彼／彼女はあまりに多くの水を飲んだ。⇨誤り。
イ 彼／彼女はあまりに多くの水分を失った。⇨正しい。
ウ 彼／彼女は長い間病気で横になっていた。⇨誤り。
エ 彼／彼女は頭や胸，腹部に痛みがあった。⇨誤り。

(4) **ア** 暑さは自然災害と同じく人を死に至らしめると述べられているので，合致しない。
ウ 地球温暖化については述べられていないので，合致しない。
エ そのような記述はない。

(5)「暑さで疲労を感じたらどうすればよいですか。」
ア「水を飲んで，冷水で体を湿らせ，涼しい場所で休む。」
イ「困難な状況でも懸命に働き続ける。」
ウ「たとえ難しくとも普通に歩く。」
エ「たくさん汗をかくのは良いことなので，より多く発汗する。」

和訳　極端に暑い気候は世界中の多くの地域で見られる。暑い気候でたいていの人々は暑さを感じるだけだが，それによって深刻な医学上の問題や，中には死さえ引き起こしてしまう可能性がある。洪水，嵐など自然災害が毎年，何千もの人々を死に至らしめる。極端な暑さもまたそうだ。専門家によると，暑さは自然界の最も決定的な致死因子かもしれないと言う。例えば，昨年の夏，アメリカの東海岸の街や都市の中には気温の史上最高記録を出したところがあった。気温は42℃ の高さに上昇したのである。

極端な暑さによる危険から自分を守るために人間は多くのことができると医師は言う。可能なら日差しを避けなさい。冷水をたくさん飲みなさい。自然の素材でできた淡い色の服を着なさい。その服がゆったりしていて，自由に動く余裕があるか確かめなさい。さらに，暑さに関連する医学上の問題の危険な徴候を知っておきなさい。

極端な暑さで，熱中症と呼ばれる重大な問題を引き起こすことがある。熱中症にかかっている人は，発汗によってあまりにも多くの水分を失う。そういった人は脱水症状となる。熱中症患者は衰弱と極端な疲労を感じる。普通に歩くことが困難になるかもしれない。熱中症は吐き気がしたり，心拍が速くなったり，呼吸困難や頭，胸，腹部が痛くなったりするという状態を引き起こすおそれもある。このような症状の人はすぐに涼しい場所で休み，水をたくさん飲むべきだと医師は言う。また，冷水で（体を）湿らすことが助けとなるかもしれないとも言う。

331

(1) he recommended Ben to be a printer
(2) bear
(3) **ア**
(4) 印刷屋であるベンの兄のところで働くこと
(5) **イ**
(6) articles
(7) ① **ウ** ② **ア** ③ **ウ** ④ **イ**
(8) ① × ② × ③ × ④ ○
⑤ ○

和訳　ベンジャミン－フランクリンはボストンに生まれ，彼の家は大家族であった。彼は17人の子供のうちの15番目であった！

ベンは10歳の時，学校をやめなくてはならなかった。当時，少年はまだ小さいうちに仕事を覚えなければならなかった。ベンは父親のもとに働きに出た。父親は，ろうそくと石けんを作っていた。しかし，ベンにはこの仕事はとてもつまらなかった。ベンは，読むことと，頭を使うことが好きだった。

ある日，ベンは，父親のところへ行き言った。「父さんの仕事を僕が手伝うのを父さんが当てにしているってことはわかっているよ。でも，父さん，僕はこの仕事を生涯ずっとやりたくはないんだ」

ベンの父親は，しばらく考えて言った。「ベン，印刷工になるっていうのはどうだい？」「それはいいね」ベンは答えた。「そうだなあ，兄さんのジェームズが印刷工だ。おまえがあいつと働けるようなんとかしてみよう」

ベンは，この考えがとても気に入った。ついに，自分が好きになると確信の持てることができるのであった。そうして彼は父親の家から兄の家に移った。当時ベンはまだ12歳であった。

ジェームズの印刷所は汚なかったが，印刷用インクのさわやかなにおいがした。ベンは，インクを混ぜ合わせたり，活字を組んだり，きめの荒い手引き印刷された紙を編集したりすることを楽しんだ。彼には本を読む時間がいっぱいあった。彼は偽名を使って記事をも書いた。それらの記事が実はベンジャミンの書いたものとは知らずに，彼の兄は印刷した。それらは「空想的な社会改良紙」として知られた。

ベンの兄は，いかにして植民地は管理されるべきかについていくつか非常に強硬な意見を持っていた。このため彼は，「急進的」となり，彼の見解を出版することで政府ともめごとを起こした。ジェームズが投獄されたとき，ベンジャミンは印刷所の仕事を運営し，ザ・カーラントと呼ばれる新聞を出版した。それはたちまちとてもよく読まれるようになった。

332

(1) knowing
(2) **ウ**
(3) 貧しい人々が買うには塩は高価すぎた
(4) paid
(5) iceboxes
(6) invention
(7) **エ**
(8) sell
(9) **ア** ○ **イ** × **ウ** × **エ** ×
オ ○ **カ** × **キ** × **ク** ○
ケ × **コ** ○

和訳　私たちのほとんどは，毎日塩を使う。私たちは料理をするときに塩を使う。しかし私たちは，欲しいときにいつでも店やスーパーマーケットで塩を手に入れられるので，塩について少しも考えない。塩はそこにあって，私たちはそれがどこから生じたのか知ることなしに使っている。

しかし大昔のギリシャでは，塩は今日ほど大衆的ではなかった。塩を得ることは容易ではなく，とりわけ海から遠い所に住んでいる人々にはそうだった。ほとんどの人々は当時料理に塩を使わなかった。貧しい人々にとって，塩は高価すぎて買えなかったので，裕福な人のみがそれを使うことができた。

塩はかつて手に入れることが難しかったので，お金として使われていた。ローマの労働者は昔，給料のすべてか賃金の一部が塩だった。英単語の“salary”はラテン語のsalarium からきている。それは“塩のお金”という意味だ。

古代中国では塩は金とほとんど同じくらい価値のあるものだった。冷蔵庫が発明される前のヨーロッパでは，塩は肉や魚を腐らせないようにするために使われた。アフリカのいくつかの地域では塩はかたまりで市場に運ばれる。市場ではそのかたまりは売るために小さく砕かれる。世界のいくつかの部分では，塩を見たり味わったりしたことが一度もない人々がまだいる。

333

(1) ① エ　③ ア　⑤ イ　⑥ ウ

(2) 永久的なものになる点。

(3) 離れた場所から即時通信が可能であるから。

(4) 書き言葉の流儀を無視すべきではないという点。

(5) 今日，活字の力はコンピュータによって徐々に衰えつつある。

解説

(1) ① (just) to be on the safe side「念のため，大事をとって」

③ elicit「引き出す，誘い出す」

⑤ jargon「用語，専門用語」

⑥ duplicate「複写する」

(2) 第1段落に書き言葉と話し言葉の違いが述べられているため，この点を簡潔にまとめればよい。

(3) 電子メールの会話がどのようなものかは第2段落に述べられている。

(4) 最終段落の，特に最後の4行を踏まえた内容であればよい。この文章の要点は，電子メールは話し言葉にずっと近いものではあるが，あくまでも書き言葉であるため，書き言葉の習慣を無視すべきではないということである。

(5) be ～ing「～しつつある」

和訳　言葉が話されるとき，それらは永久的な記録として残らない。ほとんどの人は自分が話しているとき，言葉について考えていない。しかしながら，書くときにはより注意深くなる。おそらく，「念のため」書いたものを読み返すだろう。言葉を書くことで，メッセージはより永久的なものになる。それにより私たちは結果について考えさせられる。

②今日，活字の力はコンピュータによって徐々に衰えつつある。電子メールは手紙を書く際の書式や語調に革命的変化をもたらした。電子メールは即時通信を可能にするので，それは素早く即座に反応を引き起こす。そして，そのコミュニケーションは書き言葉よりも話し言葉にずっと近い。時々，人々はメッセージをわざわざ読み直そうとはせずにとげのある返答を送信してしまう。④電子メールは長距離の話し言葉である。

電子メールの速さと即時性は手紙の作法の習慣を変えた。コンピュータ用語において，「フレーム（ネット上で喧嘩する)」という新しい動詞は電子メールの通信に対し素早く意地の悪い返事をすることを意味する。とげのある返事は「フレームメール」と呼ばれている。フレームメールの頻度が増すことは，コンピュータ使用者によりよいコンピュータマナーが必要であることを示している。

今日，コンピュータ改革は活字がここ5世紀半の間持っていた力を変化させつつある。私たちが見てきたように，コンピュータの書き言葉はしばしば書き言葉よりもむしろ話し言葉を模倣している。電子メールの即時性は話し言葉の自発性を複写するけれども，コミュニケーションの媒体は口頭ではなく，文書なのである。電子メールを使う人々は，書き言葉の流儀を無視すべきではない。

334

(1) ウ　(2) イ　(3) イ

(4) エ　(5) ア　(6) イ，ウ，オ

解説

(1) 空欄を含む文は「猫が人間なしで生きていくことができる」ということと「鶏はそ

れができない」ということを述べているので，逆接の although（〜だけれども）でつなぐのが自然である。

⑵ think of A as B「AをBとみなす，考える」，be classified as …「…として分類される」

⑶「この鶏種は食肉を私たちに提供してくれることを求められているが，卵は求められていない。」

第２段落第４文に挙げられたコーニッシュのことを指しているので，English である。

⑷ 空欄直前の文が some people で始まっていることから，「〜の人もいれば」の後にくるのは Others …「…の人もいる」となる。

⑸ 空欄の直前の部分「The place where they are kept」が主語だと考えられるので，空欄には動詞が入ると予想できる。後に now maintained at a temperature which 〜「〜の温度に現在保たれている」が続いているから，現在形の be 動詞 is が正しい。

⑹ **ア**「概して，猫は鶏と同様，人間から独立している。」⇨猫は人間なしで生きていけるが鶏は生きられないと述べられているため，本文の内容と合致しない。

no less 〜 than O「Oに劣らず，Oと同様に」

イ「人間はより強い闘鶏を望んだので，初めて鶏を育て始めた。」⇨合致する。

ウ「私たちがスーパーで買う卵はホワイト・レグホンから来ている場合が多い。」⇨合致する。

エ「鶏の体調や食べるエサの種類，卵の色が，卵の栄養に同じように影響を与える。」⇨卵の栄養は色ではなく，鶏の体調や食べるエサの種類によって決まると述べられているので，合致しない。

オ「養鶏家はより新しく良質な品種を作り出すために，異なる鶏種を交配させる方法を知る努力をしてきた。」⇨合致する。

カ「従来の鶏は周りで見つけたものを食べただけだったが，そのエサは必要な栄養が不足することがしばしばあったので，今よりも産む卵の数が少なかった。」⇨食べるエサの栄養価と産む卵の数の因果関係については述べられていないので，合致しない。

キ「飼育する鶏が食肉用か卵用かによって鶏には異なるエサが与えられる。」⇨そのような記述はないので，合致しない。

ク「おりで飼われていると，鶏はストレスを感じて産む卵の数が少なくなるのは極めて当然のことである。」⇨ストレスに関することは述べられていない。また，最終段落において，産卵する雌鶏をおりに入れておくと，より多く卵を産むとあるので，合致しない。

和訳 鶏は人によって最も完全に飼いならされてきた動物の１つである。実際，猫は人間なしでも生きていくことができるけれども，鶏はできない。鶏は食と住みかを人間に頼っている。私たちは鶏を食肉と卵の源だと考えているが，鶏を育てる元々の理由は闘鶏のためだった。このスポーツが禁止になってから，卵と食肉の生産に，より重要性が置かれるようになった。

現在，鶏の品種はたくさんある。それらは，米国種，英国種，アジア種，地中海種として分類されるのが一般的である。主な米国種はすべて赤卵を産み，卵だけでなく食肉のために飼育されている。最も重要な英国種はコーニッシュで，それらは食肉用として育てられているものである。しかしながら，その種は産む卵が少ないのだ。世界でもずばぬけて有力な卵生産を誇るのはホワイト・レグホンで，それは白卵を産む。スーパーマーケットで目にする卵のほとんどはその種からのものである。

あなたは赤卵と白卵のどちらを好むだろうか。赤卵の方が栄養があるという人もいれば，より美しく見えるからと言って白卵を好む人もいる。実際にはそれぞれの栄養はほぼ同じで，卵の色ではなくて，鶏の体調や食べるエサの種類によって決まる。

鶏の品種改良（繁殖）は，複雑な科学となってきた。いかに異なる品種の鶏を一緒に飼育することで，より多くの卵を産みより多くの肉を生み出すことのできる，より新しくてより良い品種を作り出すかというのが良い例だ。科学的な品種改良の結果として，鶏は以前のものより早く成長し，より多くの肉をつけるようになった。

かつての鶏は，農家の庭で見つけたものは何でも食べることを許されていた。現在では，栄養のある卵を産み，健康的で，食用向けの良質な鶏を生産するのに必要な栄養のすべてを鶏が受けられるよう，それが科学になっている。鶏が飼育される場所は現在，卵を産むのに最適な温度に保たれている。鶏は針金でできたおりの中で飼われている。スペースを確保するため，おりはそれぞれの上に置かれる。おりの中に産卵する雌鶏を入れることで，より多くの卵を産むということもわかってきた。

335

⑴ ① エ　② イ　③ オ　④ ウ　⑤ ア

⑵ A ウ　B ア　C ア

⑶ influence　⑷ worse

⑸ ウ　⑹ エ

⑺ ① ○　② ×　③ ×　④ ○　⑤ ○

解説

⑴ ① carry out ～「～を実行する」
② in a row「連続的に」
③ plan for ～「～の計画」
④ instead of ～「～ではなくて，～しないで」
⑤ combine A with B「AをBと組み合わせる，AとBとを結びつける」

⑵ A be the first to do「最初に～する」
B way have＋過去分詞「～したのかもしれない」
C people who ～「～する（である）人」

⑷ bad-worse-worst

⑸ make sense of ～「～を理解する」

⑹ ア「彼は私に会いに来ると思う」
イ「車にいた人々は全員，事故で死亡した。」
ウ「メアリーに初めて会ったのは，去年のパーティだった。」
エ「私たちは英語を学ぶのに易しい方法はないという結論に達した。」

下線部 d の that は「～という」の意で用いられているのでエが同じ用法。アは「～ということ」の意で接続詞，イは関係代名詞，ウは強調構文である。

⑺ ①「ある研究では悪い経験について書くことで健康を改善するということが述べられている。」⇨合致する。
②「この研究では何百もの疾患を調べた。」⇨喘息とリューマチ性関節炎の患者について100人以上を対象に調べたとあるので，合致しない。
③「研究の間に，参加した患者の全てが自分の書きたいことについて書いたあと健康を改善させた。」⇨書きたいことではなく，書くよう求められた内容を書いたので，合致しない。
④「例えば車の事故のような，悪い経験について書いた患者のほぼ半数は，健康を改善させた。」⇨47％がそうなったので，合致する。
⑤「感情を表現することは，患者の健康を手助けするときに薬と同じくらい重要かもしれないということを研究が示唆している。」⇨合致する。

和訳 精神と肉体の強力な関連が新たな研究により証明された。米国の研究者によると，ひどい経験について書くというだけの単純なことで患者の健康が回復できるということを発見したという。

この研究は，そのような経験について書くことがどのように病気に影響を与えうるのかを初めて調査したものだと考えられている。結果は米国医師会発行による機関誌上で報告された。この研究はニューヨーク州立大学ストニーブルック校で行われた。喘息という呼吸の疾患やリューマチ性関節炎という骨の疾患で深刻な状態にある100人以上の患者がその研究に関わった。

研究者たちはグループの全員に連続3日間20分間書くように頼んだ。ある患者たちは，人生において最悪の経験について感じたことを書くよう求められた。例えば，この患者たちは自動車事故や離婚，愛する人の死，子どもの時に起きたひどい出来事について書いた。その日の計画について書くよう言われた人たちもいた。

患者の健康は４か月間検査された。悪い経験について書いた多くの人の健康が４か月後に改善したと研究者は言う。そのような経験について書いたあと，これらの患者の47％は体調が良くなったそうだ。他のグループの24％にも同様の改善がみられた。

ノースダコタ州立大学のジョシュア・スミス氏がこの研究をまとめた。患者が自分の感情を表現し，経験を理解できたから回復したのかもしれないと彼は考えている。スミス氏は，この結果が患者の体調が改善し続けるかどうかを示すものではないと言う。また，あまり具合がよくない人が，治療法を捜さずに，書くという考えを検討すべきではないとも言う。

初期の研究では，感情が病気の進行に影響する可能性があることが示されていた。

機関誌はこの研究の解説を公表した。カリフォルニア州スタンフォード大学のデイヴィッド・スピーゲル氏は，書くことによる強力な効果に驚かされたといい，投薬治療がストレス感情の表現と強く結びつくと，より効果的になるという証拠を研究者が提供してくれたと述べた。